After the Trade:

Dealer and Clearing Bank Operations
in Money Market
and Government Securites

After the Trade:
Dealer and Clearing Bank Operations in Money Market and Government Securites

MARCIA STIGUM

DOW JONES-IRWIN
Homewood, Illinois 60430

Production editor: Karen Smith
Copyediting coordinator: Jean Roberts
Production manager: Bette Ittersagen
Artist: The Artforce
Compositor: Carlisle Graphics
Typeface: 10/12 Helvetica Light
Printer: Arcata Graphics/Kingsport

ISBN 0-87094-937-3
Library of Congress Catalog Card No. 87–50773
Printed in the United States of America
2 3 4 5 6 7 8 9 0 K 5 4 3 2 1 0 9 8

To my good friend,
Ira Haupt,
with many thanks for many things

Preface

THIS BOOK DESCRIBES the clearing of money market securities. The focus of the book is on the tasks that must be done to clear money market trades, *not* on the details of how these tasks are done. There's a good reason for this: The "how" story changes constantly as the Fed, the dealers, the clearing banks, and the custodial banks introduce new computer hardware and software that permit them to interface better with each other and do their appointed tasks more quickly, more accurately, and with less manpower.

Clearing personnel

The book is written primarily for people who work in dealer and clearing bank operations. Anyone coming into this area needs, especially if he lacks previous experience in the money market, both a short introduction to the instruments of the money market and a longer introduction to clearing: what clearing is, how it's done, and why doing it correctly is crucial to the successful operation of a broad range of money market institutions.

Managers

Many other people could also benefit from reading this book. All too often, to money market dealers, portfolio managers, and other Wall Street professionals, clearing is a stepchild, one that they neglect at their peril and, sometimes, to their great cost. Chaos in the back office, a common by-product of swift mergers, has felled—or close to it—more than one Wall Street firm, not only in the 1960s but more recently; Mosely, Hallgarten, Estabrock & Weeden Inc., an old line Boston broker, is a case in point.

Investors

Investors, too, can benefit from a crisp and accurate clearing operation. For example, an institutional portfolio run by someone who understands clearing will *earn money* on fails, whereas one run by someone who neglects clearing will, especially if the portfolio invests

in GNMAs, repeatedly *lose money* due to large and unnecessary fails. Any investor who, by reading this book, saves himself from even *one* fail will have paid for this book many, perhaps hundreds of, times over.

Investors also need to think hard about where they leave their valued securities. No investor who leaves securities in dealer safekeeping and who thinks doing so is prudent—perhaps because he believes it is an accepted industry practice—should skip Chapter 14, which defines dealer safekeeping and describes how it works. After reading the chapter, perhaps he will still use dealer safekeeping, but at least he'll know that when he does so, he's making *the risk equivalent of an unsecured loan* to his dealer, a point that too few portfolio managers appreciate.

Corporate equity and bond people

Although this book primarily concerns the clearing of money market securities, it should also prove valuable to people who deal in corporate stocks and bonds. In particular, Chapter 16 describes in detail the workings of DTC and NSCC, two organizations through which over 90% of the nation's trades in corporate stocks and bonds are cleared. Traders of corporate stocks and bonds should also find Chapter 9's discussion of the Fed wire interesting. Currently, there's talk of either moving DTC to settlement in Fed funds or of giving DTC dual-funds capability.

Lawyers

Lawyers, too, may find this book of interest. Both dealer bankruptcies and the use of trading in governments to shelter income have produced endless court cases in which questions about how trades are cleared arise. In particular, lawyers often ask: What is and what is not a "real trade"? As we note, the *indicia* of a *real* money market trade, if they exist at all, are not to be found in clearing. Some trades in governments clear over the Fed wire; other equally good trades do not. And so it goes.

STRUCTURE OF THE BOOK

This book describes in detail the book-entry system, the operation of the Fed wire, the clearing of book-entry securities, and the clearing of physical securities such as BAs and CDs. Special chapters are devoted to instruments, the clearing of which involves some instrument-specific quirks: commercial paper, mortgage-backed securities, and municipal securities. There is also a chapter on safekeeping and custody.

It is expected that many readers of this book will be new to the money market. Part One provides background that should help such readers

understand the rest of the book. It describes clearly the instruments traded in the money market, how yields and prices of such securities are calculated, and how money market dealers and brokers operate. Part Two focuses on various aspects of clearing: the clearing of wireable securities, the clearing of physical securities, the issuance of commercial paper, the clearing of pass-throughs, and so on.

In every area of life, people develop special terms or give common terms special meanings to communicate precisely and concisely with each other their particular interests and activities; hence *jargon*. The money market is no exception, and this book uses money market jargon extensively. To aid the reader, each piece of jargon used is carefully defined the first time it appears in the text. Also, at the end of the book, there is a *Glossary* in which a wide range of money and bond market terms are defined.

People who become fascinated, as I have, by the money market may find it useful to read any or all of the following:

Marcia Stigum, *The Money Market,* 2nd ed. (Homewood, Ill.: Dow Jones-Irwin, 1983).

Marcia Stigum in collaboration with John Mann, *Money Market Calculations, Yields, Break-Evens, and Arbitrage* (Homewood, Ill.: Dow Jones-Irwin, 1981).

Marcia Stigum and Rene Branch, *Managing Bank Assets and Liabilities* (Homewood, Ill.: Dow Jones-Irwin, 1983).

Marcia Stigum, *The Repo and Reverse Markets: Borrower and Investor Practices* (Homewood, Ill.: Dow Jones-Irwin, 1988).

The pronoun *he* is used frequently through this book. This pronoun has long been used in English to mean *person*. Any attempt to avoid this use of *he* leads, in my opinion, to nothing but bad and awkward English. Therefore, I make no such attempt.

In conclusion, I would like to thank the many persons—clearing bankers, Fed officers, and people in dealer operations in particular—who have answered with great grace and patience my endless questions. I would also like to thank Laurain Moncheck and Debbie Bromberg who have done, with good cheer, multifarious tasks that made the writing of this book possible.

Marcia Stigum

Acknowledgments

THERE WAS ONLY ONE WAY that research for this book could be conducted. That was by interviewing market participants at length. To the following people, I would like to express a very heartfelt thanks for the patient and thoughtful answers they proferred to my many questions. A particular thank you also goes to those listed below, who volunteered to read and criticize those chapters that covered their area of specialty. Needless to say, the author bears full responsibility for any remaining errors of fact, which I hope are few.

John Astrino
Carol Barrett
Jorge Brathwaite
Allen Clark
Walter Cushman
Baigio Desantis
Donald Donahue
Frank Elleo
Richard Flintoft
Michael Frieband
Herbert Friedman
Michael Farrell
Raymond Gottardi
Frank Guerin
Gary Haverman
Ann Hoagland
Joesph Janosi
James Koster

Donald Lagos
George Maloney
John Mann
William Melton
Charles Moran
Charles Morton
John Murray
Louis Musanti
John Perini
James Pauline
Ralph Peters
Donald Ringsmuth
Anthony Rudley
Mary Sue Sullivan
Robert Schultz
William Tierney
Barbara Walter
Paul Zintl

Contents

Abbreviations

EXAMPLES AND QUOTES in this book often contain "street" abbrevia-
tions of the names of various institutions. The most common are:

Bank of America...B of A
Bank of New York...BONY
Chase Manhattan Bank...Chase
Citibank...Citi
Goldman Sachs...Goldman
Irving Trust Company...Irving
Merrill Lynch...Merrill
Manufacturers Hanover Trust Co...Manny
Morgan Guaranty Trust Co...Morgan
Salomon Brothers...Sali
Security Pacific...Sec Pac

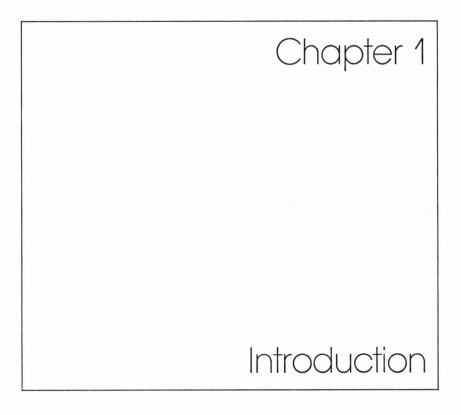

Chapter 1

Introduction

THIS IS A BOOK ABOUT THE CLEARING OF SECURITIES TRADES, about what goes on *after the trade*. It describes the wiring of money—sometimes tens, even hundreds, of millions of dollars—over Fed wire; the wiring of book-entry securities; the delivery of physical securities, often in bearer form; the tracking of everyone's credits and debits in the Street's computers; and the occurrence now and then, after the trade, of fraud. Yes, that too.

Memories are short indeed. One day, perhaps too long after bad, back-office problems put dealer bankruptcies, complete and near misses, in the headlines, a nonoperations person from a big dealership queried the author, "Why are you writing about clearing? Is clearing important?" "Yes," I replied, "for many firms—in particular, dealers, brokers, and clearing banks—clearing is a matter of life and death."

A dealer's shop is long *three* sorts of people: *traders* who trade, *salespeople* who sell, and *operations people* who clear trades. These three groups exist in a symbiotic relationship. One group cannot be healthy and robust, if the others, on whom their activities depend, are not. Perhaps this exaggerates a bit. Some trading-oriented shops do get

along OK with only a skeletal sales force. *No dealer, however, gets along OK for long without excellent execution, a good back office.*

Since this book is written partly for people new to the money market, it calls for two introductions, one to the money market and one to clearing. People who know the money market may skip to the second introduction.

THE MONEY MARKET

The U.S. money market is a huge and significant part of the nation's financial system in which banks and other participants trade hundreds of billions of dollars every working day. Where those billions go and the prices at which they are traded affect how the U.S. government finances its debt, how business finances its expansion, and how consumers choose to spend or save.

The money market is a wholesale market for low-risk, highly liquid, short-term IOUs. It is a market for various sorts of debt securities rather than equities. The stock-in-trade of the market includes a large chunk of the U.S. Treasury's debt and billions of dollars worth of federal agency securities, negotiable bank certificates of deposit, bankers' acceptances, municipal notes, and commercial paper. Within the confines of the money market each day, banks—domestic and foreign—actively trade in multimillion-dollar blocks billions of dollars of Federal funds and Eurodollars, and banks and nonbank dealers are each day the recipients of billions of dollars of secured loans through what is called the "repo market." State and municipal governments also finance part of their activities in this market.

The heart of the activity in the money market occurs in the trading rooms of dealers and brokers of money market instruments. During the time the market is open, these rooms are characterized by a frenzy of activity. Each trader or broker sits in front of a battery of direct phone lines linking him to other dealers, brokers, and customers. The phones never ring, they just blink at a pace that makes, especially in the brokers' market, for some of the shortest phone calls ever recorded. Despite the lack of ringing phones, a dealing room is anything but quiet. Dealers and brokers know only one way to hang up on a direct-line phone; they BANG the off button. And the more hectic things get, the harder they bang. Banging phones, like drums in a band, beat the rhythm of the noise generated in a trading room. Almost drowning that banging out at times is the constant shouting of quotes and tidbits of information.

Unless one spends a lot of time in trading rooms, it's hard to get a feel for what is going on amid all this hectic activity. Even listening in

on phones is not very enlightening. One learns quickly that dealers and brokers swear a lot (it's said to lessen the tension), but the rest of their conversations is unintelligible to the uninitiated. Money market people have their own jargon, and until one learns it, it is impossible to understand them.

Once adjusted to their jargon and the speed at which traders converse, one observes that they are making huge trades—$5, $50, $250 million—at the snap of a finger. Moreover, nobody seems to be particularly awed or even impressed by the size of the figures. A Fed funds broker asked to obtain $100 million in overnight money for a bank might—nonchalant about the size of the trade—reply, "The buck's yours from the B of A," slam down the phone, and take another call. Fed funds brokers earn only $1 per $1 million on overnight funds, so it takes a lot of trades to pay the overhead and let everyone in the shop make some money.

Despite its frenzied and incoherent appearance to the outsider, the money market efficiently accomplishes vital functions every day. One is shifting vast sums of money between banks. This shifting is required because major money market banks all need a lot more funds than they obtain in deposits, while many smaller banks have more money deposited with them than they can profitably use internally.

The money market also provides a means by which the surplus funds of cash-rich corporations and other institutions can be funneled to banks, corporations, and other institutions that need short-term money. In addition, in the money market the U.S. Treasury can fund huge quantities of debt with ease. And the market provides the Fed with an arena in which to carry out open market operations destined to influence interest rates and the growth of the money supply. The varied activities of money market participants also determine the structure of short-term interest rates, for example, what the yields on Treasury bills of different maturities are and how much commercial paper issuers have to pay to borrow. The latter rate is an important cost to many corporations, and it influences in particular the interest rate that a consumer who buys a car on time will have to pay on the loan. Finally, one might mention that the U.S. money market is increasingly becoming an international short-term capital market. In it, the oil imports of the nationalized French electric company, Electricite de France, as well as those of Japan—and a lot of other non–U.S. trade too—are financed.

Anyone who observes the money market soon picks out a number of salient features. First and most obvious, it is not *one* market but *a collection* of markets for several distinct and different instruments. What makes it possible to talk about *the* money market is the close interrelationships that link all these markets. A second salient feature is the

numerous and varied cast of participants. Borrowers in the market include foreign and domestic banks, the Treasury, corporations of all types, the Federal Home Loan Banks and other federal agencies, dealers in money market instruments, and many states and municipalities. The lenders include almost all of the above plus insurance companies, pension funds—public and private—and various other financial institutions. And often standing between borrower and lender is one or more of a varied collection of brokers and dealers.

Another important characteristic of the money market is that it is a *wholesale* market. Trades are big, and the people who make them are almost always dealing for the account of some substantial institution. Because of the sums involved, skill is of the utmost importance, and money market participants are skilled at what they do. In effect the market is made by extremely talented specialists in very narrow professional areas. A bill trader extraordinaire may have only vague notions as to what the Euromarket is all about, and the Euro specialist may be equally vague on other sectors of the market.

Another key characteristic of the money market is *honor*. Every day traders, brokers, investors, and borrowers do hundreds of billions of dollars of business over the phone, and however a trade may appear in retrospect, people do not renege. The motto of the money market is: *My word is my bond*. Of course, because of the pace of the market, mistakes do occur, but, typically, no one ever assumes that they are intentional, and they are ironed out in what seems the fairest way for all concerned.

They say exceptions prove the rule. A few bad-apple dealers have caused a number of too-trusting, money market investors to lose hundreds of millions of dollars. Perhaps, these dealers were able to do so not, principally, because the investors they defrauded were too naive, but rather because the market was too accustomed to operating in an atmosphere of honor and trust: my word is my bond.

The most appealing characteristic of the money market is innovation. Compared with our other financial markets, the money market is lightly regulated. If someone wants to launch a new instrument or to try brokering or dealing in a new way in existing instruments, he does it. And when the idea is good, which it often is, a new facet of the market is born.

CLEARING

In essence, clearing is a simple operation. A dealer buys and sells securities over the phone. To effect a buy, the dealer must accept delivery of the securities and pay out money; to effect a sell, the dealer must deliver out securities and accept money. A dealer could do these things for himself, and some dealers do, partially or totally, self-clear certain of their trades. However, in most instances, dealers do not want to get in-

volved in making and receiving what are likely to amount, over a month, to many thousands of deliveries and receipts of money and securities. Instead they hire a clearing bank to do all this receiving and delivering of money and securities for them. This being the case, a major function of a dealer's back office is to give to the dealer's clearing bank, each time the dealer does a trade, accurate instructions as to what money and securities the clearing bank must receive or deliver on the dealer's behalf to effect that trade.

On a buy by the dealer, the clearing bank is responsible for collecting the securities bought and for paying for these securities. On a sell by the dealer, the clearing bank is responsible for delivering the securities sold and collecting payment for them. For each trade a dealer does, the clearing bank either makes a payment out of or receives a payment into a *money account* that it maintains for the dealer. Simultaneously, it either accepts a delivery into or makes a delivery out of a *securities account* that it also maintains for the dealer. A dealer's money and securities accounts at its clearing bank together comprise its *clearing account*. Securities in a dealer's clearing account are referred to as its *box position*. This term dates from the days when all securities were in physical form, and a clearing bank literally stored a dealer's securities in a box in its vault.

That's clearing in a nutshell. While the essence of clearing can be explained in a few sentences, to explain, in detail, how dealers and investors who trade money market securities clear their trades requires many pages, all of Part Two.

STRUCTURE OF THE BOOK

The focus of this book is twofold. Part One introduces, briefly, certain money market fundamentals; Part Two describes the multifarious tasks involved in clearing the diverse collection of instruments traded in the money market. Specifically, Part One introduces the instruments of the money market; some simple notions about yields and prices; the dealers who make markets; and the brokers who talk a lot and broadcast pictures. The purpose of Part One is to introduce newcomers to some jargon and concepts they'll need in reading Part Two. Readers familiar with the money market should skip on to Part Two, which tells the story this book was written to tell.

An aside: This book is replete with examples of how this or that trade is done or cleared. In the examples involving trades between dealers, my pattern has been, perhaps all too often, to write, "Suppose that Sali does X, that Merrill does Y. . . ." Since there are 40 primary dealers, that may seem odd to the reader. My excuse—reason—is simply that the term *Sali* or *Merrill* is **"Street-speak,"** probably because both names fall off the

tongue so easily. Ask anyone in a clearing bank or elsewhere to explain how a certain trade is done or cleared, and 9 times out of 10, they will begin, "Suppose Sali does X, that Merrill does Y. . . ." This Street-speak is never intended by the people who use it to indicate that Merrill or Sali do a particular trade any more often or any differently than do the 38 other primary dealers, all of whom are top-notch firms.

A final note: Stock and corporate bond market people may find Chapter 16, which deals with the clearing of securities traded in their bailiwick, of special interest.

Part one

Some fundamentals

Chapter 2

The instruments
in brief

HERE'S A QUICK RUNDOWN of the major money market instruments. Don't look for subtleties; just enough is said to lay the groundwork for later chapters.

DEALERS AND BROKERS

The markets for all money market instruments are made in part by brokers and dealers. *Brokers* bring buyers and sellers together for a commission. By definition, brokers never position securities. Their function is to provide a communications network that links market participants who are often numerous and geographically dispersed. Most brokering in the money market occurs between banks that are buying funds from or selling funds to each other and between dealers in money market instruments.

Dealers make markets in money market instruments by quoting bid and asked prices to each other, to issuers, and to investors. Dealers buy and sell for their own accounts; thus, assuming positions—long and short—is an essential part of a dealer's operation.

U.S. TREASURY SECURITIES

To finance the U.S. national debt, the Treasury issues several types of securities. Some are nonnegotiable, for example, savings bonds sold to consumers and special issues sold to government trust funds. The bulk of the securities sold by the U.S. Treasury are, however, negotiable.

What form these securities take depends on their maturity. Those with a maturity at issue of a year or less are known as *Treasury bills, T bills* for short or just plain *bills*. T bills bear no interest. An investor in bills earns a return because bills are issued at a discount from face value and redeemed by the Treasury at maturity for face value. The amount of the discount at which investors buy bills and the length of time bills have to be held before they mature together imply some specific yield that the bill will return if held to maturity.

T bills are currently issued in 3-month, 6-month, and 1-year maturities.[1] In issuing bills, the Treasury does not set the amount of the discount. Instead, the Federal Reserve auctions off each new bill issue to investors and dealers, with the bills going to those bidders offering the highest price, that is, the lowest interest cost to the Treasury. By auctioning new bill issues, the Treasury lets currently prevailing market conditions establish the yield at which each new issue is sold.

The Treasury also issues interest-bearing *notes*. These securities are issued at or very near face value and redeemed at face value. Notes have an *original maturity* (maturity at issue) of 2 to 10 years.[2] Currently, the Treasury issues 2-, 3-, 4-, 5-, 7-, and 10-year notes on a regular cycle. Notes of other maturities are issued periodically depending on the Treasury's needs. Interest on Treasury notes is paid semiannually. Notes, like bills, are sold through auctions held by the Federal Reserve. In these auctions participants bid yields, and the securities offered are sold to those dealers and investors who bid the lowest yields, that is, the lowest interest cost to the Treasury. Thus, the coupon rate on new Treasury notes, like the yield on bills, is determined by the market. The last exception was a 1976 subscription offering in which the Treasury sold the famed 8s of 86.

In addition to notes, the Treasury issues interest-bearing negotiable *bonds* that have a maturity at issue of 10 years or more. The only difference between Treasury notes and bonds is that bonds are issued in longer maturities. In recent years the volume of bonds the Treasury can

---

[1] For tactical debt management purposes, the Treasury occasionally meets cash flow gaps by issuing very short-term "cash management bills."

[2] A 5-year note has an *original maturity* at issue of 5 years. One year after issue it has a *current maturity* of 4 years.

issue has been limited because Congress has imposed a 4.25% ceiling on the rate the Treasury may pay on bonds. Since this rate has for years been far below prevailing market rates, the Treasury is able to sell bonds only to the extent that Congress authorizes it to issue bonds exempt from the ceiling; the current exemption, which has been successively raised, is $250 billion. Treasury bonds, like notes, are normally sold at yield auctions.

Banks, other financial institutions, insurance companies, pension funds, and corporations are all important investors in U.S. Treasury securities. So, too, are some foreign central banks and other foreign institutions. The market for government securities is largely a wholesale market, and especially at the short end, multimillion-dollar transactions are common. However, when interest rates get extremely high, as they did in 1974 and again in 1978–1982, individuals with small amounts to invest are drawn into the market.

Because of the high volume of Treasury debt outstanding, the market for bills and short-term government securities is the most active and most carefully watched sector of the money market. At the heart of this market stands a varied collection of dealers who make the market for *governments* (market jargon for government securities) by standing ready to buy and sell huge volumes of these securities. These dealers trade actively not only with investors but with each other. Most trades of the latter sort are carried out through brokers.

Governments offer investors several advantages. First, because they are constantly traded in the *secondary market* in large volume and at narrow spreads between the bid and asked prices, they are highly *liquid.* Second, governments are considered to be free from credit risk because it is inconceivable that the government would default on these securities in any situation short of destruction of the country. Third, interest income on governments is exempt from state taxation. Because of these advantages, governments normally trade at yields below those of other money market instruments.

Generally, yields on governments are higher the longer their *current maturity,* that is, time left to maturity. The reason, explained in Chapters 3 and 4, is that the longer the current maturity of a debt security, the more its price will fluctuate in response to changes in interest rates and therefore the greater the *price risk* to which it exposes the investor. There are times, however, when the yield curve *inverts,* that is, yields on short-term securities rise above those on long-term securities. This, for example, was the case during much of the period 1979–81. The reason for an inverted yield curve is that market participants anticipate, correctly or incorrectly, that interest rates will fall. As a result, borrowers choose to

borrow short-term while investors seek out long-term securities; the result is that supply and demand force short-term rates above long-term rates.

The 30-year bill, alias strip

Recently, the Treasury has permitted the creation, out of standard T bonds, of what amount to T bills with distant maturities. Here's the story.

The Treasury once issued, upon request, notes and bonds in bearer form. Some dealers came up with the idea of *stripping*—clipping off coupons from—bearer bonds and selling, at discounted prices, the resulting pieces. Each such piece was *a non-interest-bearing security with a fixed maturity and a fixed value at maturity.* Such securities are known generically as *zero-coupon securities* or simply as *zeros.*

Dealers could make money stripping bearer Treasuries because demand for the pieces was so great that the sum of the values of the pieces exceeded the value of the whole bond. Unfortunately, the Treasury and the Fed opposed, for various reasons (including possibilities for tax evasion), the stripping of bearer Treasuries.

To satisfy investors' desire for long-term zeros, Merrill got a bright idea: It bought Treasuries, placed them with a custodian in a special trust, and then sold to investors participations in its trust. Under the Merrill scheme, each such participation sold was a *zero-coupon security,* backed by unstripped Treasuries. Merrill named its product TIGRS. Soon, every other major dealer was offering its addition to the zoo. Sali sold CATS; Lehman, LIONS; and so on. Also, some dealers sold plain vanilla TRs (trust receipts).

The new "zoo" zeros sold extremely well to institutional investors and even to individuals. The Treasury, eyeing this, said, "There's money to be made in stripping, let *us* earn it." So in 1985, the Treasury introduced, for certain new T bond issues, an additional feature: Any owner of such a bond, Merrill, a small dealer, or even an individual, can ask the Treasury to cut that bond into pieces, provided it is in book-entry (electronic-record-keeping) form. Each such piece corresponds to a different payment due on the bond, and each carries its own CUSIP (ID) number.[3] On a 30-year bond, there are 61 such payments: 60 semiannual interest payments and 1 payment of *corpus* (principal) at maturity. Stripped Treasuries created in the manner we've just described were dubbed *STRIPS.*

Today on Wall Street, STRIPS are a popular item, actively traded by the same dealers who make markets in regular Treasury notes, bonds, and bills.

---

[3]The terms *CUSIP number* and *book-entry* are precisely defined in Chapter 8.

Internationalization of the market for Treasuries

A decade ago, when one spoke of *the* market for Treasuries, one was referring to a market that was almost exclusively domestic. The borrower, of course, was domestic and so too were most of the investors, except for a few foreign central banks. Today, that situation has changed dramatically. Foreigners, and most importantly Japanese investors, have become big buyers of Treasury securities.

Not surprisingly, there are now active markets for Treasuries in Tokyo, London, and, to a lesser extent, certain other foreign financial centers. Today, reflecting in part the fact that foreigners currently own approximately 16% of all outstanding marketable Treasuries, the market for these securities has in truth become a 24-hour, international market.

The dealers who make this round-the-globe market are of two sorts: big American dealers, such as Merrill and Sali, who have opened offices in major financial centers around the globe, and foreign dealers, particularly Japanese dealers, who have opened offices in the U.S. and become big factors in the domestic trading of Treasury securities.

FINANCIAL FUTURES AND OPTIONS MARKETS

In discussing the market for governments, we have focused on the *cash market,* that is, the market in which existing securities are traded for same- or next-day delivery. In addition, there are markets in which Treasury bills, Treasury notes, Treasury bonds, bank CDs, and other money market instruments are traded for *future* delivery. The futures contracts in Treasuries that are most actively traded are for 3-month bills with a face value of $1 million at maturity and for notes and long bonds with a par value of $100,000.

Interest rate futures markets offer institutions that know they are going to borrow or lend in the future a way to *hedge* that future position, that is, to lock in a reasonably fixed borrowing or lending rate. They also provide speculators with a way to bet money on interest rate movements that provides greater leverage—bang for the buck—than going short or long in cash securities.

Since being introduced in 1976, futures markets for financial instruments have grown at an unforeseen and astonishing rate. In fact, futures contracts for Treasury bills and bonds have been among the most successful contracts ever launched on commodities exchanges. Their success has led to the introduction of trading of like contracts on a number of commodity exchanges in foreign financial centers.

The rapid growth and internationalization of markets for financial futures has, not surprisingly, created situations in which the relationship between the rates on different futures contracts or between the rates on a futures contract and the corresponding cash instrument get, as the Street would say, "out of sync," that is, out of synchronization or line. Thus, yet another major class of traders in financial futures has been arbitrageurs who seek to establish positions from which they will profit when a reasonable relationship between the out-of-line rates is inevitably reestablished.

Another recent innovation in the money market is the introduction of trading in *options,* rights to buy or to sell at a fixed price over a preset period, certain money market securities and futures contracts for such securities. Options, like futures, are actively traded by hedgers, speculators, and arbitrageurs.

FEDERAL AGENCY SECURITIES

From time to time Congress becomes concerned about the volume of credit that is available to various sectors of the economy and the terms on which that credit is available. Congress's usual response is to set up a federal agency to provide credit to that sector. Thus there are the Federal Home Loan Bank System, which lends to the nation's savings and loan associations as well as regulates them; the Government National Mortgage Association, which funnels money into the mortgage market; Banks for Cooperatives, which make seasonal and term loans to farm cooperatives; Federal Land Banks, which give mortgages on farm properties; Federal Intermediate Credit Banks, which provide short-term financing for producers of crops and livestock; and a host of other agencies.

Initially, all the federal agencies financed their activities by selling their own securities in the open market. Today, all except the largest borrow from the Treasury through an institution called the Federal Financing Bank. Those agencies still borrowing in the open market do so primarily by issuing notes and bonds. These securities (known in the market as *agencies*) bear interest, and they are issued and redeemed at face value. Instead of using the auction technique for issuing their securities, federal agencies look to the market to determine the best yield at which they can sell a new issue, put that yield on the issue, and then sell it through a syndicate of dealers. Some agencies also sell short-term discount paper that resembles commercial paper (see below).

Normally, agencies yield slightly more than Treasury securities of the same maturity for several reasons. First, agency issues are smaller than Treasury issues and are therefore less liquid. Second, while all agency issues have *de facto* backing from the federal government (it's inconceivable that the government would let one of them default on its obligations), the securities of only a few agencies are explicitly backed

by the full faith and credit of the U.S. government. Third, interest income on some federal agency issues is subject to state taxation.

The market for agencies, while smaller than that for governments, has, in recent years, become an active and important sector of the money market. Agencies are traded by the same dealers that trade governments and in much the same way.

FEDERAL FUNDS

All banks and other *depository institutions* (savings and loan associations, savings banks, credit unions, foreign bank branches, and so on) are required to keep reserves on deposit at their district Federal Reserve Bank.[4] The reserve account of a depository institution (*DI* for short) is much like an individual's checking account; the DI makes deposits into its reserve account and can transfer funds out of it. The main difference is that, while an individual can let the balance in his checking account run to zero and stay there, each DI is required by law to maintain some *minimum* average balance in its reserve account over the week—Wednesday to Wednesday. Under *contemporaneous reserve accounting,* introduced by the Fed in February 1984, that minimum average balance is based on the total deposits of various types held by the DI during the current settlement week.

The category of DIs that holds by far the largest chunk of the total reserves that all DIs together maintain at Federal Reserve Banks is commercial banks. Funds on deposit in a bank's reserve account are referred to as *Federal funds* or *Fed funds.* Any deposits a bank receives add to its supply of Fed funds, while loans made and securities purchased reduce that supply. Thus, the basic amount of money any bank can lend out and otherwise invest equals the amount of funds it has received from depositors minus the reserves it is required to maintain.

For some banks, this supply of available funds roughly equals the amount they choose to invest in securities plus that demanded from them by borrowers. But for most banks it does not. Specifically, because the nation's largest corporations tend to concentrate their borrowing in big money market banks in New York and other financial centers, the loans and investments these banks must fund exceed the deposits they receive. Many smaller banks, in contrast, receive more money from local depositors than they can lend locally or choose to invest otherwise. Because large banks have to meet their reserve requirements regardless

---

[4]The Federal Reserve System, which comprises 12 district Federal Reserve Banks, is the United States's central bank, and as such it is responsible for the implementation of domestic monetary policy. [See Marcia Stigum, *The Money Market,* 2nd ed. (Homewood, III.: Dow Jones-Irwin, 1983), chap. 8, "The Fed."] Prior to passage of the Monetary Control Act of 1980, only *member banks* in the Federal Reserve System were required to hold reserves at the Fed.

of what loan demand they face and because excess reserves yield no return to smaller banks, it was natural for large banks to begin borrowing the excess funds held by smaller banks.

This borrowing is done in the *Federal funds market*. Most Fed funds loans are overnight transactions. One reason is that the amount of excess funds a given lending bank holds varies daily and unpredictably. Some transactions in Fed funds are made directly, others through New York brokers. Despite the fact that transactions of this sort are all loans, the lending of Fed funds is referred to as a *sale* and the borrowing of Fed funds as a *purchase*. While overnight transactions dominate the Fed funds market, transactions for longer periods also occur there. Fed funds traded for periods other than overnight are referred to as *term* Fed funds.

DIs other than domestic commercial banks also participate in the Fed Funds market. Foreign banks are particularly active buyers and sellers of funds.

The rate of interest paid on overnight loans of Federal funds, which is called the *Fed funds rate,* is a key interest rate in the money market; all other short-term rates relate to the funds rate. This rate used to be closely pegged by the Fed, but starting in October 1979, the Fed allowed the Fed funds rate to fluctuate over a wide band.

EURODOLLARS

Many foreign banks will accept deposits of dollars and grant the depositor an account *denominated in dollars*. So, too, will the foreign branches of U.S. banks. The practice of accepting dollar-denominated deposits outside of the United States began in Europe, so such deposits came to be known as *Eurodollars*. The practice of accepting dollar-denominated deposits later spread to Hong Kong, Singapore, the Mideast, and other centers around the globe. Consequently today a *Eurodollar deposit is simply a deposit denominated in dollars in a bank or bank branch outside the United States,* and the term *Eurodollar* has become a misnomer. To make things even more confusing, in December 1981, domestic and foreign banks were permitted to open *international banking facilities (IBFs)* in the United States. Dollars deposited in IBFs are also Eurodollars.

Most Eurodollar deposits are for large sums. They are made by corporations—foreign, multinational, and domestic; foreign central banks and other official institutions; U.S. domestic banks; and wealthy individuals. With the exception of *call money*,[5] all Eurodeposits have a fixed

---

[5] Call money is money deposited in an interest-bearing account that can be called (withdrawn) by the depositor on a day's notice.

term, which can range from overnight to 5 years. The bulk of Euro transactions are in the range of 6 months and under. Banks receiving
Eurodollar deposits use them to make loans denominated in dollars to
foreign and domestic corporations, foreign governments and government
agencies, domestic U.S. banks, and other large borrowers.

Banks that participate in the Eurodollar market actively borrow and
lend Euros among themselves, just as domestic banks borrow and lend
in the Fed funds market. The major difference between the two markets
is that in the market for Fed funds, most transactions are on an overnight basis, whereas in the Euromarket, interbank placements (deposits)
of funds for longer periods are common.

For a domestic U.S. bank with a reserve deficiency, borrowing
Eurodollars is an alternative to purchasing Fed funds. Also, for a domestic
bank with excess funds, a *Europlacement* (i.e., a deposit of dollars in the
Euromarket) is an alternative to the sale of Fed funds. Consequently, the
rate on overnight Euros tends to closely track the Fed funds rate. It is
also true that, as one goes out on the maturity scale, Euro rates continue to track U.S. rates, though not so closely as in the overnight market.

Currently, futures for 3-month Eurodollar deposits are actively traded
in Chicago and abroad as well.

CERTIFICATES OF DEPOSIT

The maximum rate banks may pay on savings deposits and time
deposits (a time deposit is a deposit with a fixed maturity) used to be
set by the Fed through *Regulation Q.* Essentially, what Reg Q did was
to make it impossible for banks and other depository institutions (who
were each subject to their own versions of Reg Q) to compete with each
other for small deposits by offering depositors higher interest rates.[6] One
exception to Reg Q was that, on large deposits, $100,000 or more, banks
used to be able to pay any rate they chose so long as the deposit had
a minimum maturity of 14 days. This exception led, so to speak, to the
invention in 1961 of negotiable certificates of deposit.

There are many corporations and other large investors that have hundreds of thousands, even millions, of dollars they could invest in bank
time deposits. Few do so, however, because they lose liquidity by making a deposit with a fixed maturity. The illiquidity of time deposits and
their consequent lack of appeal to investors led banks, who were free

---

[6]The rates banks and thrifts may pay depositors were gradually deregulated under the
Monetary Control Act (MCA) of 1980. Also the Banking Act of 1982 permitted depository
institutions to begin offering unregulated rates on super-NOW and money market deposit
accounts.

to bid high rates for large deposits, to begin to offer big investors *negotiable certificate of deposit,* or *CD* for short.

CDs are normally sold in $1 million units. They are issued at face value and typically pay interest at maturity. CDs can have any maturity longer than 14 days, and some 5- and even 7-year CDs have been sold (these pay interest semiannually). Most CDs, however, have an *original maturity* of 1 to 6 months.

The quantity of CDs that banks have outstanding depends largely on the strength of loan demand. When demand rises, banks issue more CDs to fund the additional loans they are making. The rates banks offer on CDs depend on the maturity of the paper they write, on how badly the banks want to write new CDs, and on the general level of short-term interest rates.

Most bank CDs are sold directly by banks to investors. Some, however, are issued through dealers for a small commission. The same dealers make an active secondary market in CDs.

Yields on CDs exceed those on bills of similar maturities by varying spreads. One reason for the higher yield on CDs is that buying a bank CD exposes the investor to some credit risk—would he be paid off if the issuing bank failed? A second reason CDs yield more than bills is that they are less liquid.

A futures market for 3-month CDs was started in Chicago. For various reasons, including differences in the credit ratings of the top banks whose paper could be delivered by sellers of the contract, the CD contract proved unsuccessful.

Eurodollar CDs

A Eurodollar time deposit, like a domestic time deposit, is an illiquid asset. Since some investors in Eurodollars wanted liquidity, banks in London that accepted such deposits began to issue *Eurodollar CDs.* These resemble domestic CDs except that, instead of being the liability of a domestic bank, they are the liability of the London branch of a U.S. bank, of a British bank, or of some other foreign bank with a branch in London.

Many of the Eurodollar CDs issued in London are purchased by other banks operating in the Euromarket. A large proportion of the remainder are sold to U.S. corporations and other U.S. institutional investors. Many Euro CDs are issued through dealers and brokers who also make a secondary market in these securities.

The Euro CD market is younger and smaller than the market for domestic CDs, but it has grown rapidly since its inception. For the investor, a key advantage of buying Euro CDs is that they offer a higher return than do domestic CDs. The offsetting disadvantages are that they

are less liquid and expose the investor to some extra risk because they are issued outside of the United States.

The most recent development in the Eurodollar CD market is that some large banks have begun offering such CDs through their Caribbean branches. Note that a CD issued, for example, in Nassau is technically a Euro CD because the deposit is held in a bank branch outside the United States.

Yankee CDs

Foreign banks issue dollar-denominated CDs not only in the Euromarket but also in the domestic market through branches established there. CDs of the latter sort are frequently referred to as *Yankee CDs;* the name is taken from Yankee bonds, which are bonds issued in the domestic market by foreign borrowers.

Yankee, as opposed to domestic, CDs expose the investor to the extra (if only in perception) risk of a foreign name; they are also less liquid than domestic CDs. Consequently, Yankees trade at yields close to those on Euro CDs. The major buyers of Yankee CDs are corporations that are yield buyers and that "fund to dates" (that is, invest in short-term securities maturing on the date funds will be needed).

COMMERCIAL PAPER

While some cash-rich industrial firms participate in the bond and money markets only as lenders, many more must, at times, borrow to finance either current operations or expenditures on plant and equipment. One source of short-term funds available to a corporation is bank loans. Large firms with good credit ratings, however, have an alternative source of funds that is cheaper, namely, the sale of commercial paper.

Commercial paper is an unsecured promissory note issued for a specific amount and maturing on a specific day. All commercial paper is negotiable, but most paper sold to investors is held by them to maturity. Commercial paper is issued not only by industrial and manufacturing firms but also by finance companies. Finance companies normally sell their paper directly to investors. Industrial firms, in contrast, typically issue their paper through dealers. Recently foreign bank holding companies, municipalities, and municipal authorities have joined the ranks of commercial paper issuers.

The maximum maturity for which commercial paper may be sold is 270 days, since paper with a longer maturity must be registered with the Securities and Exchange Commission (SEC), a time-consuming and costly procedure. In practice, very little 270-day paper is sold. Most paper sold is in the range of 30 days and under.

Since commercial paper has such short maturities, the issuer rarely will have sufficient funds coming in before the paper matures to pay off his borrowing. Instead, he expects to *roll* his paper, that is, sell new paper to obtain funds to pay off his maturing paper. Naturally the possibility exists that some sudden change in market conditions, such as when the Penn Central went "belly up" (bankrupt), might make it difficult or impossible for him to sell paper for some time. To guard against this risk, commercial paper issuers back all or a large proportion of their outstanding paper with lines of credit from banks.

The rate offered on commercial paper depends on its maturity, on how much the issuer wants to borrow, on the general level of money market rates, and on the credit rating of the issuer. Almost all commercial paper is rated with respect to credit risk by one or more of several rating services: Moody's, Standard & Poor's, and Fitch. While only top-grade credits can get ratings good enough to sell paper these days, there is still a slight risk that an issuer might go bankrupt. Because of this, and because of illiquidity, yields on commercial paper are higher than those on Treasury obligations of similar maturity.

BANKERS' ACCEPTANCES

Bankers' acceptances (BAs) are an unknown instrument outside the confines of the money market. Moreover, explaining them isn't easy because they arise in a variety of ways out of a variety of transactions. The best approach is to use an example.

Suppose a U.S. importer wants to buy shoes in Brazil and pay for them four months later after he has had time to sell them in the United States. One approach would be for the importer to borrow from his bank; however, short-term rates may be lower in the open market. If they are, and if the importer is too small to go into the open market on his own, then he can go the bankers' acceptance route.

In that case, he has his bank write a letter of credit for the amount of the sale and sends this letter to the Brazilian exporter. Upon export of the shoes, the Brazilian firm, using this letter of credit, draws a time draft on the importer's U.S. bank and discounts this draft at its local bank, thereby obtaining immediate payment for its goods. The Brazilian bank, in turn, sends the time draft to the importer's U.S. bank, which then stamps "accepted" on the draft (that is, the bank guarantees payment on the draft and thereby creates an *acceptance*). Once this is done, the draft becomes an irrevocable primary obligation of the accepting bank. At this point, if the Brazilian bank did not want cash immediately, the U.S. bank would return the draft to that bank, which would hold it as an investment and then present it to the U.S. bank for payment at maturity. If, on the other hand, the Brazilian bank wanted cash immediately, the

U.S. bank would pay it and then either hold the acceptance itself or sell it to an investor. Regardless of who ends up holding the acceptance, it is the importer's responsibility to provide its U.S. bank with sufficient funds to pay off the acceptance at maturity. If the importer fails to do so, the bank is still responsible for making payment at maturity.

Our example illustrates how an acceptance can arise out of a U.S. import transaction. Acceptances also arise in connection with U.S. export sales, trade between third countries (e.g., Japanese imports of oil from the Mid East), the domestic shipment of goods, and domestic or foreign storage of readily marketable staples. Currently, most BAs arise out of foreign trade; they may be in manufactured goods but more typically are in bulk commodities, such as cocoa, cotton, coffee, and crude oil. Because of the complex nature of acceptance operations, only large banks that have well-staffed foreign departments act as accepting banks.

Bankers' acceptances closely resemble commercial paper in form. They are short-term, non-interest-bearing notes sold at a discount and redeemed by the accepting bank at maturity for full face value. The major difference is that payment on commercial paper is guaranteed only by the issuing company. In contrast, bankers' acceptances, in addition to carrying the issuer's pledge to pay, are backed by the underlying goods being financed and also carry the guarantee of the accepting bank. Consequently, bankers' acceptances are less risky than commercial paper and thus sell at slightly lower yields.

The big banks through which bankers' acceptances are originated generally keep some portion of the acceptances they create as investments. The rest are sold to investors through dealers or directly by the bank itself. Major investors in BAs are other banks, foreign central banks, money market funds, corporations, and other domestic and foreign institutional investors. BAs have liquidity because dealers in these securities make an active secondary market in those that are eligible for purchase by the Fed.

REPOS AND REVERSES

A variety of bank and nonbank dealers act as market makers in governments, agencies, CDs, and BAs. Because dealers, by definition, buy and sell for their own accounts, active dealers inevitably end up holding some securities. They will, moreover, buy and hold substantial positions if they believe that interest rates are likely to fall and that the value of these securities is therefore likely to rise. Speculation and risk taking are an inherent and important part of being a dealer.

While dealers have large amounts of capital, the positions they take are often several hundred times that amount. As a result, dealers have to borrow to finance their positions. Using the securities they own as

collateral, they can and do borrow from banks at the dealer loan rate. For the bulk of their financing, however, they resort to a cheaper alternative, entering into *repurchase agreements* (*RPs or repos,* for short) with investors.

Much RP financing done by dealers is on an overnight basis. It works as follows: The dealer finds a corporation, money fund, or other investor who has funds to invest overnight. He sells this investor, say, $10 million of securities for roughly $10 million, which is paid in Federal funds to his bank by the investor's bank against delivery of the securities sold. At the same time, the dealer agrees to repurchase these securities the next day at a slightly higher price. Thus, the buyer of the securities is in effect making the dealer a one-day loan secured by the obligations sold to him. The difference between the purchase and sale prices on the RP transaction is the interest the investor earns on his loan. Alternatively, the purchase and sale prices in an RP transaction may be identical; in that case, the dealer pays the investor some explicit rate of interest.

Often a dealer will take a speculative position that he intends to hold for some time. He might then do an RP for 30 days or longer. Such agreements are known as *term* RPs.

From the point of view of investors, overnight loans in the RP market offer several attractive features. First, by rolling overnight RPs, investors can keep surplus funds invested without losing liquidity or incurring a price risk. Second, because RP transactions are secured by top-quality paper, investors expose themselves to little or no credit risk.

The overnight RP rate generally is less than the Fed funds rate. The reason is that the many nonbank investors who have funds to invest overnight or very short term and who do not want to incur any price risk, have nowhere to go but the RP market because (with the exception of S&Ls) they cannot participate directly in the Fed funds market. Also, lending money through an RP transaction is safer than selling Fed funds because a sale of Fed funds is an unsecured loan.

On term, as opposed to overnight, RP transactions, investors still have the advantage of their loans being secured, but they do lose some liquidity. To compensate for that, the rate on an RP transaction is generally higher the longer the term for which funds are lent.

Banks that make dealer loans fund them by buying Fed funds, and the lending rate they charge—which is adjusted daily—is the prevailing Fed funds rate plus a one-eighth to one-quarter markup. Because the overnight RP rate is lower than the Fed funds rate, dealers can finance their positions more cheaply by doing RP than by borrowing from banks.

A dealer who is bullish on the market will position large amounts of securities. If he's bearish, he will *short* the market, that is, sell securities he does not own. Since the dealer has to deliver any securities he sells

whether he owns them or not, a dealer who shorts has to borrow securities one way or another. The most common technique today for borrowing securities is to do what is called a *reverse RP,* or simply a *reverse.* To obtain securities through a reverse, a dealer finds an investor holding the required securities; he then buys these securities from the investor under an agreement that he will resell the same securities to the investor at a fixed price on some future date. In this transaction, the dealer, besides obtaining securities, is extending a loan to the investor for which he is paid some rate of interest.

An RP and a reverse are identical transactions. What a given transaction is called depends on who initiates it; typically, if a dealer hunting money does, it's an RP; if a dealer hunting securities does, it's a reverse.

A final note: The Fed uses reverses and RPs with dealers in government securities to adjust the level of bank reserves.

MUNICIPAL NOTES

Debt securities issued by state and local governments and their authorities are referred to as *municipal securities.* Such securities can be divided into two broad categories: bonds issued to finance capital projects and short-term notes sold in anticipation of the receipt of other funds, such as taxes or proceeds from a bond issue.

Municipal notes, which are an important money market instrument, are issued with maturities ranging from a month to a year or more. They bear interest, and minimum denominations are highly variable ranging anywhere from $5,000 to $5 million.

Most muni notes are general obligation securities; that is, payment of principal and interest is secured by the issuer's pledge of its full faith, credit, and taxing power. This sounds impressive, but as the spectacle of New York City tottering on the brink of bankruptcy brought home to all, it is possible that a municipality might default on its securities. Thus, the investors in evaluating the credit risk associated with publicly offered muni notes rely on ratings provided principally by Moody's and by Standard & Poor's.

The major attraction of municipal notes to an investor is that interest income on them is exempt or at least partially exempt from federal taxation and usually also from any income taxes levied within the state in which they are issued. The value of this tax exemption is greater the higher the investor's tax bracket, and the muni market thus attracts relatively highly taxed investors—commercial banks, cash-rich corporations, and wealthy individuals.

Large muni note issues are sold to investors by dealers who obtain the securities either through negotiation with the issuer or through com-

petitive bidding. The same dealers also make a secondary market in muni notes.

The yield a municipality must pay to issue notes depends on its credit rating, the length of time for which it borrows, and the general level of short-term rates. It used to be that a good credit risk could normally borrow at a rate well below the yield on governments of equivalent maturity because of the value to the investor of the tax exemption on municipal securities. Currently, numerous complex changes and proposed changes in the federal tax code have lessened the value of the tax exemption attached to municipal securities. As a result, muni securities have, at times, actually traded at rates above Treasuries, which is precisely where they would trade were it not for the tax advantages they offer. Because of the ever-changing federal tax code and the consequent changing nature of the spread of Treasury to muni yields, some municipal bodies have begun, in recent times, to issue fully taxable securities and even to tap the Euromarket for money. Today, the muni market is an innovative place, and some muni issuers have even experimented with issuing zero-coupon securities.

MORTGAGE-BACKED, PASS-THROUGH SECURITIES

Mortgage-backed, pass-through securities are a hybrid debt instrument, one that has correctly been called the most complex security ever traded on Wall Street. Strictly speaking, pass-throughs are not a money market instrument, since their average life, a variable number at best, exceeds by far that of true money market instruments. Nonetheless, because pass-throughs are so actively traded, we introduce such securities here and describe in Chapter 18 how trades in them are cleared.

The securities

Total residential mortgage debt outstanding is roughly one and a half trillion dollars, a sum far greater than total Treasury and federal agency debt outstanding. About a fifth of total residential mortgage debt has been used to back various types of negotiable securities, which in turn have been sold to investors. Of the more than $300 billion of mortgage-backed securities outstanding, all but about $20 billion are pass-throughs.

Pass-through securities are formed when mortgages are pooled and undivided interests in the pool are sold. *Pass-through* means that the cash flow from the underlying mortgages is *passed through* to the holders of the securities via *monthly payments of interest and principal*. *Undivided* means that each security holder has a proportionate interest in each cash flow generated by the pool. Payments of principal on a pass-

through include *prepayments;* the latter occur when a mortgage holder prepays the remaining principal on his mortgage because he moves, refinances his mortgage, or less commonly, dies.

Pass-throughs have existed for decades, but they first made sense on a broad scale when several federal credit agencies began to provide credit guarantees and standards of uniformity for pass-throughs issued through them. This made pools of mortgages underlying pass-throughs readily marketable; in particular, the standardization of mortgage characteristics within pools made the resulting securities easier to analyze and, thus, more suitable for nontraditional mortgage investors. Also, the credit guarantee by a federal agency lessened investor concerns about collection of amounts due.

Mortgage originators such as savings and loans, commercial banks, and mortgage companies are active in pooling mortgages to back pass-throughs. An originator can either issue a private pass-through or file the necessary documents with a guarantor to issue a pass-through backed by the latter. The sale of a pass-through security represents a sale of assets; thus a pass-through is not a debt obligation of the originator.

The issuers

Pass-throughs come in four flavors: there are Ginnie Mae, Freddie Mac, and Fanny Mae pass-throughs issued by federal or quasi-federal credit agencies; also, there are private pass-throughs. All pass-throughs are structured similarly, but differences exist among the four types with respect to the nature of the credit guarantee, if any; the size of the pools used; and the nature of the underlying mortgages. Because of these, different types of pass-throughs trade at varying spreads to each other.

Ginnie Mae pass-throughs are guaranteed by the *Government National Mortgage Association (GNMA),* known to the Street as Ginnie Mae. The mortgage pools underlying GNMA pass-throughs are made up of mortgages that are either insured by the Federal Housing Administration (FHA) or guaranteed by the Veterans Administration (VA). GNMA pass-throughs are backed by the full faith and credit of the U.S. government. Pass-throughs issued by GNMA are fully modified: regardless of whether mortgage payments are received, the holders of GNMAs receive full and timely payment of principal and interest due them.

The *Federal Home Loan Mortgage Corporation (FHLMC),* created by the Federal Home Loan Banks, also issues pass-throughs. These pass-throughs, the second largest class of pass-throughs, have been dubbed *Freddie Macs.* Freddie Macs are based on *conventional mortgages:* single-family residential mortgages that are neither guaranteed by the VA nor insured by the FHA. Whereas GNMA and FNMA (discussed next)

guarantee the timely payment of interest and principal, FHLMC guarantees only the timely payment of interest and the ultimate payment (within a year) of principal. Because of the difference in guarantee, Freddie Macs trade at a spread above Ginnie Maes.

A third type of pass-through, *Fannie Maes,* is issued by the *Federal National Mortgage Association (FNMA).* Fannie Maes are similar to Freddie Macs except that they carry a guarantee like the one on GNMAs.

The fourth type of pass-through security is private pass-throughs. In terms of volume outstanding, this type pass-through is the least important of the four types discussed.

Pass-throughs are based on mortgages with a 30-year life, but due to prepayments, they have, in normal times, if such exist, an expected life of only 12 years. Prepayments rates on pass-throughs vary with the level of mortgage rates. In years when mortgage rates are high, people chose not to move or to refinance, which cuts prepayment rates sharply. In contrast, low mortgage rates in 1986 brought forth a flood of refinancings of existing high-rate mortgages. The resulting high rate of prepayment on some high-coupon Ginnies caused these securities to be viewed and traded as odd-ball, short-term (2-year in some cases) Treasuries.

Pass-throughs are attractive to investors; they carry little or no credit risk but yield more than Treasuries of approximately similar maturity. Pass-throughs are bought by banks, savings and loan associations, GNMA mutual funds, and a range of other investors.

THE NEXT CHAPTER

In the next chapter, we discuss, with a little simple math, non-interest-bearing IOUs, T bills and other short-term paper, which the Street refers to as discount securities or *discount paper.*

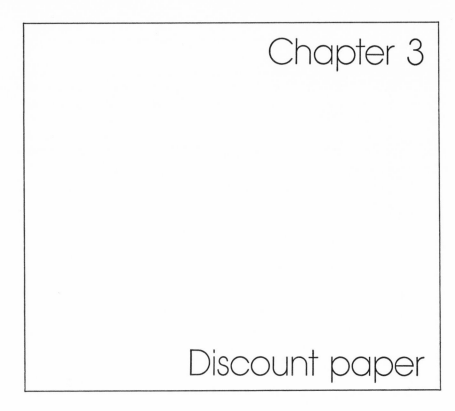

Chapter 3

Discount paper

THE MONEY MARKET DEALS IN TWO TYPES of instruments, *interest-bearing securities* and *discount paper*. Yields on these two types of instruments are calculated and quoted in quite different ways. Thus, a discussion of the clearing of money market securities should be prefaced by some simple math that shows how yields and prices on these different instruments are calculated. We start with discount securities.[1]

TREASURY BILLS

To illustrate how a discount security works, we assume that an investor who participates in an auction of new Treasury *year bills* picks up $1 million of them at 10%. What this means is that the Treasury sells the investor $1 million of bills maturing in one year at a price approximately 10% below their face value. The "approximately" qualifier takes a little explaining. Offhand one would expect the amount of the discount to be the face value of the securities purchased times the rate of discount times the *fraction of the year* the securities will be outstanding. In our

---

[1]For a complete description, see Marcia Stigum in collaboration with John Mann, *Money Market Calculations: Yields, Break-Evens, and Arbitrage* (Homewood, III.: Dow Jones-Irwin, 1981).

example, the discount calculated this way would equal $1 million times 10% times one full year, which amounts to $100,000. That figure, however, is incorrect for two reasons. First, the year bill is outstanding not for a year but for 52 weeks, which is 364 days. Second, the Treasury calculates the discount as if a year had only 360 days. So the fraction of the year for which the security is outstanding is 364/360, and the true discount on the security is:

$$\left(\begin{array}{l}\text{Discount on \$1 million of}\\ \text{year bills issued at 10\%}\end{array}\right) \begin{array}{l}= \$1{,}000{,}000 \times 0.10 \times \dfrac{364}{360}\\[2mm] = \$101{,}111.11\end{array}$$

Because the Treasury calculates the discount as if the year had 360 days, our investor gets his bills at a discount that exceeds $100,000 even though he invests for only 364 days. The price he pays for his bills equals *face value minus the discount*, that is,

$$\left(\begin{array}{l}\text{Price paid for \$1 million of}\\ \text{year bills bought at 10\%}\end{array}\right) \begin{array}{l}= \$1{,}000{,}000 - \$101{,}111.11\\[2mm] = \$898{,}888.89\end{array}$$

Generalizing from this example, we can construct formulas for calculating both the discount from face value and the price at which T bills will sell, depending on their current maturity and the discount at which they are quoted. Let

$$D = \text{Discount from face value}$$
$$F = \text{Face value}$$
$$d = \text{Rate of discount}$$
$$t = \text{Days to maturity}$$
$$P = \text{Price}$$

Then

$$D = F\left(\frac{d \times t}{360}\right)$$

and

$$P = F - D = F\left(1 - \frac{d \times t}{360}\right)$$

EQUIVALENT BOND YIELD

If an investor lent $1 million for one 365-day year and received at the end of the year $100,000 of interest plus the $1 million of principal invested, we would—calculating yield on a *simple interest basis*—say that he had earned 10%.[2] Using the same approach—return earned divided

---

[2] By *simple interest* we mean interest paid once a year at the end of the year. There is no compounding as, for example, on a savings account.

by principal invested—to calculate the return earned by our investor who bought a 10% year bill, we find that, on a simple interest basis, he earned significantly *more than* 10%. Specifically,

$$\left(\begin{array}{c}\text{Return on a simple interest basis on}\\ \text{\$1 million 10\% year bills held to maturity}\end{array}\right) = \frac{\$101,000.11}{\$898,888.89} \div \frac{364}{365}$$

$$= 11.28\%$$

In this calculation, because the bill matures in 364 days, it is necessary to divide by the fraction of the year for which the bill is outstanding to annualize the rate earned.

Treasury notes and bonds, which—unlike bills—are *interest bearing,* pay the holder interest equal to the face value times the interest (i.e., *coupon*) rate at which they are issued. Thus, an investor who bought $1 million of Treasury notes carrying a 10% coupon would receive $100,000 of interest during each year the securities were outstanding.

The way yields on notes and bonds are quoted, 10% notes selling at *par* (i.e., face value) would be quoted as offering a 10% yield. An investor who bought these notes would, however, have the opportunity to earn *more than* 10% simple interest. The reason is that interest on notes and bonds is paid in semiannual installments, which means that the investor can invest, during the second six months of each year, the first semiannual interest installment.

To illustrate the effect of this on return, consider an investor who buys at issue $1 million of 10% Treasury notes. Six months later, he receives $50,000 of interest, which we assume he reinvests at 10%. Then at the end of the year, he receives another $50,000 of interest plus interest on the interest he has invested; the latter amounts to $50,000 times 10% times the one-half year he earns that interest. Thus, his total dollar return over the year is:

$$\$50,000 + (0.10)(\$50,000)(0.5) + \$50,000 = \$102,500$$

and the percentage return that he earns, expressed in terms of simple interest, is

$$\frac{\$102,500}{\$1,000,000} = 10.25\%$$

Note that what is at work here is *compound interest;* any quoted rate of interest yields more dollars of return, and is thus equivalent to a higher simple interest rate, the more frequently interest is paid and the more compounding that can thus occur.

Because return can mean different things depending on the way it is quoted and paid, an investor can meaningfully compare the returns offered by different securities only if these returns are stated on a com-

parable basis. With respect to *discount* and *coupon* securities, the way yields are made comparable in the money market is by restating yields quoted on a *discount basis*—the basis on which T bills are quoted—in terms of *equivalent bond yield*—the basis on which yields on notes and bonds are quoted.

We calculated above that an investor in a year bill would, on a simple interest basis, earn 11.28%. This is slightly higher than the rate he would earn measured on an equivalent bond yield basis. The reason is that equivalent bond yield understates, as noted, the true return on a simple interest basis that the investor in a coupon security would earn if he reinvested interest. When adjustment is made for this understatement, the equivalent bond yield offered by a 10% year bill turns out to be something less than 11.28%. Specifically, it is 10.98%.

The formula for converting yield on a bank discount basis to equivalent bond yield is complicated for discount securities that have a current maturity of longer than 6 months, but that is no problem for investors and other money market participants because bill yields are always restated on dealers' quote sheets in terms of equivalent bond yield at the *asked* rate (Table 3–1).

On bills with a current maturity of 6 months or less, equivalent bond yield is the simple interest rate yielded by a bill. Let

$$d_b = \text{Equivalent bond yield}$$

Then, on a security quoted at the discount rate *d*, equivalent bond yield is given by

$$d_b = \frac{365 \times d}{360 - (d \times t)}$$

TABLE 3–1
Selected quotes on U.S. Treasury bills, June 22, 1987

Billions outstanding	Days to maturity	Maturity	Discount (%) Bid	Discount (%) Asked	Dollar price	Equivalent bond yield
14.2	1	6/25/87	4.80	4.76	99.987	4.840
13.6	29	7/23/87	5.40	5.36	99.568	5.473
13.0	64	8/27/87	5.50	5.46	99.029	5.605
6.4	92	9/24/87	5.66	5.62	98.564	5.797
6.6	120	10/22/87	5.76	5.72	98.093	5.928
6.4	148	11/19/87	5.85	5.81	97.611	6.051
9.75	183	12/24/87	5.95	5.93	96.986	6.216
9.50	239	2/18/88	6.07	6.05	95.983	6.361
9.75	267	3/17/88	6.13	6.11	95.468	6.441
9.75	351	6/9/88	6.25	6.23	93.926	6.638

Source: The Morgan Bank.

For example, on a 3-month bill purchased at 8%, equivalent bond yield is

$$d_b = \frac{365 \times 0.08}{360 - (0.08 \times 91)} = 8.28\%$$

From the examples we have considered, it is clear that the yield on a discount security is *significantly less* when measured on a discount basis than when measured in terms of equivalent bond yield. The absolute divergence between these two measures of yield is, moreover, not constant. As Table 3–2 shows, the greater the yield and the longer the maturity of the security, the greater the divergence.

TABLE 3–2
Comparisons, at different rates and maturities, of rates of discount and equivalent bond yields

Yields on a discount basis (%)	Equivalent bond yields (%)		
	30-day maturity	182-day maturity	364-day maturity
4	4.069	4.139	4.183
6	6.114	6.274	6.375
8	8.166	8.453	8.639
10	10.227	10.679	10.979
12	12.290	12.952	13.399
14	14.362	15.256	15.904

MONEY MARKET YIELD

Equivalent bond yield on a bill is calculated on the basis of a 365-day year. Bill rates are—to make them directly comparable to rates on CDs and other interest-bearing, money market instruments—often converted to a simple interest rate on a 360-day-year basis. That number, dubbed *money market yield,* is obtained by substituting 360 for 365 in the above equation for equivalent bond yield; specifically,

$$\left(\begin{array}{c}\text{Money market yield} \\ \text{on a bill}\end{array}\right) = \frac{360 \times d}{360 - (d \times t)}$$

FLUCTUATIONS IN A BILL'S PRICE

Normally, the price at which a bill sells will rise as the bill approaches maturity. For example, to yield 9% on a discount basis, a 6-month bill must be priced at $95.45 per $100 of face value. For the same bill three

months later (three months closer to maturity) to yield 9%, it must have risen in price to $97.72. The moral is clear: If a bill always sold at the same yield throughout its life, its price would rise steadily toward face value as it approached maturity.

A bill's yield, however, is unlikely to be constant over time; instead, it will fluctuate for two reasons: (1) changes may occur in the general level of short-term interest rates, and (2) the bill will move along *the yield curve.* Let's look at each of these factors.

Short-term interest rates

T bills are issued through auctions in which discounted prices (yields) are bid. The rate of discount determined at auction on a new bill issue depends on the level of short-term interest rates prevailing at the moment of the auction. The reason is straightforward. Investors who want to buy bills at the time of a Treasury auction have two alternatives—to buy new bills or to buy existing bills from dealers. This being the case, investors will not bid for new bills at a rate of discount lower than that available on existing bills. If they did, they would be offering to buy new bills at a price higher than that at which they could buy existing bills. Also, investors will not bid substantially higher rates of discount (lower prices) than those prevailing on existing bills. If they did, they would not obtain bills, since they would surely be underbid by others trying to get just a slightly better return than that available on existing securities. Thus, the prevailing level of short-term rates determines, within a narrow range, the discount established on new bills at issue.

However, the going level of short-term rates is not constant over time. It rises and falls in response to changes in economic activity, the demand for credit, investors' expectations, and monetary policy as set by the Federal Reserve System. Figure 3-1, which plots auction rates on 6-month T bills for the period January 1981 to February 1987, portrays vividly the volatility of short-term interest rates. It shows both the sharp ups and downs that occurred in these rates as the Fed successively eased and tightened and the myriad of smaller fluctuations over the period in response to short-lived changes in other determinants of these rates.

If the going level of short-term rates (which establishes the rate at which a bill is initially sold) falls after a bill is issued, then this bill—as long as its price doesn't change—will yield more than new bills. Therefore, buyers will compete for this bill, and in doing so, they will drive up its price and thereby force down its yield until the bill sells at a rate of discount equal to the new, lower going interest rate. Conversely, if short-term rates rise after a bill is issued, the unwillingness of buyers to purchase any bill at a discount less than that available on new issues will drive down its price and thereby force up its yield.

FIGURE 3-1
Average auction rate on 6-month T bills (*weekly historical data*)

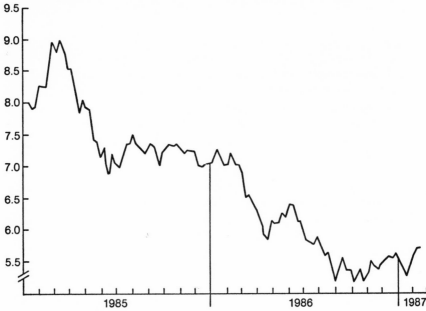

Source: The Morgan Bank.

The yield curve

Even if the going level of short-term interest rates does not change while investors hold bills, it would be normal for the rate at which they could sell their bills to change. The reason lies in the *yield curve*. How this works is a function of several factors, described below.

Price risk. In choosing among alternative securities, an investor considers three things: risk, liquidity, and return. Purchase of a money market instrument exposes an investor to two sorts of risk: (1) *credit risk:* Will the issuer pay off at maturity? and (2) *price risk:* If the investor later sold the security, might he have to do so at a loss because interest rates had subsequently risen? Most money market investors are risk averse, which means that they will accept lower yields to obtain lower risk.

The price risk to which bills and other money market instruments expose the investor is *larger* the *longer* their current maturity. To see why, suppose that short-term interest rates rise a full percentage point across the board; then the prices of all bill issues will drop, *but the price drop will be greater, the longer an issue's current maturity.* For example, a 1 percentage point rise in market rates would cause a 3-month bill to fall

only $2,500 in price per $1 million of face value, whereas the corresponding price drop on a 9-month bill would be $7,600 per $1 million of face
value.

The slope of the yield curve.   Because a 3-month bill exposes the
investor to less price risk than a 9-month bill does, it will normally yield
less than a 9-month bill. In other words, the bill market yield curve, which
shows the relationship between yield and current maturity, normally
slopes upward, indicating that the longer the time to maturity, the higher
the yield. We say "normally" because other factors, such as the expectation that interest rates are going to fall, may, as explained below, alter
this relationship.

To illustrate the concept of the yield curve, we have used the bid quotes
in Table 3-1 to plot a yield curve in Figure 3-2; each dot is one quote.
Our results show a normal upward-sloping yield curve. Lest you try doing the same and be disappointed, we should admit that we cheated a
bit in putting together our demonstration yield curve. On April 27, 1987,
there were many more bill issues outstanding than those quoted in Table
3-1. Had we plotted yields on all of these in Figure 3-2, we would have
found that yield did not rise quite so consistently with maturity; the points
plotted for some bill issues would have been further off a smooth yield
curve. Yields may be out of line for various reasons. For example, a bill

FIGURE 3-2
Yield curve for Treasury bills—April 27, 1987

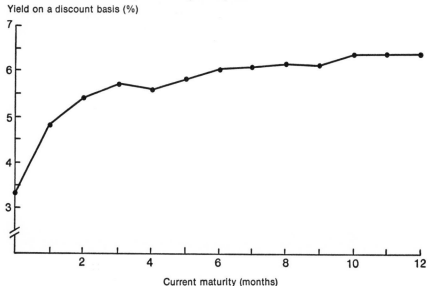

issue maturing around a tax date might be highly desired by investors who had big tax payments to make and, for this reason, trade at a yield that was relatively low compared to yields on surrounding issues.

While the yield curve for short maturities normally slopes upward, its shape and slope vary over time. Thus, it is difficult to pinpoint a "normal" spread between, say, 1-month and 6-month bills.

Yield spreads between different securities are always measured in terms of basis points. *A basis point is 1/100 of 1 percentage point.* Thus, if 5-month bills are quoted at 10.45 and 6-month bills at 10.56, the spread between the two is said to be 11 basis points. A yield spread between two securities of 100 basis points would indicate a full 1% difference in their yields. A basis point is also frequently referred to as an 01 (pronounced oh one).

BANKERS' ACCEPTANCES AND COMMERCIAL PAPER

In talking about discount securities, we have focused on bills since they are the most important discount security traded in the money market. All we have said about yields on bills is, however, equally applicable to yields on BAs and commercial paper, both of which are sold on a discount basis with the discount being calculated on a 360-day year.

THE NEXT CHAPTER

In the next chapter, we shift our focus to interest-bearing notes and bonds. We also introduce several key concepts: (1) the relationship, for a bond, of current maturity and coupon to price volatility, and (2) the yield curve as measured in the Treasury market.

Chapter 4

Interest-bearing securities

THE STOCK-IN-TRADE OF THE MONEY MARKET includes, besides discount securities, a variety of *interest-bearing* instruments: Treasury and federal agency notes and bonds, municipal notes and bonds, and bank certificates of deposit. Notes, bonds, and other interest-bearing debt securities are issued with a fixed *face value;* they mature at some specified date and carry a *coupon rate,* which is the annual interest rate the issuer promises to pay the holder on the security's face value while the security is outstanding.

Some notes and bonds are issued in *registered* form; that is, the issuer keeps track of who owns its outstanding IOUs, just as a corporation keeps track of who owns its common stock. Most notes and bonds, however, are issued in *bearer* form. To prove ownership of a bearer security, the owner must produce or bear it. An issuer with $50 million of bearer bonds outstanding does not know where to send interest when a payment date comes along. Consequently, such securities carry *coupons,* one for each interest date. On the interest date, the investor or his bank clips the appropriate coupon from the security and sends

it to the issuer's paying agent, who, in turn, makes the required payment.[1] Generally, interest payments are made semiannually on coupon securities. Because notes and bonds carry coupons, the return paid on face value is called the *coupon rate* or simply the *coupon.*

Notes and bonds with a short current maturity are referred to as *short coupons,* those with an intermediate current maturity (2 to 7 years) as *intermediate coupons,* and those with a still longer current maturity as *long coupons.*

CALL PROVISIONS

Once a bond issue is sold, the issuer might choose to redeem it early. For example, if interest rates fell, the borrower could reduce his interest costs by refunding his loan: paying off outstanding high-coupon bonds and issuing new lower-coupon bonds.

For the investor, early repayment on a bond is almost always disadvantageous because a bond issuer will rarely be tempted to repay early when interest rates are rising, a time when it would be to the bondholder's advantage to move funds out of the issuer's bonds into new, higher-yielding bonds. On the other hand, early payment looks attractive to the issuer when interest rates are falling, a time when it is to the investor's advantage to keep funds invested in the issuer's high-coupon securities.

To protect investors making long-term commitments against frequent refundings by borrowers out to minimize interest costs, most bonds contain call provisions. A bond issue is said to be *callable* when the issuer has the option to repay part or all of the issue early by paying some specified redemption price to bondholders. Most bonds offer some call protection to the investor. Some are noncallable for life, others for some number of years after issue. Thirty-year Treasury bonds are callable by the Treasury only during the final five years of their life.

Call provisions usually specify that the issuer who calls a bond must pay the bondholder a price above face value. The call premium frequently equals the coupon rate on early calls and then diminishes to zero as the bond approaches maturity.

Price quotes

Note and bond prices are quoted in slightly different ways depending on whether they are selling in the new issue or the secondary market. When notes and bonds other than governments are issued, the price

---

[1]The procedure is different on Treasury and agency securities, which are now being issued in *book-entry* form; computerized records of ownership maintained by the Fed and banks have been substituted for actual securities.

which they are offered to investors is normally quoted as a percentage of face value. To illustrate, the two Fannie Mae bond issues announced in Figure 4-1 were offered at prices of 100% and 99.875%, respectively, which means that the investor had to pay $100 for each $100 of face value on the 8.55% debentures and $99.875 for each $100 of face value on the 9.20% debentures. This percentage price is often called the bond's *dollar price*. The securities described in Figure 4-1 happened to be offered at par, so the actual yields offered by these securities equaled their respective coupon rates. Often on a new offering this is not the case.

Once a note or bond issue is distributed and trading in it moves to the secondary market, prices are also quoted on a percentage basis but always, depending on the security, in 32nds, 8ths, 4ths, or halves. Table 4-1 reproduces, by way of illustration, a few quotes on Treasury notes and bonds posted by a dealer on April 27, 1987. The first bid is 101-4, meaning that this dealer was willing to pay $101-4/32, which equals $101.125 per $100 of face value for that issue. The advantage of dollar pricing of notes and bonds is that it makes the prices of securities with different denominations directly comparable.

TREATMENT OF INTEREST IN PRICING

There's another wrinkle with respect to note and bond pricing. Typically, interest on notes and bonds is paid to the holder semiannually on the coupon dates. This means that the value of a coupon security rises by the amount of interest accrued as a payment date approaches and falls thereafter by the amount of the payment made. Since notes and bonds are issued on every business day and consequently have coupon dates all over the calendar, the effect of accrued interest on the value of coupon securities would, if incorporated into the prices quoted by dealers, make meaningful price comparisons between different issues difficult. To get

TABLE 4-1
Quotations for selected Treasury notes—April 27, 1987

Millions of $s publicly held	Coupon rate	Maturity	Bid*	Asked	Yield to maturity	Yield value of 1/32	Issue date
9250	8⅞	10/31/87	101- 4	101- 5	6.511	.0631	10/31/85
9500	8½	11/30/87	101- 0	101- 1	6.645	.0542	12/2/85
9500	7⅞	12/31/87	100-20	100-21	6.815	.0478	12/31/85
9750	6⅝	4/30/88	99-17	99-18	7.066	.0328	4/30/86
3381	10⅜	11/15/09-04†	111-26	111-30	9.007	.0033	11/15/79

*Prices quoted in 32nds.
†Issue matures in 2009 but is callable in 2004.
Source: The Morgan Bank.

FIGURE 4-1
Pricing announcement for two new Fannie Mae debentures

NEW ISSUES   June 3. 1987

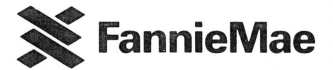

FannieMae

$900,000,000
8.55% Debentures

Dated June 10, 1987   Due June 10, 1991
Interest payable on December 10, 1987 and semiannually thereafter.

Series SM-1991-K   Cusip No. 313586 XF 1
Non-Callable

Price 100%

$600,000,000
9.20% Debentures

Dated June 10, 1987   Due June 10, 1997
Interest payable on December 10, 1987 and semiannually thereafter.

Series SM-1997-C   Cusip No. 313586 XG 9
Non-Callable

Price 99.875%

The debentures are the obligations of the Federal National Mortgage Association. a corporation organized and existing under the laws of the United States, and are issued under the authority contained in Section 304(b) of the Federal National Mortgage Association Charter Act (12 U.S.C. 1716 et seq.).

The debentures. together with any interest thereon, are not guaranteed by the United States and do not constitute a debt or obligation of the United States or of any agency or instrumentality thereon other than Fannie Mae.

This offering is made by the Federal National Mortgage Association through its Senior Vice President-Finance and Treasurer with the assistance of a nationwide Selling Group of recognized dealers in securities.

Debentures will be available in *Book-Entry* form only.
There will be no definitive securities offered.

Gary L. Perlin
Senior Vice President-
Finance and Treasurer

Linda K. Knight
Vice President and
Assistant Treasurer

3900 Wisconsin Avenue. N.W.. Washington. D.C. 20016

This announcement appears as a matter of record only.

Source: *The Wall Street Journal.*

around this problem, the actual prices paid in the new issue and secondary markets are always the quoted dollar price *plus* any accrued interest. For example, if an investor—three months before a coupon date—bought $100,000 of 12% Treasury notes quoted at 104, he would pay $104,000 plus $3,000 of accrued interest:

$$\$104,000 + 0.5\left[\frac{(0.12)(\$100,000)}{2}\right] = \$104,000 + 0.5(\$6,000)$$
$$= \$107,000$$

where (0.12)($100,000)/2 represents the $6,000 semiannual interest due on the notes.

FLUCTUATIONS IN A COUPON SECURITY'S PRICE

When a new note or bond issue comes to market, the coupon rate on it is, with certain exceptions, set so that it equals the yield prevailing in the market on securities of comparable maturity and risk. This permits the new security to be sold at a price equal or nearly equal to par.

The price at which the security later trades in the secondary market will, like that of a discount security, fluctuate in response to changes in the general level of interest rates.

Yield to maturity

To illustrate, let's work through a simple example. Suppose a new 6-year note with an 8% coupon is issued at par. Six months later, the Fed tightens, and the yield on comparable securities rises to 8.5%. Now what is this 8% security worth? Since the investor who pays a price equal to par for this "seasoned issue" is going to get only an 8% return, while 8.5% is available elsewhere, it is clear that the security must now sell at *less* than par.

To determine how much less, we have to introduce a new concept—*effective yield*. When an investor buys a coupon security at a *discount* and holds it to maturity, he receives a two-part return: the promised interest payment *plus* a capital gain. The capital gain arises because the security that the investor bought at less than par is redeemed at maturity for full face value. The investor who buys a coupon issue at a *premium* and holds it to maturity also receives a two-part return: interest payments due plus a capital *loss* equal to the premium paid.

For dollars invested in a coupon issue that sells at a discount or premium, it is possible to calculate the overall or effective rate of return received, which is the rate that the investor earns on his dollars when both interest received *and* capital gains (or losses) are taken into account. Naturally, an investor choosing between securities of similar risk and

maturity will do so not on the basis of coupon rate but on the basis of effective yield, referred to in the financial community as *yield to maturity.*

To get back to our example, it is clear that once rates rise to 8.5% in the open market, the security with an 8% coupon has to be priced at a discount sufficiently great so that its yield to maturity equals 8.5%. Figuring out how many dollars of discount this requires involves complicated calculations. Dealers used to use bond tables, but all have now switched to bond calculators. A trader can thus determine in a few seconds that, with interest rates at 8.5%, a $1,000 note with an 8% coupon and a 3½-year current maturity must sell at $985.13 (a discount of $14.87) to yield 8.5% to maturity.

Current maturity and price volatility

A capital gain of $14.87, which is what the investor in our discounted 8% note would realize if he held it to maturity, will raise effective yield more the faster this gain is realized (the shorter the current maturity of the security). Conversely, this capital gain will raise effective yield less the more slowly it is realized (the longer the current maturity of the security).[2]

But if this is so, then a one-half percentage point rise in the yield on comparable securities will cause a larger fall in price for a security with a long current maturity than for one with a short current maturity. In other words, the discount required to raise a coupon security's yield to maturity by one-half percentage point is *greater* the *longer* the security's maturity.

By reversing the argument above, it is easy to see that if six months after the 6-year, 8% note in our example was issued, the yield on comparable securities *fell* to 7.5%, the value of this note would be driven to a *premium;* that is, it would sell at a price above par. Note also that a one-half percentage point *fall* in the yield on comparable securities would force an outstanding high-coupon security to a *greater* premium the *longer* its current maturity.

As these observations suggest, when prevailing interest rates change, prices of long coupons respond more dramatically than prices of short coupons. Figure 4–2 shows this sharp contrast. It pictures, for a $1,000 note carrying an 8% coupon, the relationship between *current* maturity and the discount that would prevail if the yield on comparable securities rose to 8.5% or to 10%. It also plots the premium to which a $1,000 note

---

[2]If you don't see this, just think—somewhat imprecisely—of the capital gain as a certain number of dollars of extra interest paid out in yearly installments to the investor as his security matures. Clearly, the shorter the security's current maturity, the higher these extra annual interest installments will be and, consequently, the higher the overall yield to the investor.

FIGURE 4-2
Premiums and discounts at which a $1,000 note with an 8% coupon would sell, depending on current maturity, if market yields on comparable securities were 6%, 8.5%, and 10%

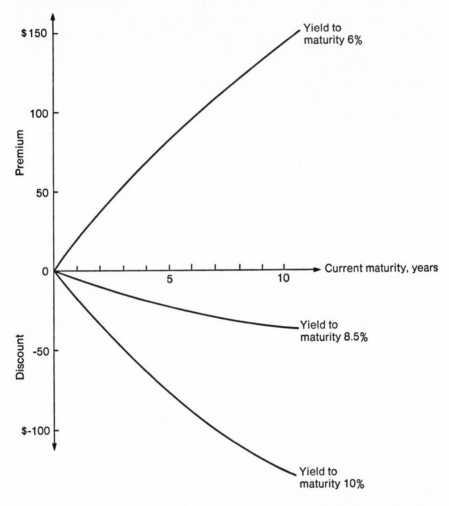

with an 8% coupon would, depending on its current maturity, be driven if the yield on comparable securities fell to 6%.

Coupon and price volatility

The volatility of a note or bond's price in the face of changing interest rates also depends on its coupon; the *lower* the coupon, the *greater* the percentage change in price that will occur when rates rise or fall. To

illustrate, consider two notes with 4-year current maturities. Note A has an 8% coupon and note B a 6% coupon. Both are priced to yield 8%. Suppose now that interest rates on comparable securities rise to 10%. Note A will fall in price by $6.46; since it was initially priced at $100, that works out to a 6.46% fall in value. Note B's dollar price drops from $93.27 to $87.07—a $6.20 fall, which equals a 6.64% loss of value. The reason for the greater percentage fall in the price of the low-coupon note is that capital appreciation represents a greater proportion of promised income (capital appreciation plus coupon interest) on the low coupon than on the high coupon. Therefore, for the low-coupon note's yield to maturity to rise two percentage points, its price has to fall relatively *more* than that of the high-coupon note.

Zeros. As the reasoning in the preceding paragraph suggests, *zero-coupon* securities (securities with a zero coupon) are far more volatile in price than securities paying even as low a coupon as 6%.

Yield value of ⅟₃₂. Prices of government and federal agency securities are quoted in 32nds. The greater the change in yield to maturity that results from a price change of ⅟₃₂, the less volatile the issue's price will be in the face of changing interest rates. As a result, dealers include on their quote sheets for such securities a column titled *Yield value of ⅟₃₂*. Looking back at Table 4–1, we see that the yield value of ⅟₃₂ on the 12¾s Treasury notes maturing on 2/15/87 was .0530, which means that a fall in the asked price on this security from 103–26 to 103–25 (a ⅟₃₂ fall) would have raised yield to maturity by 0.0530%, from 5.95 to 6.03. The yield value of ⅟₃₂ drops sharply as current maturity lengthens. Thus, on the 14s Treasury bonds maturing on 7/15/88 (the next to last line of the table), the yield value of ⅟₃₂ was only .0156, indicating that these notes would have had to fall in value by approximately 64/32 (2 points) for their yield to rise 1%.

Current yield

So far we have focused on yield to maturity, which is the yield figure always quoted on coupon securities. When the investor buys a note or bond, he may also be interested in knowing what rate of return interest payments per se will give him on the principal he invests. This measure of yield is referred to as *current yield*.

To illustrate, consider our earlier example of a note with an 8% coupon selling at $985.13 to yield 8.5% to maturity. Current yield on this note would be: ($80/$985.13) × 100, or 8.12%. On a discount note or bond, current yield is always less than yield to maturity; on a premium bond it exceeds yield to maturity.

THE YIELD CURVE

From the examples we have worked through, it is clear that investors in notes and bonds expose themselves, like buyers of discount securities, to a *price risk*. Moreover, even though longer-term rates fluctuate less violently than do short-term rates (Figure 4–3), the price risk associated with holding debt securities tends to be greater the longer the current maturity. Thus, one would expect the yield curve to slope upward over the full maturity spectrum. And often it does.

Price risk, however, is not the only factor affecting the shape of the yield curve. Borrowers' and investors' *expectations* with respect to future interest rates are also an important—at times dominant—factor.

If the general expectation is that interest rates are going to rise, investors will seek to keep their money in short coupons to avoid getting locked into low-yield, long coupons. Borrowers, on the other hand, will try to lengthen the maturity of their outstanding debt to lock in prevailing low rates for as long as possible. Both responses tend to force short-term rates down and long-term rates up, thereby accentuating the upward slope of the yield curve. The expectation that interest rates would

FIGURE 4–3
U.S. government security yields (*monthly historical data*)

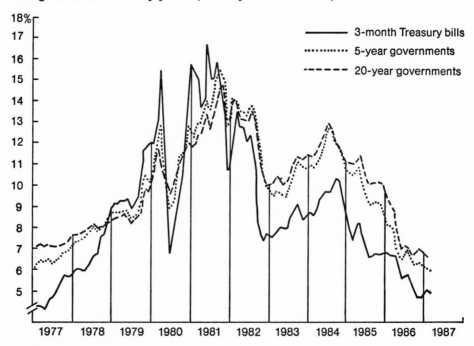

Source: The Morgan Bank.

rise was widespread in August 1975, the time of the yield curve pictured in Figure 4–4; this expectation explains in part why the yield curve sloped so steeply upward.

People, of course, may expect interest rates to fall. When this is the case, investors respond by buying long coupons in the hope of locking in a high yield. In contrast, borrowers are willing to pay extremely high short-term rates while they wait for long rates to fall so that they can borrow more cheaply. The net result of both responses is that, when interest rates are expected to fall, the yield curve (or at least some part of it) may be *inverted,* with short-term rates above long-term rates. Figure 4–5 pictures the yield curve on February 4, 1980, when people anticipated a fall in rates. Note that after a current maturity of 1 month, the slope of this curve becomes negative.

Figure 4–6 pictures the yield curve on April 27, 1987. It was upwardly sloping, but the bulk of the rise was in the 1- to 5-year range. Also, it wiggled a bit.

If, inspired by our yield curves, you start poring over dealer quote sheets on governments, you are bound to discover some out-of-line yields. The reasons are varied.[3] For one thing, sale of a large new issue may cause a temporary upward bulge in the yield curve in the maturity range of the new issue. Also, a security with an out-of-line yield may have some special characteristic. Some government bonds (*flower bonds* to the Street) are acceptable at par in payment of federal estate taxes when owned by the decedent at the time of death. These bonds, which all sell at substantial discounts, have yields to maturity much lower than those on straight government bonds.

Yields are not always directly comparable

In calculating the yield on discount securities, we found a considerable discrepancy between yield measured on a discount basis and equivalent bond yield. There are also many discrepancies—albeit smaller ones—between the ways that interest is measured and quoted on different interest-bearing securities. For example, interest on Treasury notes is calculated for actual days on the basis of 365-day year, while interest on CDs is calculated for actual days on the basis of a 360-day year. Thus, a 1-year CD issued at 10% would yield a higher return than a 10% year note selling at par. Partially offsetting this advantage, however, is the fact that a 1-year CD would pay interest only at maturity, whereas a 1-year note would pay it semiannually. The latter disadvantage disappears, however,

---

[3]One trivial reason may be a mistake in the quote sheet. These are typically compiled daily in great haste with the result that errors creep in. For this reason, such sheets often carry a footnote stating that the quotes are believed to be reliable but are not "guaranteed."

FIGURE 4-4
Yield curve for U.S. Treasury securities—bills, notes, and bonds—August 19, 1975*

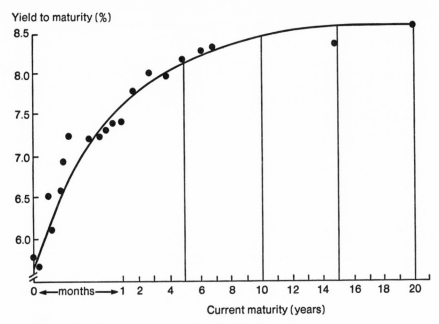

*Dots represent observed yields; yield curve is fitted to them.

FIGURE 4-5
Yield curve for U.S. Treasury securities—bills, notes, and bonds—February 4, 1980

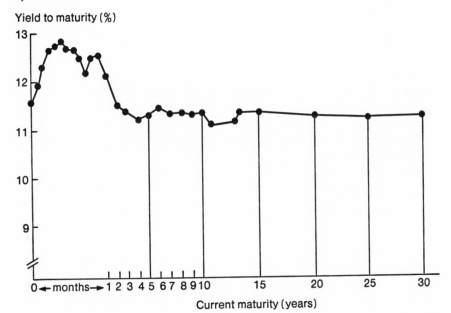

FIGURE 4-6
Yield curve for U.S. Treasury securities—bills, notes, and bonds—April 27, 1987

Yield to maturity (bond equivalent basis, %)

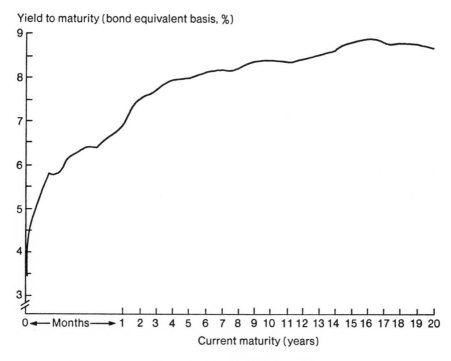

Current maturity (years)

on CDs with a maturity longer than 1 year, since such CDs pay interest semiannually.

Another discrepancy: When government notes and bonds are sold, accrued interest is calculated between coupon dates on the basis of actual days passed since a coupon date, while on agency securities it accrues as if every month had 30 days. Thus, for example, agency securities accrue no interest on October 31, but they do accrue interest on February 30!

These and the many other minor discrepancies among yields on interest-bearing securities have little importance for understanding the workings of the money market, but they are important to the market participant out to maximize return.

THE NEXT CHAPTER

In the next chapter, we turn to *dealers,* those key players who make the markets that together comprise the money market.

Chapter 5

The market makers:
Dealers

THAT A COLLECTION OF MARKETS is called *the* money market suggests that the participants in this market trade in a single market where at any time one price reigns for any one instrument. This description is accurate, but that is startling. Money market instruments, with the exception of futures contracts, are traded not on organized exchanges but strictly over the counter. Moreover, money market participants, who vary in size from small to gargantuan, are scattered over the whole United States—*and* throughout Canada, Europe, the Mid East and the Far East. Thus one might expect fragmentation of the market, with big New York participants dealing in a noticeably different market from their London or Wichita counterparts. However, money market lenders and borrowers can operate almost as well out of Dearborn, Michigan, Washington, Singapore or Tokyo as they can from Wall Street. Wherever they are, their access to information, bids, and offers is (time zone problems excepted) essentially the same. That the money market is a single market is due largely to the activities of the dealers and brokers who weld the market's many participants into a unified whole and to the modern communication techniques that make this possible.

THE DEALERS

Money market dealers are a mixed bag. Some are tiny, others huge. Some specialize in certain instruments, others cover the waterfront. One is also tempted to say that some are immensely sharp and others are not so sharp, but the not-so-sharp players lead short lives. Despite dealers' diversity, one can generalize about their operations.

Activities

The hallmark of a dealer is that he buys and sells for his own account; that is, trades with retail and other dealers off his own position. In addition, dealers engage in various activities that come close to brokering.

The prime example of the latter is commercial paper dealers. Each day they help their customers borrow hundreds of millions of dollars from other market participants. Commercial paper dealers' responsibilities are: (1) to advise their clients on market conditions, (2) to ensure that their clients post rates for different maturities that give them the lowest possible borrowing costs but are still high enough to get their paper sold, and (3) for a ⅛ commission, to show and sell that paper to retail. Positioning is part of a commercial paper dealer's operation but only marginally so. Paper dealers will position any of their clients' paper that goes unsold, but that amounts to little. One reason is that dealers are careful to ensure that their clients post realistic rates. A second reason is that commercial paper dealers as a group feel that it is not in their best interest or in that of their clients for them to position large amounts of paper. Commercial paper dealers do, however, stand ready to bid for paper bought from them by retail and thus make a secondary market in paper. Such activity leads them at times to position paper, but the amounts are small because the secondary market in commercial paper is inactive. Thus dealers in commercial paper act more like brokers than like true dealers.

Dealers also act at times like brokers in the CD market. A bank that wants to do a large program in one fast shot may call one or more dealers and offer then an 05 (5 basis points) on any CDs they can sell to retail. Finally, smaller dealers who are hesitant about the market or who are operating outside their normal market sector at times act more or less as brokers, giving a firm bid to retail only if they can cross the trade on the other side with an assured sale.

As noted, however, brokering is not what dealing is all about. *The crucial role dealers play in the money market is as market makers, and in performing that role, they trade off their own positions.*

Part of the dealers' role as market makers involves underwriting new issues. Most large municipal note issues are brought up at issue by dealers or syndicates of them who take these securities into position and sell them off to retail. In the market for governments there is also underwriting, though of a less formal nature; frequently dealers buy large amounts of new government issues at auction and then distribute them to retail.

In the secondary market dealers act as market makers by constantly quoting bids and offers at which they are willing to buy and sell. Some of these quotes are to other dealers. In every sector of the money market, there is an *inside market* between dealers. In this market dealers quote price *runs* (bids and offers for securities of different maturities) to other dealers, often through brokers. Since every dealer will *hit* a bid he views as high or take an offering he views as low, trading in the inside market creates at any time for every security traded a prevailing price that represents dealers' consensus of what that security is worth.

Dealers also actively quote bids and offers to retail. In doing so they consistently seek to give their customers the best quotes possible because they value retail business and they know that other shops are competing actively with them for it. This competition between dealers ensures that dealers' quotes to retail will never be far removed from prices prevailing in the inside market. Thus, all the money market's geographically dispersed participants can always trade at close to identical bids and offers.

As the above suggests, through their trading activities, the dealers give the secondary market for money market instruments two important characteristics. First, they ensure that at any moment a single price level will prevail for any instrument traded in it. Second, by standing ready to quote firm bids and offers at which they will trade, they render money market instruments liquid.

Profit sources

Dealers profit from their activities in several ways. First, there are the 05s and ⅛s they earn selling CDs and commercial paper. Particularly for firms that are big commercial paper dealers, these commissions amount to a substantial sum, but in total they represent only a small part of dealers' profits.

A second source of dealers' profits is *carry*. As noted below, dealers finance the bulk of their long positions (muni notes excepted) in the repo market. Their RP borrowings are of shorter maturity than the securities they position. Thus their financing costs are normally less than the yields on the securities they finance, and they profit from *positive* carry.

Carry, however, is an undependable source of profit because, when the yield curve inverts, carry turns negative.¹ As one dealer commented, "Back in 1974 when Fed funds were 10 to 14%, there was nothing you could position at a positive carry. You might position because you thought rates were going to fall, but not for carry. And you knew *ex ante* that, if you positioned and the market did not appreciate, you would lose money on two levels: carry and depreciation of values. This led to the phenomenon of the Friday night bill trader. At one point, to carry bills over the weekend cost 5 basis points. So traders would attempt on Friday to sell the 90-day bill for cash settlement and buy it back for regular settlement." The late 1970s and early 1980s were also characterized often by negative carry.

A third source of dealer profits is what might be called day-to-day trading profits, buying securities at one price and reselling them shortly at a slightly higher price, or shorting securities and covering in at a slightly lower price. How traders seek to earn 02s and 32nds from such trading is discussed later.

The sources of profit mentioned so far suffice to pay dealers' phone and light bills—to cover their overhead. Dealers earn really big money on position plays, that is, by taking into position huge amounts of securities when they anticipate that rates will fall and securities prices will rise or by shorting the market when they are bearish.

Being willing to position on a large scale is characteristic of all dealers, although the appetite of some shops for such *speculation* is stronger than that of others.² One might argue that positioning done specifically to speculate as opposed to the positioning that arises out of a dealer's daily trading activities with retail and other dealers is not an inherent part of being a market maker. But such speculation serves useful functions. It guarantees that market prices will react rapidly to any change in conditions, economic or in demand, supply, or rate expectations. Also, and more important, the profits dealers can earn from correct position plays are the prime incentive they have for setting up the elaborate and expensive operations they use daily to trade with retail and each other. Position profits help to oil the machinery that dealers need to be effective market makers.

¹The yield curve is said to be *inverted* when short-term rates exceed long-term rates. For an inverted yield curve, see Figure 4–5.
²The term *speculation* as used here and throughout the book is *not* meant to carry pejorative connotation. *Speculation is taking an unhedged position, short or long.* A homeowner who buys a house financed with a mortgage is assuming a speculative, levered position in real estate. A dealer who buys governments with RP money is assuming a speculative, levered position in governments. The only difference between the two is that the dealer knows he's speculating; the homeowner used not to think of it that way.

Dealers possess no crystal balls enabling them to perfectly foresee the future. They position on the basis of carefully formulated expectations. When they are right, they make huge profits; when they are wrong, their losses can be staggering. Thus the successful shops and the ones that survive are those that are right on the market more often than wrong.

DEALER FINANCING

The typical dealer runs a highly levered operation in which securities held in position may total a large multiple of their capital. Some dealers rely heavily on dealer loans from New York banks for financing, but as one dealer commented, "The state of the art is that you don't have to." RP money is cheaper, and sharp dealers rely primarily on it to meet their financing needs. For such dealers the need to obtain RP money on a continuing basis and in large amounts is one additional reason for assiduously cultivating their retail customers. The money funds, corporations, state and local governments, and other investors that buy governments and other instruments from them are also big suppliers of RP money to the dealers.

Much of the borrowing dealers do in the RP market is done on an overnight basis. The overnight rate is typically the lowest RP rate. Also, securities "hung out" on RP for one night only are available for sale the next day. Nonbank dealers have to clear all their RP transactions through the clearing banks, which is expensive. As a result they also do a lot of *open repos* at rates slightly above the overnight rate. Open or demand repos have an indefinite term; either the borrower or the lender can each day choose to terminate the agreement.

The financing needs that nonbank dealers do not cover in the RP market are met by borrowing from banks at the dealer loan rate. Even dealers who look primarily to the RP market for financing will use bank loans to finance small pieces they hold in inventory. A typical nonbank dealer commented, "The smallest RP ticket I will write is 2 [million]. On a transaction of less than 2, writing the tickets and making deliveries is not worth the cost and trouble. I can combine small pieces, but generally I let such junk just sit at the bank."

In financing, bank dealers have one advantage over nonbank dealers— they can finance odd pieces they do not RP by buying Fed funds.

While much dealer financing is done using open or very short repos, dealers will sometimes finance speculative positions they anticipate holding for some time with term RP, taking in money for 30, 60, or 90 days, or even longer.

Fails and the fails game

If, on the settlement date of a trade, a seller does not make timely delivery of the securities purchased, delivers the wrong securities, or fails in some other way to deliver in proper form, the trade becomes a *fail*. In that case the buyer does not have to make payment until proper delivery is made, presumably the next day; *but* he owns the securities as of the initially agreed-upon settlement day. Thus, on a fail the security buyer (who is *failed to*) receives, overnight, a free loan equal to the amount of the purchase price, that is, one day's free financing. And if the fail persists, the free loan continues. Fails occur not only in connection with straight trades but in connection with repos; on a repo the lender has to make timely return of the collateral he is holding to unwind the transaction and get his money back.

Dealers often play some portion of their financing needs for a fail; that is, they estimate on the basis of past experience the dollar amount of the fails that will be made to them and reduce their RP borrowing accordingly. If their estimate proves high, more securities will end up in their box at the clearing bank than they had anticipated, and that bank will automatically grant them a box loan against that collateral. On such last-minute loans the clearing banks charge the dealer a rate that's a margin above their posted dealer loan rate to encourage dealers to track their positions and run an orderly shop. A dealer who plays the *fails game* is in effect using his clearing bank as a lender of last resort.

INTEREST RATE PREDICTIONS

The key rate in the money market is the Fed funds rate. Because of the role of this rate in determining dealers' cost of carry (the RP rate is usually slightly below the funds rate), the 90-day bill rate settles close to the Fed funds rate, and other short-term rates key off this combination in a fairly predictable way (Figure 5–1). Thus when a dealer positions, he does so on the basis of a strongly held view with respect to where money supply numbers and Fed policy are headed; and *every long position he takes is based on an implicit prediction of how high Fed funds and other money market instruments might trade* within the time frame of his investment. In formulating expectations about short-term interest rates, dealers engage in constant and careful Fed watching.

CONFIDENCE LEVEL IN POSITIONING

Positioning is a form of gambling, and the dealers most skilled in this art attempt, first, to express their expectations about what might occur in terms of probabilities of various outcomes and, second, to estimate

FIGURE 5-1
Other short-term money rates key off the Fed funds rate.

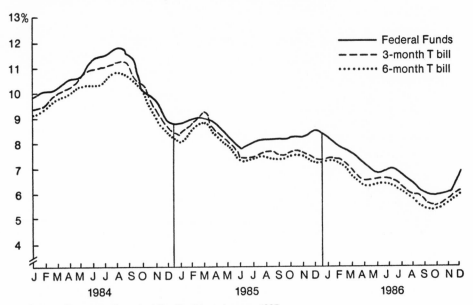

Source: *Economic Report of the President,* January 1987.

the payoff or loss that a given strategy would yield if each of these outcomes were to occur. Then on the basis of these numbers, they decide
whether to bet and how much to bet.

Probabilists who have theorized about gambling like to talk about a
fair gamble or a *fair game.* A fair game is one that, if played repeatedly,
will yield the player neither net gains nor losses. For example, suppose
a person plays the following game: A coin is flipped; if it lands heads
up, he wins $1; if it lands heads down, he loses $1. The probability that
the coin will land heads up is ½. So half the time he bets our player
will lose $1; half the time he will win $1; and his *expected winnings* or
return, if he plays the game repeatedly, is *zero.*

There is nothing in it for a dealer to make a fair bet. What he looks
for is a situation in which expected return is *positive;* and the more
positive it is, the more he will bet. For example, if a dealer believed (1)
that the probabilities that the Fed would ease and tighten were 60 percent and 40 percent, respectively, and (2) that a given long position would
return him $2 if the Fed eased and would cause him to lose $1 if the
Fed tightened, then his *expected* winnings would be

$$0.6 \times \$2 - 0.4 \times \$1 = \$0.80$$

In other words, the gamble is such that, if the dealer made it 10 times, his expected winnings would be $8. That degree of favorableness in the bet might suffice to induce the dealer to position.

If the game were made still more favorable, for example by an improvement in the odds, then he would gamble still more.

All this may sound a bit theoretical, but it is the way good dealers think, explicitly or intuitively; and such thinking disciplines them in positioning. Noted one dealer, "The alternative is a sloppy operation in which a dealer runs up his position because he sort of likes the market now or runs it down because he doesn't like the market."

Quantifying his thinking about the market also helps a dealer provide retail with useful suggestions. Most customers can find fair bets on their own. What they appreciate is a dealer who can suggest to them a favorable bet.

In quantifying expectations and payoffs and acting on them, fleet-footedness is essential since everyone on the Street is playing the same game, and the market therefore frequently anticipates what the Fed is going to do.

THE MATURITY CHOICE

We suggested that the more favorable the gamble a dealer faces, the more securities he's likely to position. There is one more wrinkle to the dealer's positioning decision. A classic part of a bullish strategy is for a dealer to extend to longer maturities. The reason he is tempted to extend is that the longer the maturity of the securities he positions, the more price play he will get—and the more risk.

Dealers are very conscious that extending to longer maturities exposes them to greater *price risk*. They also tend to think that extending to longer maturities exposes them to greater risk for another reason; namely, the predictability of long-term rates is less than that of short-term rates. Short rates relate directly to Fed policy; long rates do so to a much lesser extent because they are also strongly influenced by the *slope* of the yield curve. Thus the dealer who extends must be prepared not only to predict Fed policy but to predict shifts in the slope of the yield curve—an art that is separate from and, in the eyes of many dealers, more difficult than successful Fed watching.

To protect against the risks posed by extending maturity, some dealers confine their unhedged positions largely to securities of short current maturity. A dealer typical of this group noted, "We are accused of being an inch wide and a mile deep—the mile deep being in securities with a maturity of a year and under. There are various arts in this business: predicting spreads, predicting the yield curve, predicting the trend in in-

terest rates. You go with the learning curve of the organization you have, and ours is strong in predicting short-term spreads and yields."

Other dealers are more willing to extend maturity to reach for gains, but in doing so they seek to control carefully the price risk they assume. The guidelines used to control price risk—frequently they take the form of smaller position limits on longer maturities—vary considerably from shop to shop. One reason is that there is no objective way a dealer can compare the risk he assumes in holding 6-year notes to that he assumes in holding 6-month bills. Another is that in establishing position limits by instrument and maturity, a dealer is inevitably making subjective judgments about the ability of each of his traders.

SHORTING

When money market dealers are bullish, they place their bets by positioning securities; when they are bearish, they do so by shorting. One might expect that the quantity of securities a dealer would short, if he were confident that securities prices would fall, would be as great as the quantity of securities he would position if he were confident that securities prices would rise. But in fact dealers will, at a given confidence level, short smaller amounts of securities than they would position. There are several reasons. First, the only instruments dealers can short are governments and agencies; other instruments, such as commercial paper, BAs, CDs, and muni notes, are too heterogeneous with respect to name, maturity, and face amount to short. Second, shorting securities tends to be more cumbersome and expensive than going long because the short seller must find not only a buyer, but—since the shorted securities must be delivered—a source of these securities.

In recent years it has become increasingly common for dealers to *reverse in* securities shorted rather than to borrow them. One reason is that the reverse may be cheaper. When a dealer borrows securities, he gives up other securities as collateral and pays the lender a borrowing fee, which typically equals ½ of 1% but may be more if many people want to short an issue at once. On a reverse the dealer obtains the securities shorted by buying them from an investor with an agreement to repurchase. In effect the dealer is extending a collateralized loan to the owner of these securities. The owner takes the loan because he needs cash or, more typically, because he can reinvest the loan proceeds at a higher rate, and the reverse thus becomes to him part of a profitable arbitrage.

Whether a dealer borrows securities or reverses them in, he must make an *investment*—in the first case in collateral, in the second case in a loan to the institution on the other side of the reverse. To figure which

investment would yield more, he compares the rate he could earn on the collateral *minus* the borrowing fee with the reverse rate. For example, suppose a dealer has some short-dated paper yielding 9.25% he could use as collateral. If he did so, he would own that paper at 9.25% minus the 0.5% borrowing fee; that is, at an effective rate of 8.75%. If the reverse rate were 9%, he would do better on the reverse.

A dealer's overall cost on a short is (1) the interest that accrues on the securities shorted (rise in value in the case of a discount security) over the period the short is outstanding, *minus* (2) the yield on the off-setting investment he makes. If the reverse rate exceeds the net rate he could earn on collateral backing a borrowing, reversing will be the cheaper way to support his short.

A dealer who borrows securities to support a short can never know with certainty how long he can have those securities because borrowed securities can be called by the lender on a day's notice. If, alternatively, a dealer reverses in securities for a fixed period, he knows he will have the securities for that time. Thus a dealer who anticipates maintaining a short for some time may choose to cover through a reverse rather than a borrowing partly because a reverse offers him certainty of availability.

RP AND REVERSE BOOK

A large dealer who is known to the Street can borrow more in the repo market and at better rates than can a small dealer or a corporate portfolio manager. Thus a large dealer finds knocking at his doors not only customers who want to give him repo money but would-be borrowers who want to reverse out securities to him because that is the cheapest way they can borrow. In response to the latter demand, large dealers have taken to doing repo and reverse not just to suit their own needs but as a profit-making service to customers. In providing that service, the dealer takes in securities on one side at one rate and hangs them out on the other side at a slightly more favorable (lower) rate; or to put it the other way around, the dealer borrows money from his repo customers at one rate and lends it to his reverse customers at a slightly higher rate. In doing so, the dealer is acting like a bank, and dealers know this well. As one noted, "This shop *is* a bank. We have customers lining up every morning to give us money. Also we are in the business of finding people who will give us securities at a little better rate than we can push them out the repo door. So we are a bank taking out our little spread, acting—if you will—as a financial intermediary."

A dealer who seeks to profit by borrowing in the repo market and lending in the reverse market ends up in effect running a *book* in repo. And,

he can mismatch that book to increase his profit, that is, borrow short and lend long.

POSITIONING AND PROFITS

Ever since the Fed turned monetarist with a vengeance in October 1979, interest rates—short- and long-term—have displayed a degree of volatility far exceeding anything experienced in past years (Figure 5–1).

The recent volatility in interest rates has altered both the relative importance that many dealers assign to positioning as a source of profits and also the size and ways in which they are willing to position. Prior to the big run up in interest rates that began in 1979, it was hard to find a big dealer who did not claim to make his real profits from big position plays that were on the mark. There are still shops that operate this way: They might be satisfied to lose money for four months in small amounts and then to make it big in the fifth month.

Among dealer shops today, however, a more typical attitude is that the first step in building a successful, long-term operation is to establish a mix of dependable profit sources that can be counted on to be there in good markets and bad. For such a shop, position profits are icing on the cake not the cake itself. Typical of this attitude is a bank dealer who noted, "Our focus has changed from one where we were always trying to make large amounts of money from guessing right the big swings in the market to one where we are trying to develop in our department a base of operations that makes money day in and day out. If you can build a business that makes money consistently, then you can afford to speculate with money that you have made as a department, as opposed to speculating with the bank's capital."

One base for earning consistent profits that is getting much attention from dealers these days is retail business. In describing operations, one dealer after another will stress the importance they place on building a solid retail business by providing good markets to retail. Noted one manager, "For us to make money, we had to focus on the real nuts and bolts of the business—service. We look at our business as one in which we provide our clients access to the market, investment advice, risk transfer, and execution."

No dealer can stand ready to make markets with customers without holding inventory and being willing to take securities into position on which customers want to bid. Shops that stress making markets to retail realize this and emphasize techniques to minimize the risks inherent in being a market maker. One technique is hedging. Hedging, which used

to be a sometimes affair, now gets a lot of attention especially with the development in Chicago of large and liquid futures markets in governments and other securities. Using these markets, a dealer can transfer the risk generated by customer business back into the markets a lot faster than formerly, and agile shops do just that.

Dealers trying to make money regularly on retail business also strive to develop techniques to anticipate order flow. Said one dealer, "We put a lot of effort into developing relations with major buyers and sellers of securities so that they will give us the inquiry. When we look at the brokers' screens and there is a lot of activity in a sector, we want to know who is participating and what they are doing. This is a crucial part of our business. Now we *all* know what the Fed is doing. What is really tough is to keep on top of and anticipate what retail is or will be doing."

Arbitrage is another base that more dealers are seeking to develop as a source of consistent profits—not spectacular gains but 10 basis points here and 30 there earned by observing an anomaly in the market, taking a position against it, and then having the patience to wait until natural market forces eliminate that anomaly and permit the arbitrage to be unwound at a profit.

ARBITRAGES

Pure *arbitrage* means to buy at a low price in one market and simultaneously resell at a higher price in another market. Money market participants use the term *arbitrage* to refer not only to pure arbitrage, but to various transactions in which they seek to profit by *exploiting anomalies* either in the yield curve or in the pattern of rates established between different instruments. Typically the anomaly is that the yield spread between two similar instruments is too wide or too narrow: one instrument is priced too generously relative to the other. To exploit such an anomaly, the arbitrager *shorts* the expensive instrument and goes *long* in its underpriced cousin.

If the arbitrager is successful, he will be able to unwind his arbitrage at a profit because the abnormal yield spread will have changed in one of several ways: (1) the security shorted will have fallen in price and risen in yield, (2) the security purchased will have risen in price and fallen in yield, or (3) a combination of the two will have occurred.

In the money market, yield spread arbitrages are often done (1) between identical instruments of similar maturity (one government is priced too generously relative to another of similar maturity) and (2) between different instruments of the same maturity (an agency issue is priced too generously relative to a government issue of the same maturity).

In a strictly defined yield spread arbitrage (the long and the short positions in similar maturities), the arbitrager exposes himself to *no market risk.* If rates rise, the resulting loss on his long position will be offset by profits on his short position; if rates fall, the reverse will occur. Thus the arbitrager does not base his position on a prediction of the direction of market rates; he is concerned about a possible move up or down in interest rates only insofar as such a move might alter yield spreads in the money market.

A pure arbitrage involves *no* risk, since the sale and purchase are assumed to occur simultaneously or almost so. An arbitrage based on a yield spread anomaly involves no market risk, but it does involve risk of another sort: The arbitrager is speculating on a yield spread. If he bets that a given spread will narrow and it widens, he will lose money. Thus even a strictly defined yield spread arbitrage offers no locked-in profit.

Most money market dealers, with the exception of commercial paper and muni note dealers, actively play the arbitrage game. They have input to a computer all sorts of information on historical yield spreads and have programmed the computer to identify anomalies in prevailing spreads as they feed into it data on current yields. Dealers used the resulting "helpful hints to the arbitrager" both to set up arbitrages themselves and to advise clients of arbitrage opportunities.

Generally in a dealer shop, arbitrage is done in an account that is separate from the *naked trading* account. Arbitrage and naked trading are distinctly different lines of business. The trader who seeks to profit from a naked position long or short is a specialist in one narrow sector of the market, and the positions he assumes are based on a prediction of interest rate trends and how they are likely to affect yields in his sector of the market. The arbitrager, in contrast, has to track yields in a number of market sectors, and if he engages in strictly defined yield-spread arbitrage, he is not much concerned with whether rates are likely to rise or fall.

Anomalies in yield spreads that offer opportunities for profitable arbitrage arise due to various temporary aberrations in market demand or supply. For example, if the Treasury brings a big 4-year note issue to market, it might trade for a time at a higher rate than surrounding issues because investors were loath to take the capital gains or losses they would have to in order to swap into the new issue. In this case the cause of the out-of-line yield spread would be, for the time it persisted, that the new issue had not been fully distributed. Alternatively, an anomaly might be created by a particular issue being in extremely scarce supply.

Bull and *bear market arbitrages* are based on a view of where interest rates are going. A bull market arbitrager anticipates a fall in interest rates

and a rise in securities prices. Thus he might, for example, short 2-year Treasuries and go long in 10-year Treasuries on a one-for-one basis, hoping to profit, when rates fall, from the long coupon appreciating more than the short coupon. If, alternatively, the arbitrager were bearish, he would do the reverse: short long governments and buy short ones.

An arbitrage can also be set up to profit from an anticipated change in the slope of the yield curve. For example, an arbitrager who anticipated a flattening of the yield curve might buy notes in the 7-year area for high yield and short notes in the 2-year area not necessarily on a one-to-one basis. If the yield curve flattened with no change in average rate levels, the 7-year note would appreciate, the 2-year note would decline in price, and the arbitrage could be closed out at a profit.

Money market practitioners are wont to call any pair of long and short positions an arbitrage; as the maturities of the securities involved in the transaction get further and further apart, however, price risk increases, and at some point the "arbitrage" becomes in reality two separate speculative positions, a naked long and a naked short.

Money market arbitragers normally put on both sides of an arbitrage simultaneously, but they rarely take them off simultaneously. As one dealer noted, "The compulsion to *lift* a leg [unwind one side of an arbitrage before the other] is overwhelming. Hardly anyone ever has the discipline to unwind both sides simultaneously. Instead they will first unwind the side that makes the most sense against the market. If, for example, the trader thinks the market is going to do better, he will lift a leg by covering the short."

RELATIVE VALUE

We have said that a dealer will position securities if he is bullish. In choosing which securities to buy, he considers relative value.

Every rational investor is interested in risk, liquidity, and return. Specifically he wants maximum return, maximum liquidity, and minimum risk. When he shops for securities, however, he finds that the real world presents him with nothing but trade-offs; securities offering higher returns tend to be riskier or less liquid than securities offering lower returns. That is as true in the money market as elsewhere, and it is the reason money market dealers think first of *relative* value when they decide to position.

If the spread at which one security is trading relative to another more than adequately compensates for the fact that the high-yield security is riskier or less liquid than the low-yield security, the high-yield security has greater relative value and should be bought in preference to the low-yield security. If, alternatively, the spread is inadequate, then the low-yield security has greater relative value and should be bought in preference

to the high-yield security. When dealers talk about relative value, they are really talking about the management of credit risk, market risk, and liquidity.

How relative value considerations affect a dealer's decisions as to what to position was put rather nicely by one dealer, "When we are all bullish, my bill trader, my CD trader, and my BA trader all want to take on stuff, and my reverse trader wants to take on 90-day collateral. At that point we have to sit down and get our heads together about relative value theory. Say we want to position $100 million in 6 months and under. Our most obvious options are CDs and bills. If, because of unusual supply conditions in the CD market, CDs are trading at a narrow spread—8 basis points—to bills, we are not going to buy CDs. Now picture a slightly different situation. Loans are not increasing at major New York banks, and additionally CDs are trading in the 6-month area 35 basis points off bills. We expect market rates to fall, and we also expect the spread between CDs and bills to narrow. In this situation CDs have greater relative value, so we will buy some. *But* putting all our eggs in one basket might be terribly unwise because we can only make an intelligent guess about supply in the CD market. Morgan might do a large Euro loan and fund the first 6 months with domestic CDs. If so, bing, we get knocked out of the water. We do not get the price action we expected out of the CD market even though the market as a whole rallies. Because that's possible, we might go 60% CDs and 40% bills—hedge our bets by diversifying. That way we will not miss the entire flip. I have seen it happen on numerous occasions, when we have done half bills and half CDs, that bills rallied 30 basis points—a nice flip we had anticipated—and CDs just sat there like a rock."

Relative value considerations arise not only in choices between different instruments but in choices between different maturity sectors of the same market. A dealer might ask whether he should position 6-month or 1-year bills. If the yield curve were unusually steep out to 1 year and the dealer expected it to flatten, then the year bill would have more relative value than the 6-month bill.

THE NEXT CHAPTER

In the next chapter, we turn to the *brokers* and other communications networks that enable each of the decentralized, over-the-counter sectors of the money market to operate in truth as a single, competitive, and efficient market.

Chapter 6

The market makers: Brokers and other information networks

FOR A MARKET OR SET OF MARKETS TO BE COMPETITIVE, a key requisite is that information on market prices be widely disseminated among market participants. In the money market, this condition is more than met; throughout the day, money market brokers and other vendors of information busily beam into trading rooms current money market prices as well as a wealth of other information: prices in related markets, latest values of economic indicators, money supply numbers, and so on.

THE BROKERS

A broker is a firm that brings buyers and sellers together for a commission. Unlike dealers, brokers by definition do not position. Brokers are everywhere in the money market. They are active in the *interdealer* markets in governments, agencies, CDs, bankers' acceptances, repo, and reverse, and in the *interbank* markets for Fed funds and Euro time deposits.[1]

---

[1] Some people call money market brokers *brokers' brokers* in order to distinguish them from stock brokers. This cumbersome bit of jargon is not needed in the money market, since no one there would confuse a broker of governments with Merrill Lynch, the parent of Merrill Lynch's GSI (Government Securities Inc.).

Volume and commissions

The volumes of funds and securities that are brokered each business day are staggering. Unfortunately, because statistics on brokered trades are not collected in most sectors of the market, it is impossible to put precise dollar figures on these amounts. Currently, almost all interdealer trades in governments and agencies are done through brokers.

Brokers could not survive without a huge volume of trades because the commissions they receive per $1 million of funds or securities brokered are small. In the bill market, brokerage on 90-day bills works out to $12.50 per $1 million; in the Fed funds market, on overnight trades it's only $0.50 per $1 million. In some sectors of the market (Fed funds and Euros) brokerage is paid by both the buyer and the seller; in others (governments and agencies), it is paid only by the dealer who initiates a trade by either hitting a bid or taking an offer quoted by the broker.

The service sold

Much of what a broker is selling his clients is a fast information service that tells the trader where the market is—what bids and offers are and how much they are good for. Speed of communication is thus crucial to a money market broker, and each has before him a board of direct phone lines through which he can contact every important trader he services by merely punching a button. Over those lines brokers constantly collect bids and offers throughout the day. They pass these on to other traders either by phone calls or more commonly over display screens, referred to throughout the industry as *CRTs*—short for cathode ray tubes.

In many sectors of the market (governments, Euro time deposits) the broker gives runs: bids and offers for a number of issues or maturities. In others (the market for overnight Fed funds), just one bid and offer are quoted. In some sectors of the market, bids and offers are good until withdrawn; in others they are understood to be good for only a few minutes.

The pace at which brokering is done in all sectors of the money market is hectic most of the time and frantic at certain crucial moments—in the Fed funds market on Wednesday afternoon when the banks settle with the Fed, in the government market on Thursday afternoon after the Fed announces money supply figures.

Brokerage operations vary a lot in size. Since shops dealing in CDs have a single CD trader, CDs can be brokered by just a couple of people sitting in a small room with a battery of direct phone lines. Brokering governments or Euros takes more personnel because there are many more traders to be covered and many more bids and offers to be quoted. Some brokerage outfits are large because they broker a number of

different instruments. A Euro broker, for example, often brokers foreign exchange, and some firms that broker Fed funds also broker a potpourri of other instruments.

A broker has to be not only quick but *careful* because he is normally expected to substantiate any bid or offer he quotes. This means that, if he quotes a market inaccurately to a trader, he must either (1) pay that trader an amount equal to the difference between the price he quoted and the price at which the trade can actually be got off or (2) buy securities from or sell securities to that trader at the quoted price and then cover, typically at a loss, his resulting long or short position.

The ethics of brokering are strict in all sectors of the money market. A broker is not supposed to and never will give up the names of the dealers or banks that are bidding or offering through him. He simply quotes prices and size. However, in certain markets, once a bid is hit or an offer taken, names are given up. In the Fed funds market, for example, before the seller can agree to a trade, he must know to whom he is selling because he has to check that he has a line to the buyer and that that line is not full. Also, the buyer has to know who the seller is because the two institutions clear the transaction directly with each other over the Fed wire. In many brokered securities trades, in contrast, the seller never knows who the buyer is, and vice versa.

There are certain rules of ethics that brokers' clients are expected to observe. In particular, in markets in which names are given up, the customer is not supposed to then go around the broker and do the trade direct. Also, brokers feel it is unfair of a trader to use them as an information service and just do small trades through them. Traders who make a practice of this get to be known and ignored by brokers.

Usefulness of brokers

In recent years brokerage has been introduced to almost every sector of the money market; and in those market sectors where it did exist, the use of brokers has increased dramatically. One reason is that in all sectors of the market the number of dealers has expanded sharply; as a result, it has become increasingly difficult for a trader to know where other traders are quoting the market and to rapidly disseminate his own bids and offers other than through the communications network provided by the brokers. In the government market, there are 40 primary dealers, and no bill trader can possibly keep in touch with his counterparts at other shops by talking directly to each of them.

Another reason brokers are used is anonymity. A big dealer may operate in such size that simply by bidding or offering, he will affect either market quotes or the size for which they are good. A trader who would be will-

ing to buy $15 million in bills through a broker might, for example, be leery of buying the same amount at the same price from a big position house like Salomon Brothers for fear that Sali might have a lot more of these bills to sell.

A second reason anonymity is valued by traders is the "ego element." In the words of one dealer, "Anonymity is very important to those giant egos on Wall Street. When they make a bad trade, they just do not want the whole world to watch them unwind it at a loss."

Still another reason the brokers are used is because many traders literally hate each other, usually because of some underlying ethical issue, real or perceived. As one trader noted, "There are guys I would not deal with personally, but if it happens through a broker, well OK. Money is green whatever the source."

A final reason brokers are used, particularly in the government market, is that the brokers' screens provide an arena in which a trader can paint pictures and play other trading games.

Agent or principal?

All brokers of governments claim that, whenever they broker a trade in governments, they are acting *not as a principal, but as an agent for undisclosed principals.* Some dealers on the Street and certain lawyers take the position that any entity that acts in a transaction as an agent for an undisclosed third party assumes in that transaction—like it or not—the role of principal.

So long as all goes smoothly, whether a broker of governments or of other securities is acting as agent or principal has no impact on the outcome of the transaction. Where the legal position of the broker does matter is if the principal on one side of a brokered trade or other transaction—a reverse, a borrowing of securities or whatever—fails to fulfill its obligation under that transaction and, as a result, the principal on the other side stands to lose money. As noted, if the amount of the loss is small and the problem has perhaps arisen out of a misunderstanding, the broker will absorb the loss in the interests of customer relationships. But if the foulup is not the broker's fault and if making the "injured party" whole would cost the broker hundreds of thousands of dollars or more, the broker is likely to go to court and have his lawyer argue, "Broker XYZ has *no* responsibility for any losses incurred by one party to a trade brokered by XYZ because the second party to that trade failed to live up to his side of the bargain. Broker XYZ was acting solely as *agent*, not principal."

Personnel

Brokering is much more than quoting rates. As brokers are wont to note, it's a highly professional business. The broker is often required to make split-second decisions about difficult questions. If a trader offers at a price and the broker has x bids at that price on his pad, with which buyer does he cross the trade? Technically he attempts to decide who was there first, but the choice is often complicated by the fact that the offer is for one amount, the bids for others.

Also, in some sectors of the money market, a broker does more than quote rates. The buyer or seller may look to him for information on the tone of the market, and it's the broker's job to sense that tone and be able to communicate it—to say, for example, to a bidder, "The market's 5/16-3/8, last trade at 5, but I think it could be worth 3/8."

Being a broker is also part salesmanship, to get a buyer or seller who has done one trade to let the broker continue to work for him. This is especially the case in markets, such as those for Fed funds and Euros, where a dealer who does a trade is likely to have a lot more business to do in the same direction during the day. In one area of brokering, the reverse market, salesmanship is crucial. To get a bank or an S&L to reverse out securities, the broker almost always has to point out a profitable arbitrage and then sell the institution on doing that arbitrage.

Being a good broker requires a special mix of talents. Salesmanship is one. In addition, a broker must be able to listen with one ear on the phone and keep the other tuned to bids and offers coming in around him, to maintain a feel for his own market and for other related markets as well. A good broker also must be able to think on his feet and often use his own personality to put trades together. As one broker noted, "Brightness is not enough; anyone can quote a market."

Many brokers are ex-traders, people who have the advantage when they come to brokering of knowing a market and how traders in it operate. One reason traders become brokers is the pressure under which traders operate. Another is their own inability to do what many good traders do, forget their position when they go home. Said one successful broker, "Trading is a problem. You track the things you think might impact the market and then buy. All too often the unexpected—war in the Mid-East—happens and you end up being right for the wrong reason, or vice versa. Once as a trader, I was down three-quarters of a million. I made 2 million the next month, but accepting the fact that I had done something stupid at one point in time was too much. It's part of the reason I became a broker."

Consolidation of brokers

In recent years there has been a strong tendency for brokers to merge. The reasons are various. For a big broker, a marriage that adds to capital can look extremely attractive. A second reason for broker mergers is that a shop that handles a wide menu of securities has a better chance of getting its foot into a dealer's door and, once there, can better service the dealer's needs. Institutions that reverse out securities often do so, for example, as part of an arbitrage in which they invest in another security; a broker that offers one-stop shopping can put together the whole arbitrage package.

In Euro and foreign exchange brokering, both cross-market and transatlantic mergers made sense. The foreign exchange and Euromarkets could not be separated, and no broker could provide an international service without having an office or tie of some sort in at least both New York and London.

The advent of Liberty

The major brokers of governments, of which there are six or seven, show their quotes to and do business with only the big primary dealers recognized by the Federal Reserve Bank of New York. These brokers form what economists would call an oligopoly. It's possible to enter their business, but it's expensive and tough enough to discourage most people from trying. All this means that, until recently, brokers of governments were nicely insulated from price competition.

Over the last decade, several developments occurred that tended to increase brokers' profits. First, there were technological changes that lowered the cost of brokering. Second, huge increases occurred in the average size and number of brokered interdealer trades; brokers could, moreover, accommodate this extra business at limited additional cost. Despite these developments, no broker cut his rates; interbroker price competition was nil. The upshot was that brokers earned increasingly high profits, profits that dealers finally came to regard as absurd. A dealer's definition of what constituted an absurd level of brokers' profits was simple: at the old brokerage rates ($78 per million on a trade of government bonds), a big broker who assumed *no risk* was earning, on an $80 billion-volume day, more profit than was the average dealer who—to make any money—had to assume *lots of risk*.

To introduce some price competition to the world of government brokering, in 1986 Salomon Brothers, together with a group of 30 other dealers, formed a new government bond broker, Liberty Brokerage, Inc. The advent of Liberty caused brokerage rates on government notes and bonds to fall immediately by 50%, and then yet more.

Forcing a cut in brokerage rates was not the sole objective of the dealers who formed Liberty. Another was to create the possibility for more netting of interdealer trades at the broker level, a change that would decrease the volume of trades that dealers must clear through their clearing banks. Doing the latter, not an easy task, would offer dealers two advantages: it would cut their normal operating costs, and it would decrease the opportunities for the costly, occasional mistakes that inevitably creep into any clearing operation.

Who may tune in

Most brokers of governments will accept as clients only *primary dealers* (dealers with whom the Fed does business) and *"aspiring" dealers* (dealers who report to the Fed and are seeking primary-dealer status.)[2] The exception is Cantor Fitzgerald, who has opened its screens to other dealers and major investors who meet its credit standards. Dealers denied access to the market that the activities of the principal brokers of governments and the primary dealers create have criticized this "inside market" as monopolistic; and one nonprimary dealer, Lazard Freres & Co. is suing to end what it terms the "private club approach" to the dissemination of bond price information. The U.S. General Accounting Office, in consultation with the Fed, the Treasury, and the SEC, is also looking into the question of whether access to brokers' electronic screens should be widened.

Naturally, the primary dealers oppose the giving by the brokers of wider access to their screens. In doing so, the primary dealers argue that widening access to the brokers' screens would reduce liquidity in the government market.

COMMUNICATIONS

In a discussion of the makers of the money market, ignoring the phone company, Telexes, CRTs, computers, and other communications facilities would be a serious omission. Without Ma Bell and her foreign counterparts, the money market would be utterly different. That the money market is a single market that closely approaches the economist's assumption of perfect information is currently due in no small part to the fact that New York brokers and traders are one push of a direct-phone-line button away from the B of A and often only a four-digit extension from London, Singapore, and other distant spots. All this is extremely expensive. Banks

---

[2] In May 1987, there were 40 primary dealers, including several Japanese dealers, and 13 aspiring dealers.

spend well over half a billion on phone bills; and the nonbank dealers and brokers spend huge amounts in addition to that. To cut costs, the banking industry has considered setting up a private interbank phone network, which would be the most ambitious private phone network in the country.

The phone bill is one reason for the concentration of the money market in New York. The brokers in particular have to be there to minimize communications costs. It is cheaper to be in New York with one direct phone line to the B of A than to be in San Francisco with 30 direct lines to New York.

Phones, while ubiquitous, are not enough. Giving and receiving quotes over the phone takes more time than money market participants have; thus the growing role of CRTs.

Years ago, the only way money market participants could get current quotes was by calling brokers and dealers. Moreover, to get a range of quotes they had to make several calls because no quote system covered the whole market. In 1968 a new organization, *Telerate*, began to remedy this situation by quoting commercial paper rates on a two-page, CRT display system; it then had 50 subscribers. From this modest start, the system was quickly expanded because people wanted more information.

Today several hundred pages of information on credit market quotes and statistics are available to Telerate subscribers; the subscriber gets the page he wants by pressing a series of numbered buttons. Information on current quotes, offerings, and bids are inputted into the system through computers around the country, and the system is dynamically updated; that is, if GMAC changed its posted rate while a viewer is looking at the commercial paper quotes, the quotes change as GMAC inputs its new rates into the system. A wide range of institutions now use Telerate; its advent has not only eliminated a lot of phone calls but vastly improved communications within the money market. On the international scene, there is a similar *Reuters* system that flashes information on the Euromarket, the foreign exchange market, and other related markets into foreign countries and the United States. Since the money market is international in scope, it was to be expected that both Telerate and Reuters invaded each others' turf both geographically and in terms of information provided.

Many brokers in the government and other markets have also replaced endless phone quotes with CRTs that they have placed before the traders at dealer shops. Today every trading room is literally strewn with CRTs.

Deathknell of the dumb terminal?

When Telerate and other quote systems first hit money market trading rooms with their CRTs, the latter were regarded as incredibly useful, *high-*

tech gadgets—a paradigm of the marvels that modern technology could produce. Alas, no love affair is forever.

With the advent of the IBM PC in 1981, the CRTs of information vendors began to be described disparagingly as "dumb" terminals. A dumb terminal gives you quotes but that's it; to massage a quote, you must copy it down from your CRT. From there on in, you're on your own.

The power and the cheapness of the IBM PC, combined with the fact that most young people today feel as comfortable with a computer as secretaries of yore felt with a typewriter, created a need and niche for a new sort of information system: one that fed quotes into a smart terminal. With such a system, for a tidy annual fee, the customer gets an IBM PC, current quotes, access to a database of past quotes, and an analytic software package all in one fell swoop.

For investors, traders, and arbitragers, this innovation offers the opportunity to do a lot of analysis that's highly useful, especially if doing it doesn't require much time and effort. For example, if a user sees an instrument whose price looks attractive, he can, using his smart terminal, calculate the instrument's yield on any of a variety of bases, its duration, its past spread to some other instrument. The possibilities are endless. The computer's response time is, of course, rapid. This is a crucial advantage to a user because markets move so fast today that a trader or investor can't wait long for analysis, lest he find that the quote that interested him is history before he's set to act.

Smart terminals have even permitted some traders to change their lifestyles outside of business hours. If a user likes to look at technical charts, he can pick the technical indicators that he wants to follow and then instruct, as often as he wants, his computer to update and print these indicators. Said one trader, "I live in Jersey but used to sleep weeknights in New York, so I'd have time to do my charts. Now, a machine does them for me, and I see my wife seven nights a week." That's one guy who doesn't decry the onward march of technology.

Our remarks on smart terminals are not meant to indicate that the days of dumb terminals are necessarily numbered. Users of smart terminals often like to have an old, read-only Telerate sitting around for various reasons—they need other information it provides or they feel that, when markets move fast, Telerate's quotes stay more current.

The black box

While impressive, the various present CRT systems are not the ultimate state of the art. In the view of some participants, the money market is on the threshold of a communications revolution. One London dealer noted, "We are working on a system by which we will show our offerings and rates on a CRT. Say Ford in Dearborn, Michigan, hits our code.

They will be able to type on a machine, like a Telex, a message that will come up on our CRT in London: 'Want to buy your 5 million Chases, Oct. 17th, bid you ⅞.' We are offering at ¹³⁄₁₆ and decide to hit their bid. So we type in, 'OK, done.' Then they type in, 'Deliver to Morgan,' and the confirmations come out of the machine. We are going to put on the screen actual offerings; Cantor Fitzgerald already does that in governments, but they do not trade off the machine."

Said another dealer, envisioning much the same sort of development, "The firms like us without branch offices will introduce machines to the world to undercut the branch office franchises of the Merrills and the Salis. It is clear that for firms like us that lack branch offices, this is the cost-effective way to compete. We will trade off those machines; the *black box* is coming, and when it does, the market will go central marketplace."

THE NEXT CHAPTER

In the next chapter, we begin the heart of this book's story of how money market securities are cleared. Chapter 7 describes the development of the Fed's book-entry system: the Street's first steps toward trading, at least certain securities, *without moving paper.*

Part two

Clearing trades in money market securities

Chapter 7

The book-entry system: Background and history[1]

WE BEGIN CHAPTER 7 WITH A FEW WORDS OF PREFACE AND BACKGROUND: several brief definitions and then a description of the far-reaching institutional changes wrought by the *Depository Institutions Deregulation and Monetary Control Act of 1980* (Monetary Control Act or MCA).

REGISTERED, BEARER, AND BOOK-ENTRY SECURITIES

Prior to the introduction of what's called the *book-entry system,* all securities were issued in *physical form* and were evidenced by a *certificate.* In the case of notes and bonds, this certificate has always been an engraved, elaborate affair. In the case of BAs and CDs, in contrast, the certificate is a not-so-impressive slip of paper.

---

[1]The Federal Reserve plays a key role in the book-entry system. For the benefit of any readers unfamiliar with the Fed, we present, in the appendix to this chapter, a short description of this weighty, financial lady.

77

Physical securities come in *two* forms, registered and bearer. In the case of *registered* securities, the issuer (more likely, his *agent*) maintains a list of the holders of record of its issue; and it transmits, automatically to those holders, any payments due them. A *bearer* security does not have the name of its owner inscribed on it. A bearer security is assumed to be owned by he who bears it. Bearer notes and bonds (except for *zero-coupon* bonds, which are non-interest-bearing bonds) always have attached to them dated *coupons,* which look like oversize postage stamps. When a coupon date arrives, the owner of the bond clips the appropriate coupon and presents it, often via a commercial bank, for payment of interest due him. Registered notes and bonds have no attached coupons, since the issuer or his agent always maintains a record of who owns such securities and to whom periodic payments of coupon interest are therefore due. While the payment of coupon interest to the holder of a registered security is automatic, the owner of such a security must, when his security matures, present his certificate to receive payment of principal. All physical securities have certificate numbers.

Today, all Treasury securities, most federal agency securities, many municipal notes, and some other securities as well are no longer issued in physical form. Instead, they have been converted to book-entry form. In this chapter, we describe how and why this conversion occurred. In Chapter 8, we discuss the operation of the book-entry system today.

TWO BRIEF DEFINITIONS

The book-entry system is a scheme whereby, first, the Treasury and, later, federal credit agencies substituted, for physical securities (bearer and registered), computerized records of ownership and other interests in securities held in the system. Book-entry records are maintained by the Federal Reserve, by commercial banks, and by other parties who figure in the tiered structure of the book-entry system (Figure 8–1, p. 95).

Fedwire is a communications network and means of settlement that links Federal Reserve Banks to any bank or other depository institution that wants and is willing to pay fees to link up to it. Fedwire is used, by institutions linked to it, to direct the Fed, usually via a computer-to-computer message, to transfer money (Fed funds), book-entry securities, or both.

THE MONETARY CONTROL ACT OF 1980

As background for a discussion of the book-entry system and, later, of the Fed wire, a few words must be said about reserve requirements, Fed services, and the Monetary Control Act of 1980. Anyone whose study of economics predates 1980 will surely recall, from the discussion of

monetary policy, that in textbook discussions banks used to appear in *two* flavors. Some banks—the group comprised all nationally chartered banks and a number of big, state-chartered banks—were *member banks,* that is, members of the Federal Reserve System (FRS). Many other small-to-medium-size, state-chartered banks were *nonmember banks.* All member banks were required to hold at the Fed reserves equal to a percentage—the percentage varied with the type of deposit—of the total deposits, by type, made with them. Nonmember banks were not subject to reserve requirements.

Reserve requirements

The Fed used to offer member banks various services *free of charge,* and the most important service was check clearing. Also, only member banks had direct access to the Fedwire for money and securities transfers. These were the pluses a member of the Fed enjoyed—the big minus was that club dues were high: a member bank was required to hold reserves in a non-interest-bearing account at the Fed.

Congress legislated reserve requirements because its members observed that runs on banks often led banks that had exhausted their liquidity to shut their doors. Requiring banks to hold reserves, Congress reasoned, would contribute to bank liquidity and, thereby, decrease bank closings. That made as much sense as Congress writing a hunger-prevention statute that stated: henceforth, every citizen is required to keep a $100-minimum balance in his checking account so that he will always have enough money on hand to buy groceries. The fallacy of such a law is that, once a citizen got down to his last $100, he would have, if he wanted to abide by the law, one choice: to starve. Required reserves do not and never did contribute to bank liquidity.

In the minds of many, required reserves are also supposed to serve a second useful function: to make it possible for the Fed to carry out monetary policy by raising or lowering the supply of reserves available to banks relative to the amount of reserves that banks are required to hold. This notion, too, is incorrect. The Fed, it's easy to show, could tighten or ease credit through open market operations just as well whether required reserves were 0% (no required reserves) or 10%.

The above facts are understood, vaguely at least, by the powers that be in Washington; but required reserves, like the poor, are still with us—and probably always will be. In practice, requiring banks to hold non-interest-bearing reserves at the Fed has turned out to be something its originators never envisioned: a *hidden tax* on banking, the proceeds of which go to the Treasury.

The mechanics of this tax are simple. The Fed enforces reserve requirements and invests all the free funds banks give it in interest-bearing

Treasuries and agencies. By doing so, the Fed has acquired a $180-billion portfolio of securities. In 1986, the Fed earned over $17 billion on this portfolio; it spent $1 billion on operating costs and transmitted the balance to the Treasury.

As the numbers above make clear, eliminating required reserves—or requiring the Fed to pay interest on bank reserves, a proposal that has also been bandied about—would be, from the point of view of the federal government, equivalent to a tax cut or a rise in government spending, depending on the measure adopted. Since the federal budget is constantly in deficit, the Treasury has been more interested in measures that would raise taxes and cut spending than in those that would do the reverse. Thus there has been little enthusiasm in Washington for tinkering either with required reserves or with the zero rate of return paid by the Fed on them.

Small bankers have always understood that meeting reserve requirements costs them money. With respect to FRS membership, they made a simple calculation: reserve requirements cost us X; the free services we get from the Fed are worth Y; X exceeds Y; therefore, we will opt out of the FRS; and any services, such as check clearing and access to the Fedwire, that we need we will buy from a correspondent bank who is a FRS member.

Changes under MCA

During the 1970s, more and more banks left the FRS, and that trend worried the Fed. It argued that the exit of these banks from the system was impairing its ability to implement monetary policy. At the same time, big money center banks complained that the U.S. branches of foreign banks were subjecting them to unfair competition: foreign bank branches and agencies were not required to hold reserves against deposits they received. Consequently, domestic bankers argued, such banks had a lower cost of funds than did domestic banks.

These perceived problems, plus the obvious need to get rid of the last vestiges of pernicious Regulation Q[2] (before it destroyed what was left

---

[2]Reg Q, promulgated by the Fed, barred member banks from paying market (i.e., competitive) rates of interest on deposits made with them. The FDIC and regulators of non-bank DIs established similar regulations that together clamped lids on the rates that all but a handful of other uninsured DIs could pay. As interest rates soared in the late-1970s, Reg Q and its cousins spawned the $200 billion-plus money fund industry. These regs also made many individuals active investors in Treasury bills and other money market paper; to them, 10 percent T bills sounded like a far better deal than a 5% or 5¼% savings account at a bank or other DI.

of the banking and S&L industries) led to the passage in 1980 of the *Monetary Control Act.*[3]

To keep the Fed and domestic money market banks happy, MCA also had something to say about reserve requirements. Over an eight-year phase-in period, the Fed was to impose reserve requirements on all nonmember banks and on all other DIs as well. This change was not all that expensive for S&Ls and other thrifts, because during the phase-in period, reserve requirements on savings and time deposits held by individuals were eliminated.

MCA made all DIs pay the FRS dues that only member banks previously had to pay; so, logically, the law mandated that, henceforth, *all* DIs, foreign bank branches included, would have access to *all* services provided by the Fed and to loans at the discount window as well. After MCA was passed, the terms *member bank* and *nonmember bank* nearly became obsolete—many Fed regulations now apply to DIs, and Fed statistics that once described member banks now describe DIs.

Member banks were always required to buy stock in Federal Reserve Banks, which are, nominally, privately owned. Large banks still retain their Fed memberships, that is, still own stock of Federal Reserve Banks. These banks do so for prestige and to retain a voice in operational matters of concern to them.

Pricing of Fed services. In the Monetary Control Act, Congress required that the Fed price the services it had previously provided to member banks and, more recently, to other DIs free of charge. This innovation was supposed to encourage, and has in fact encouraged, more private-sector competition with the Fed; fees have increased the efficiency with which various services, of which the Fed used to be the principal supplier, are now provided to DIs.

The pricing of Fed services to reflect costs is relevant to the discussion below. Today the Fed is required to price (reflect its costs for) transfers on the Fedwire of both money and securities.

The Fed is also required to price any custodial services it provides to DIs. Banks have long been in the habit of leaving some or all of their muni portfolios with the Fed. A bank that holds in custody at the Fed securities that are *eligible* collateral for a loan at the discount window can borrow at the window simply and quickly: "First National, you say

---

[3]MCA provided for the gradual phasing out, now complete, of all regulatory ceilings on rates paid by all *depository institutions (DIs)*, which comprise banks, savings and loans *(S&Ls)*, trust companies, credit unions, savings banks, and foreign bank branches. Little DIs, in particular, small banks and small S&Ls, did not like this aspect of MCA, but they had two choices: try to live with it or die for sure. They opted for choice one.

that you want a $25 million loan at the window. Fine, you've got it. We [the Fed] will take $25 million of the collateral you have in custody with us and put it into a pledge account." That pledge account is controlled by the Fed, not the bank that owns the collateral.

Not all DIs are created equal. Fed descriptions of the book-entry system, like the one quoted below, now refer, not to member banks, but to DIs. It is true that MCA further blurred the line of demarcation between commercial banks and thrifts, but money market banks, small banks, and thrifts remain different animals. Of the 20,000 DIs in this land, only 5,500 have book-entry accounts at the Fed; of these, only 1,000 have on-line book-entry accounts. Presumably, the 14,500 DIs without book-entry accounts at the Fed figured that having such accounts would cost them more than it was worth—there are charges. DIs that lack Fed book-entry accounts, a priced Fed service, use banks that have such accounts as custodians for any book-entry securities they own or hold for customers.

THE BOOK-ENTRY SYSTEM

In brief, the book-entry system was designed to replace physical securities, which are issued by the Treasury and others, with book-entry accounting entries.

Registered and bearer Treasury securities

Until the late-1960s, the Treasury issued its securities in *definitive* form: All Treasury bills, notes, and bonds were issued as either bearer or registered securities. For registered Treasuries, of which there are still some outstanding, the Treasury maintains in Washington a record of who owns such securities and to whom periodic payments of coupon interest are therefore due.

The switch to book-entry

Physical securities are expensive to clear and to store; also, in an environment lacking tight security, they invite theft. To reduce the costs and problems associated with the trading and holding of physical securities, the Treasury and the Fed devised, beginning in 1968, a book-entry system for Treasuries. The intent was to eliminate *physical* Treasury securities by providing an alternative means for the issuance, maintenance, and transfer of such securities.

Under the book-entry system, entries are made in the accounts of Federal Reserve Banks, of commercial banks, and of other DIs to record both *ownership* of and other *"interests"* (custodial, trust, and pledges,

for example) in Treasury securities. Most, if not all, book-entry records are computerized; and most, but not all, transfers of book-entry securities are made using the Fedwire. "Fedwire," as the Fed calls its wire, is a computerized communications network that links each Federal Reserve Bank with other Federal Reserve Banks and with local institutions that maintain book-entry accounts with it.

Today, not only Treasury securities, but securities issued by most federal credit agencies (including many mortgage-backed issues) either can or can only be held in book-entry form. Both the dollar face amount and number of securities originally issued in, or convertible to, book entry are constantly growing.

HISTORY OF THE BOOK-ENTRY SYSTEM

The present book-entry system was not devised and implemented overnight; it evolved in a number of steps that spanned over a decade. The evolution of the book-entry system continues today. In 1983, the Fed completed a major upgrading of its computer facilities; that upgrading permitted the Fed to handle and process more messages and to track "interests" in a vastly greater number of book-entry issues.

CPDs

The first step toward modern clearance of Treasury securities was taken in the 1920s when Treasuries became transferable by telegraph between Federal Reserve Banks. At that time, all such transfers required approval by the Treasury's *Commissioner of the Public Debt.* Such transfers became known as *CPDs.*

Under the CPD system, the sender of securities, usually a commercial bank, delivered certificates to its local Federal Reserve office. That office, as fiscal agent of the Treasury, retired (by canceling) these certificates and sent a telegram describing the transfer to another Reserve office located near the institution receiving the securities. This second Reserve office issued new certificates to the receiving bank or deposited the securities in that bank's safekeeping account at the Fed. Thus, most CPD transfers required deliveries of paper certificates to and pickups of such certificates from the nearest Fed office.

While CPDs eliminated the need to transport physical government securities on long interstate hauls, the clearing of a sale of bonds, between a buyer and a seller located in the same city, remained cumbersome and time-consuming. Under the old system for doing this, the seller typically ordered his bank to deliver to the buyer, usually through a bank, a specified par amount of a particular issue against a specified payment. The delivering bank prepared an order authorizing the withdrawal of the

securities from its vault. Before being released from custody, these securities were counted by the delivering bank's vault personnel; they were also examined and counted once or twice more by the delivering bank's cage; they were then turned over to a messenger, sometimes armed, who went to the receiving bank. There the counting and examining of the securities for "good delivery" were repeated by the buyer's bank. Finally, the receiving bank, after preparing a deposit ticket or equivalent record, placed the securities in custody for the account of the buyer. To make payment, the buyer's bank either issued a bank check or transferred, often via the Fed wire, Fed funds to the seller's bank.

Government Securities Clearing Arrangement (GSCA)

Because of the difficulties experienced in New York City by banks and dealers making "street" deliveries (deliveries among themselves) of governments in physical form, a *Government Securities Clearing Arrangement (GSCA)* was established in New York City in 1965. Under GSCA, parties to the arrangement made (or received), toward the end of each business day, only one *net* delivery to (or from) each other. GSCA did not eliminate deliveries of physical governments within New York City, but it significantly reduced the size and frequency of such deliveries.

GSCA: history and operation. The Federal Reserve Bank of New York (FRBNY) has always been concerned about the cost, in both money and time, to itself and to N.Y.C. banks, that physical receipts and deliveries of U.S. government securities entailed. In the mid-1960s, the daily volume of incoming and outgoing, interdistrict wire transfers of governments handled by the FRBNY often totaled more than 1,500 separate receipts and deliveries. New York City, thus, provided an ideal situation for an experiment intended to reduce the physical movements of securities.

Accordingly, in 1965, the FRBNY proposed establishing a Government Securities Clearing Arrangement (GSCA). This arrangement was designed to eliminate or greatly reduce the burdensome operations performed by participating banks—counting, examining, and making physical delivery of such securities—when securities were, in connection with interdistrict transfers, withdrawn from one institution and deposited in another.

Under GSCA, a N.Y.C. bank transfering securities by wire to a Federal Reserve Bank outside the N.Y. district was not required to physically deliver securities to the FRBNY. Instead, the FRBNY *offset,* Treasury issue by Treasury issue, deliveries of securities by a N.Y.C. bank against receipts of securities, by that bank. This procedure resulted in the banks having *net* balances (plus or minus) in different issues with the FRBNY. Banks settled these net balances with the FRBNY in the afternoon. At the outset of the GSCA, it was estimated that new netting procedures would

eliminate up to 80% of the physical deliveries being made between the FRBNY and N.Y.C. banks in connection with telegraphic transfers of governments.

To operate GSCA, the FRBNY had to maintain clearing accounts, by issue, for each participating bank. In lieu of delivering and receiving securities for each individual wire transfer of securities, the FRBNY would debit (or credit) the appropriate securities accounts of each participating bank with the amounts, by issue, of all governments it sent (or received) during the day. Prior to the settlement hour, the FRBNY would inform each participating bank what amount of each Treasury issue it owed or was owed; actual settlement, accomplished by transfers of physical securities, was made at the FRBNY in the afternoon.

At this time, the Treasury held, for various fiscal purposes, at the FRBNY a stock of unissued U.S. government securities. To implement the clearing arrangement, the FRBNY had to obtain approval from the Treasury to use this stock to effect end-of-day settlements. This approval, received early in 1965, was essential to efficient clearing; it permitted the FRBNY to pay out securities "due to" participants at the settlement without awaiting receipt of securities of the same issue "due from" other participants.

The steps by which GSCA was implemented were as follows. In July of 1965, a pilot test of clearing between the FRBNY and Morgan Guaranty Trust was begun; specifically, the FRBNY began netting interdistrict CPDs received by and sent to Morgan's account. One month later, Irving Trust Co. became the second pioneer in this securities clearing arrangement. After several months of exchanging, in lieu of securities, tickets that represented transfers to and from the FRBNY, and after many meetings to iron out day-to-day operational problems, GSCA was temporarily suspended for further evaluation.

Based on the experience gained in this pilot test, all parties concluded that it would be feasible to operate efficiently under the clearing account concept. The Fed's arrangements with Morgan Guaranty and Irving Trust were resumed in January 1966 under letter agreements detailing the rights and responsibilities of the parties to the arrangement.

In August 1966, another major step was taken to reduce further the movement of physical securities between the two original participants. Morgan and Irving were permitted to "redirect" between themselves government securities originally transferred to them over the Fedwire. This step effectively "unblocked" securities that would otherwise be immobilized in the system until the settlement hour; it is believed that this was the first time that governments were transferred between N.Y.C. member banks without physical delivery.

The success of the pilot operation and the ability to "redirect" transfers to other participants induced other large N.Y.C. banks to join the group.

Bankers Trust and Manufacturers Hanover Trust became participants in late-August 1966; they were soon followed by First National City Bank (now Citibank), Chemical Bank, Chase Manhattan Bank, the Bank of New York, and other N.Y.C. banks.

The beginnings of the book-entry system

In January 1968, the Fed and the Treasury took a third crucial initiative to automate the government securities markets: the book-entry program. *This program was to replace, gradually, most of the pieces of paper representing both Treasury and federal agency securities with computerized book entries.* As this was done, it became possible to effect transactions in such securities by means of wire messages, including computer-to-computer communications.

The book-entry system was designed to improve the efficiency of operations in the government market by reducing the time, money, personnel, and space required to handle the increasing volume of transactions in government and agency securities, by ensuring adequate controls, and by minimizing the risk of loss or theft of such securities.

Introduction of the book-entry system required many changes in procedures by market participants, the introduction of new equipment, the training of personnel, and the resolution of complex tax, legal, and other issues. Consequently, the Fed and the Treasury planned that the book-entry system should be introduced in a series of carefully planned steps. Their intent was to begin using book-entry procedures for only a few types of transactions among a small number of market participants; then, gradually, the system was to be expanded by extending book-entry coverage to more types of transactions and to a wider range of participants.

Securities thefts and the insurance crisis. Things did not go according to plan. An abrupt rise in securities thefts caused an insurance crisis. Since it was the shuffling of paper securities within banks and dealerships and the transfer of such securities between institutions that invited theft, the timetable for conversion to book entry was accelerated.

The problem of securities thefts first came to public attention in late 1969 when, within a matter of weeks, $17 million in governments was stolen from three New York banks. By the end of that year, approximately $30 million in Treasury security losses had been incurred nationally; high losses due to theft continued in 1970. Looking back, one is surprised not that many millions of Treasuries were stolen, but rather that the number was not much larger. An old hand in the government market recalls working in a bank operations department that regularly sent out one unarmed messenger to deliver as much as $250 million of bearer

Treasuries. The bank added an armed guard only for trips to and from the Fed when the messenger might be carrying as much as $1 billion of bearer certificates.

The securities thefts that occurred in 1969 and 1970 led, in early 1971, to an insurance crisis that threatened the continued operation of the government market. At that time, the Continental Insurance Company announced plans to end its coverage of bearer government securities held by money center banks, dealers, and brokers. Since Continental was the major insurer of such securities, it was feared that, if Continental carried out its plans, the major participants in the government market would end operations and that trading in governments would grind to a halt.

To prevent this, the Fed, the Treasury, the insurance companies, and leaders of the banking and securities industries negotiated intensively over several months to develop a greatly accelerated program for extending the book-entry system.

The new book-entry program was designed to accelerate existing long-term plans for automation as rapidly as possible. To implement this program, the Treasury had to amend governing Treasury regulations, the Internal Revenue Service had to amend its tax rulings on dealer securities and tax-reporting requirements, and the Fed had to revise its operating rules and procedures. The program also required that New York City banks affected by the crisis begin promptly to convert their securities accounts to book entry to avert complete termination of their insurance coverage.

By April 1971, all necessary legal actions had been completed to accelerate the book-entry program. This program contemplated that the book-entry procedure would be extended in steps to cover various classes of securities: (1) securities owned by primary dealers, both bank and nonbank; (2) securities held by member banks in customer accounts; and (3) securities held by member banks in trust accounts. For step one to be implemented, special book-entry agreements, pledges, and similar arrangements had to be established; for step two to be implemented, certain legal questions under state laws had to be resolved. At this time, plans were also made for extending the book-entry program to securities issued by federal credit agencies.

The first stage of implementing the new book-entry system was limited to the New York City money market banks. These banks had the greatest problem with insurance coverage; also, it seemed a good idea for the Fed to use just a few banks to test the new procedures and to develop a pattern of book-entry accounts that could accommodate the operations of all member banks.

During the first six months of the new book-entry program, nine banks opened new book-entry accounts; these included several special ac-

counts in which customer securities were gradually deposited. Several banks—particularly banks that acted as clearing agents for nonbank dealers—encountered delays in moving to book entry because their computer systems were inadequate.

During the period, the capabilities of GSCA were further enlarged; computer switching systems came into operation, and all new book-entry accounts were integrated into the GSCA. Also, New York State enacted legislation, endorsed by the FRBNY, to permit the application of the book-entry procedure to governments held by banks as trustee.

After the new book-entry program had been tried for six months, its operations were subject to a comprehensive review; this review indicated that certain changes in the basic legal concepts underlying the book-entry procedure would be desirable and feasible. These changes, which concerned particularly transfers and pledges of customer securities, obviated certain operating complexities and resulted in a simpler system.

Transfers and pledges of Treasuries in book-entry form

The principal regulations that govern transfers and pledges of Treasury securities in book-entry form are sections 306.116(a) and 306.116(b) found in Subpart O of Treasury Circular No. 300, as amended. These regulations were designed to supersede, for book-entry securities, provisions in *states' Uniform Commercial Codes (UCCs),* which described what steps an owner of an item must take to *perfect his interest* in that item. To have a perfected interest in something is legal jargon for having an ownership claim that would stand up in court. In the case of securities, state UCCs stipulate that a buyer of a security can perfect his interest in that security either by taking possession of that security himself or by placing it with a third party under an arrangement whereby he (the buyer) can exercise direct control over the security. If, for example, a buyer purchases a security from a dealer, pays for it, and then leaves the security with his dealer who in turn leaves the security at his (the dealer's) clearing bank in a safekeeping account under his (the dealer's) control, the buyer has—at least in the view of some lawyers—not perfected his interest in the security.

Treasury subparagraphs (a) and (b), which govern ownership and other interests in book-entry securities, state:

(a) A transfer or a pledge of book-entry Treasury securities to a Reserve Bank (in its individual capacity or as Fiscal Agent of the United States), or to the United States, or to any transferee or pledgee eligible to maintain an appropriate book-entry account in its name with a Reserve Bank under this subpart, is effected and perfected, notwithstanding any provision of law to the contrary, by a Reserve Bank making an appropriate entry in its records of the securities transferred

or pledged. The making of such an entry in the records of a Reserve Bank shall (1) have the effect of a delivery in bearer form of definitive Treasury securities; (2) have the effect of a taking of delivery by the transferee or pledgee; (3) constitute the transferee or pledgee a holder; and (4) if a pledge, effect a perfected security interest therein in favor of the pledgee. A transfer or pledge of book-entry Treasury securities effected under this paragraph shall have priority over any transfer, pledge, or other interest, theretofore or thereafter effected or perfected under paragraph (b) of this section or in any other manner.

(b) A transfer or a pledge of transferable Treasury securities, or any interest therein, which is maintained by a Reserve Bank (in its individual capacity or as Fiscal Agent of the United States) in a book-entry account under this subpart, including securities in book-entry form under Sec. 306.117(a) (3), is effected, and a pledge is perfected, by any means that would be effective under applicable law to effect a transfer or to effect and perfect a pledge of the Treasury securities, or any interest therein, if the securities were maintained by the Reserve Bank in bearer definitive form. For purposes of transfer or pledge hereunder, book-entry Treasury securities maintained by a Reserve Bank shall, notwithstanding any provision of law to the contrary, be deemed to be maintained in bearer definitive form. A Reserve Bank maintaining book-entry Treasury securities either in its individual capacity or as Fiscal Agent of the United States is not a bailee for purposes of notification of pledges of those securities under this subsection, or a third person in possession for purposes of acknowledgement of transfers thereof under this subsection. Where transferable Treasury securities are recorded on the books of a depositary (a bank, banking institution, financial firm, or similar party, which regularly accepts in the course of its business Treasury securities as a custodial service for customers, and maintains accounts in the name of such customers reflecting ownership of or interest in such securities) for account of the pledgor or transferor thereof and such securities are on deposit with a Reserve Bank in a book-entry account hereunder, such depositary shall, for purposes of perfecting a pledge of such securities or effecting delivery of such securities to a purchaser under applicable provisions of law, be the bailee to which notification of the pledge of the securities may be given or the third person in possession from which acknowledgment of the holding of the securities for the purchaser may be obtained. A Reserve Bank will not accept notice or advice of a transfer or pledge effected or perfected under this subsection, and any such notice or advice shall have no effect. A Reserve Bank may continue to deal with its depositor in accordance with the provisions of this subpart, not withstanding any transfer or pledge effected or perfected under this subsection.[4]

At the time subparagraph (a) was written, only member banks might have book-entry accounts at the Fed. Subparagraph (a) describes how

---

[4]Subpart O of Treasury Department Circular No. 300, Section 306.118 (Appendix A to Operating Circular No. 21, effective March 30, 1973, Federal Reserve Bank of New York), pp. 3–4.

Bank A could transfer Treasury securities to Bank B and how such a transfer would affect, on the Reserve Bank's books, the interests of both Bank A and Bank B in the securities transferred. Since subparagraph (a) is silent concerning how a customer of Bank A could transfer Treasury securities to a customer of Bank B, subparagraph (b) was later added to cover such transfers of customer interests.

Some bright lawyers purport to read deep meaning into Treasury subparagraphs (a) and (b). Other equally bright lawyers take the view that subparagraphs (a) and (b) are incomprehensible as written. No lawyer has, to the author's knowledge, nominated either subparagraph (a) or subparagraph (b) for the Pulitzer Prize for clarity-in-writing.

Not surprisingly, subparagraphs (a) and (b) are, for various reasons, being redrafted. One hopes that one reason for the redrafting is to achieve some clarity in their meaning.

THE NEXT CHAPTER

In the next chapter, we turn to the operation of the book-entry system in its current form. It is no exaggeration to say that today's levels of trading would, absent that system, lead to total and immediate chaos in the markets for government and agency securities.

SOURCES ON THE HISTORY OF CPDs, GSCA, AND BOOK ENTRY

Debs, Richard. "The Program for the Automation of the Government Securities Market." Federal Reserve Bank of New York, *Monthly Review* 54, no. 7 (July 1972), pp. 180–81.

Federal Reserve Bank of New York. *Fedpoints 5: Book-Entry Procedure.* 1985, p. 2.

Hoey, Matthew J., and Richard Vollkomer. "Development of a Clearing Arrangement and Book-Entry Custody Procedure for U.S. Government Securities." *The Magazine of Bank Administration,* June 1971, pp. 22–23. (The authors are ex-officers of the FRBNY.)

Appendix to chapter 7
The most watched player: The Fed*

The Federal Reserve System, the nation's central bank, was established by act of Congress in 1913. The Federal Reserve Act divided the country into 12 districts and provided for the creation within each of a *district Federal Reserve Bank.* Responsibility for coordinating the activities of the district banks lies with the Federal Reserve's *Board of Governors* in Washington, D.C. The board has seven members appointed by the President and confirmed by the Senate.

The main tools available to the Fed for implementing policy are open market operations, reserve requirements, and the discount rate. On paper authority for policymaking at the Fed is widely diffused throughout the system. In practice, however, this authority has gradually been centered in the *Federal Open Market Committee* (FOMC), which was established to oversee the Fed's open market operations. Members of the FOMC include all seven governors of the system, the president of the New York Fed, and the presidents of 4 of the other 11 district banks; the latter serve on a rotating basis. Every member of the FOMC has one vote, but it has become tradition that the chairman of the Board of Governors plays a decisive role in formulating policy and acts as chief spokesman for the system, which is why that position is viewed as one of power and importance.

In establishing policy, the Fed enjoys considerable independence on paper from both Congress and the executive branch. Members of the Board of Governors are appointed to 14-year terms so that a President has only limited control over who serves on the Board during his term of office. The chairman of the board, who is designated as such by the President, serves in that capacity for only four years, but his term is not coincident with that of the President, so an incoming President may have to wait until well into his first term to appoint a new chairman.

Congress, like the President, has no lever by which it can directly influence Fed policy or the way it is implemented. In creating the Fed, Congress endowed this institution with wide powers and granted it considerable leeway to exercise discretion and judgment. Having said that, one must hasten to add that the autonomy enjoyed by the Fed is in reality much less than it appears. Presidents who are concerned that the Fed

---

*For a detailed description of how the Fed operates, see Chapter 8, Marcia Stigum, *The Money Market*, 2nd ed. (Homewood, Ill.: Dow Jones-Irwin, 1983).

is forcing interest rates too high (Presidents *never* seem to be concerned over interest being too low) attack the Fed subtly and not so subtly from the White House. Also the Fed is well aware that Congress, should it become too distressed over high interest rates, might take away the Fed's autonomy.

The book-entry
system today

THIS CHAPTER DESCRIBES THE CURRENT STRUCTURE AND OPERA-
TION of the book-entry system as well as its rapid growth over time. The
chapter ends with a description of the book-entry account that an individual may, if he so chooses, maintain at the Treasury for the purpose
of holding governments. *The reader should pay particular attention to
Figure 8-1 and to Table 8-1.*

CURRENT STRUCTURE OF THE BOOK-ENTRY SYSTEM[1]

Each of the 12 district Federal Reserve Banks and each of their 25
branches establishes and maintains book-entry accounts for depository
institutions located within its district or area. Only depository institutions
are eligible to maintain a book-entry account at a Reserve Bank, but any

[1]Material under this heading, pages 93–99, is excerpted, with numerous editorial changes
including the deletion of technical footnotes and the addition of Figure 8-1, from: Mary
Sue Sullivan, "The Treasury Book-Entry System," a Federal Reserve paper reprinted in *Government Securities: Counselling and Regulation* (New York/Washington, D.C.: Law & Business
Inc./Harcourt Brace Jovanovich, 1985), pp. 354–62. Ms. Sullivan is Assistant Counsel of

individual or entity may maintain a book-entry account at a depository institution.

The Federal Reserve book-entry system is, thus, a *tiered* system of accounts. *Interests* of a depository institution are recorded on the books of a Reserve Bank; *interests* of others are recorded on the books of a depository institution. If a customer of a depository institution is another bank or a securities dealer, that bank or securities dealer may also maintain book-entry accounts for its customers; securities in such accounts will be reflected in the book-entry account maintained, at the depository institution, by that bank or securities dealer. (Figure 8–1, added by the author, portrays the tiered book-entry system of accounts.)

Explanation of Figure 8–1

Book entry is a tiered system for recording *interests, only some of which reflect ownership,* in securities maintained in the system. Figure 8–1 depicts the relationships among different tiers of the book-entry system that, *given current market practices,* are most common.

Figure 8–1 shows, at the top tier of accounts and recordkeeping, an issuer of book-entry securities, the U.S. Treasury. The Treasury's records show, for each of its issues, what total amount is outstanding and what amounts of the issue are held by different Federal Reserve Banks.

All money market instruments used to be, and many still are, in physical form. Clearing a trade of money market instruments in physical form requires, more often than not, that securities be moved from one place to another: from one clearing bank to another or from a clearing bank to a custodial bank. Because it is *cheaper* and *quicker* to have a messenger walk two or three blocks carrying securities than it is to send securities, no matter how it is done, on cross-country jaunts, most clearing of money market trades is done in one city, New York. West Coast dealers use, as their clearing agent, a N.Y.C. bank, not the B of A. Security Pacific, the one West Coast bank that has moved into clearing in a big way, has done so through a N.Y.C. subsidiary.

Investors in money market instruments are scattered about the country. An out-of-town, hold-to-maturity investor, who buys long-lived instruments, such as GNMAs, may want his GNMAs delivered either to his local bank for custody or to himself if he has a vault, as a bank or S&L would. However, *out-of-town (outside N.Y.C.)* delivery of physical securities (as opposed to book-entry securities) is expensive and makes little sense for short-term paper such as CDs, BAs, and commercial paper; this is so even if the investor plans to hold such securities to maturity. Out-of-town delivery of physical securities makes absolutely no sense for an active portfolio manager who trades often and must, to prevent expensive fails, have his trades cleared on the day he makes them or on the following business day. A big hidden cost for a dealer on delivering paper out of town, say to Chicago, is that he must pay for the paper in N.Y.C. the day he accepts delivery of it, but he will receive payment for that paper only the next day when he delivers it in Chicago; on such a delivery, the dealer thus incurs a one-day financing cost.

All large portfolio managers—pension funds, insurance companies, nonfinancial cor-

---

the FRBNY. Her piece may be obtained, in its entirety, by writing the FRBNY, 33 Liberty Street, New York, N.Y. 10045.

All the rules and regulations under which the book-entry system currently operates are described in the following Treasury "Operating Circulars": OC No. 21 (revised December 12, 1977), Appendices A–E to OC No. 21, OC No. 21A, and First Supplement to it, Appendices A and B to OC No. 21A, and Exhibit to OC No. 21A. These circulars, too, may be obtained from the FRBNY.

FIGURE 8-1
The Federal book-entry system*

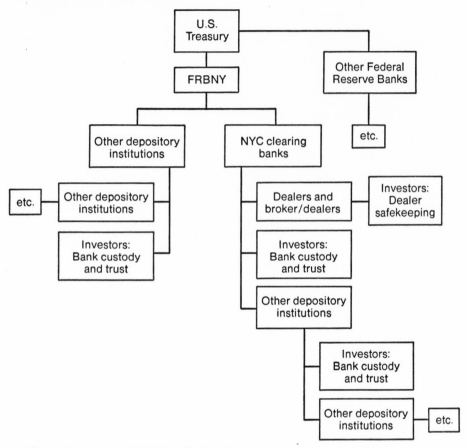

*See explanatory material; **figure added by the author.**

porations, and others—use the services of a custodial bank. This bank, acting as agent for the investor, accepts delivery of securities the investor buys against payment, safekeeps securities he sells against payment, collects coupon interest, collects principal at maturity, and prepares periodic statements of account activity as well as any other reports the investor wants. In the case of book-entry securities, clearing of both the investor trades and the collecting of interest and principal payments could be done by a local bank anywhere in the country. However, since many money market instruments are in physical form and since most physical securities never, for reasons explained above, leave New York City, the bulk of bank custodial work for money market investors continues to be done, as it was done before book entry, by N.Y.C. banks. This explains why 60% of all book-entry securities held by DIs are held in the accounts of N.Y.C. banks at the FRBNY (see Table 8-1).

Lots of John Does leave any securities, from stocks to T bills, that they buy from a broker/dealer with that broker/dealer for safekeeping. Also, many smaller institutional investors, following the John Doe pattern, safekeep any money market securities or govern-

ments, physical or book-entry, that they buy with the dealer or broker/dealer from whom they bought them.

Bearing the above in mind, look again at Figure 8–1. Federal Reserve Banks, which maintain book-entry accounts in which depository institutions hold securities in which they have interests, form tier two of the book-entry system. We have put the FRBNY in the center of tier two of Figure 8–1 because of New York City's position as the center of the national money market.

Currently, about 5,500 out of the 20,000 eligible DIs have opened book-entry accounts at a FRB. The costs associated with having such an account are such that institutions doing only a few securities trades find it cheaper to use another DI to clear their trades

TABLE 8–1

Marketable U.S. Treasury securities and portion in book-entry form 1968–81, Federal Reserve Bank of New York, (April 1982)*

End of period	Marketables[†] (billions)	Book-entry holdings[‡]			Definitive[§] outstanding (billions)
		System total (billions)	%	New York (billions)	
1968	$236.8	$ 36.5	15.4	$ 21.0	$200.3
1969	235.9	38.2	16.2	21.2	197.7
1970	247.7	121.3	48.9	96.6	126.4
1971	262.0	152.6	58.2	124.6	109.4
1972	269.5	160.2	59.4	129.2	109.3
1973	270.2	176.6	65.4	135.6	93.6
1974	281.3	201.4	71.6	151.5	79.9
1975	363.2	285.1	78.5	194.5	78.1
1976	421.3	354.1	84.0	232.4	67.2
1977	459.9	428.2	93.1	284.5	31.7
1978	487.5	457.4	93.8	307.4	30.1
1979	530.7	497.8	93.8	317.4	32.9
1980	623.1	585.2	93.9	378.4	37.9
1981	720.2	686.0	95.2	426.8	34.2

Marketable government agency securities and portion in book-entry form

1974	71.9[‖]	23.2	32.2	8.4	48.7
1975	74.4	40.5	54.4	16.1	33.9
1976	78.9	64.2	81.4	29.3	14.7
1977	84.2	77.9	92.5	38.0	6.3
1978	99.6	96.3	96.6	44.6	3.3
1979	114.1	111.8	98.0	51.0	2.3
1980	127.7	127.2	99.6	58.2	0.5
1981	147.9	147.8	99.9	65.1	0.1

*Marketable debt excludes debt issued to foreign central banks and to trust funds, such as the fund for social security, the Railroad retirement fund, etc. Unfortunately, the Fed no longer updates this table, but the table does show important past trends.

†Source: Monthly Statement of the Public Debt; excludes Federal Financing Bank for July 1974 et. seq.

‡Source: Treasury Department and FRBNY.

§Includes both bearer and registered securities.

‖Dealer quotation sheets, PD and agencies estimates.

in governments and to safekeep securities for them than to have their own book-entry account. Depository institutions that maintain accounts at the FRBNY fall into *two* categories. *Some are clearing banks* who clear each day tens of thousands of trades for client dealers and broker/dealers; a clearing bank maintains, for each of its dealer clients, a clearing account in which the dealer deposits money and both book-entry and physical securities. Clearing banks hold securities not only for dealers, but for investors and other depository institutions who have no account at the Fed.

Most N.Y.C. banks are not in the clearing business. Such institutions do not hold securities for dealers, but they do hold securities for other depository institutions and for investors. (See tier three of Figure 8–1 under FRBNY.) This pattern is repeated by depository institutions that have accounts with the FRBs other than the FRBNY (Figure 8–1, far left branch).

An investor, wherever he may be located, may hold book-entry securities in a custody account at either a N.Y.C. bank or an out-of-town bank, or he may hold such securities in a dealer safekeeping account maintained by a dealer in governments (lower tiers of Figure 8–1).

All entities at each tier of the book-entry system always maintain records that show both what securities, if any, they own and what securities they are holding, in any capacity, for entities at a lower tier of the system.

Each depository institution may establish up to seven standard book-entry accounts at its Federal Reserve Bank. These accounts are denominated "General," "Investment," "Trust," "Dealer," "Special," "Select," and "Clearance." In addition to these, a qualified DI may set up two international accounts. Although the account titles are suggestive, they exist solely for the convenience of the depository institution's own bookkeeping, and a depository institution may elect to hold all of its book-entry securities in a single account. The Fed does not monitor the character of transactions processed in each type of account. Rather, a depository institution's entire book-entry securities portfolio is "subject to the sole order of the [depository institution] depositor." In turn, the depository institutions

are expected to maintain appropriate records in regard to their customers, covering such matters as transfer of the securities, pledge interests in the securities, and redemption of the securities and payment of interest thereon.[2]

In this respect, the book-entry system closely resembles the system of nominal or "street name" registration that commonly exists for definitive securities. The depository institution acquires control over disposition of the securities in its book-entry accounts, as well as the right to receive principal and interest payments. The depository institution in turn is accountable to its customers for both the securities and payments it receives.

The "International" and "Special" accounts serve more limited purposes. The "International Account" is used exclusively for issues of foreign-targeted securities (issues designed by the Treasury to be sold,

---

[2]OC No. 21, paragraph 3(c).

at issue, exclusively to foreign investors). The "Special Account" is actually a series of subaccounts (collateral accounts) in which the Federal Reserve Banks record pledges by depository institutions to various federal, state, and local governmental entities.[3]

CURRENT OPERATION OF THE BOOK-ENTRY SYSTEM

The book-entry system is designed to handle the issuance, maintenance, and transfer of all issues put into the system.

New issues

On original issue date, the 12 Reserve Banks electronically issue book-entry debt through entries in the accounts of depository institutions. Each entry takes the form of a single dollar amount representing the portion of the aggregate principal amount of the issue designated for delivery to that depository institution. The Reserve Bank makes a simultaneous debit to the reserve account of the depository institution in the amount of the purchase price and credits that dollar amount to the Treasury's cash account. Based on delivery instructions submitted by its customers, the depository institution makes entries on its own books that identify its customers' interests in the securities issued to it by the Reserve Bank.

Payment of principal and interest

The Treasury uses a similar method to pay interest and principal. On payment date, the Fed debits the Treasury's cash account and credits the reserve account of the depository institution whose book-entry accounts contain the issue for which an interest or maturity payment is due. These payments are made at the opening of business on payment date. Thus, entitlement to payments is based on the Fed's records as of the close of business on the preceding day.

Here's an example. The coupon dates on a 30-year Treasury bond always fall on the 15th of a month; actual payments of coupon interest on book-entry securities are made, by the Treasury through the Fed, on the morning of the 15th; these payments go to *holders of record,* that is, to parties who, according to Fed and Treasury records, had interests in the issue as of the *record date,* which is the close of business on the 14th. *Aside:*

---

[3]See OC No. 21, paragraph 4. Unlike the safekeeping accounts, the collateral accounts show the name of the pledgee governmental entity, as well as the pledgor depository institution. The securities in those accounts are held subject to the order of the pledgee pursuant to statutes, regulations, court orders, and agreements. The most common collateral accounts are those securing the Treasury tax and loan deposits, Federal Reserve Bank advances at the discount window, and deposits of money subject to federal bankruptcy proceedings.

For *physical, registered* notes and bonds, in contrast to book-entry securities, the Treasury sends on the 15th a check for interest due, according to its records, to the holders of record of such securities. To get interest due them, holders of remaining *bearer* notes and bonds must clip and present coupons.

Secondary-market trades

Trades in Treasuries that occur after their original issue, that is, *secondary-market transactions,* are also completed through the book-entry system. If securities are transferred "free," the Fed debits the securities account of the sending depository institution and credits the securities account of the receiving depository institution by the principal amount specified in the transfer instruction. If the securities are transferred against payment, the Fed also credits the reserve account of the sending depository institution and debits the reserve account of the receiving depository institution by the dollar amount specified in the instruction. Transactions between depository institutions that are not located in the same Reserve district or branch territory require entries on the books of two Reserve Banks or branches.

The vast majority of book-entry transfers occur on a direct computer access (on-line) basis. In an on-line transaction, the depository institution sending securities controls the transfer by entering a command in the book-entry system that causes the debits and credits described above to occur automatically. As a result of the high level of automation in the market, Fedwire processes on average 30,000 transactions per day for securities valued at $225 billion.[4] In contrast, transactions that require manual processing by Fed personnel (off-line) average 420 transactions per day.

Financing of transactions in Treasury securities

After it receives securities transferred against payment for the account of a customer, the receiving DI can either accept the transaction or reverse it. If it accepts the transaction and the customer has insufficient funds to cover the payment, the depository institution must extend daylight credit (overdraft). If the customer's failure to pay persists, that daylight credit becomes an outright or term loan. DIs that process transactions for dealer customers extend daylight credit in an aggregate amount of billions of dollars per day. Overnight credit reaches a more modest $2.6 billion on average each week.

---

[4]Note: since one dealer's buy is another dealer's sell, the number implies that dealers together instruct on an average day their clearing banks to clear 60,000 trades.

GROWTH OF BOOK ENTRY

Once the book-entry system was introduced, it was rapidly accepted by investors (Tables 8-2 and 8-3; also refer to Table 8-1, p. 96.). Since 1977, over 90% of all governments have existed in book-entry form; today, the corresponding figure is 96%. The book-entry system was also expanded to cover an over-increasing number of issues sold by various federal credit agencies: the Farm Credit System, the Federal Home Loan Bank Board, Sallie Mae (student loans), and so on. Today, almost 100% of all eligible agencies are in book-entry form.

TREASURY BOOK-ENTRY ACCOUNTS

The last pocket of resistance to book entry has been among individuals. Some small investors want a certificate that they can see, feel, and tuck in their safe or under their mattress. For years after the book-entry system was begun, the Treasury offered investors in each new issue of Treasury bills, notes, and bonds the option of taking delivery of physical securities. Finally in 1979, the Treasury began offering new bill issues

TABLE 8-2
Total public debt outstanding—September 30, 1985

$1,823,103 million
  of which
    $1,360,179 million is interest-bearing marketable securities
      of which
        96% is in book-entry form
        2% is in registered form
        2% is in bearer form

Source: Federal Reserve Bank of New York.

TABLE 8-3
Marketable debt outstanding—September 30, 1985

$338,220 million (bills)
  of which
    $19,225 million (5.7%) is recorded at the Treasury
    in book-entry form in 880,085 accounts
    with the balance in book-entry form
    on the Federal Reserve books

$975,959 million (notes and bonds)
  of which
    $27,755 million (2.8%) is in registered form and recorded at the Treasury
    in 1,141,395 accounts
    with the balance in book-entry form
    on the Federal Reserve books or
    in coupon form

Source: Federal Reserve Bank of New York.

in book-entry form only. To make individuals more comfortable with owning book-entry securities, the Treasury allowed buyers of bills to open a book-entry account with it. The book-entry account offered by the Treasury is a degraded (with respect to services offered and speed of execution) version of the custodial account that an investor could, alternatively, open at a bank. To transfer or pledge securities in a Treasury book-entry account, an investor must (1) first figure out and then fill out a form, (2) get a notarized signature, and (3) wait days. Treasury book-entry accounts are designed to be unattractive to the investor who actively trades his portfolio.

The Treasury describes its book-entry accounts for investors in bills as follows:

> Treasury bills are issued only in book-entry form. This means that the purchaser's ownership of the bills will be recorded in a book-entry account established for the purchaser at the Treasury Department. The purchaser receives a receipt rather than an engraved certificate as evidence of the purchase. The book-entry method of recording ownership of Treasury bills protects the purchaser against loss, theft, and counterfeiting of ownership documents.
>
> When Treasury bills are purchased, the Treasury Department will establish an account for the purchaser within a period of 10 to 60 days after the issue date and will mail the purchaser Form PD 4949, a Statement of Account. This statement will include relevant information about the purchaser's transaction, such as the account number, amount of securities, amount of discount, date of issue, and date of maturity. The first copy of the statement, marked "DUPLICATE" is intended for use in corresponding with the Bureau of Public Debt, U.S. Treasury Department. The second copy is the statement that purchasers should retain for their own records. This copy does not have a carbon-back and has relevant information printed on the reverse side. The duplicate copy should be included with all correspondence and transaction requests affecting the account, except Form PD 4633-2 (computer reinvestment card).
>
> To request a change in the account, such as change in address or cancellation of a previous request for reinvestment, the purchaser should request Form PD 4633 from a Federal Reserve Bank. The completed form should be mailed to the Bureau of Public Debt, Department X, Washington, D.C., 20239–0001, along with the duplicate copy of Form PD 4949. The Treasury Department will not make an account change unless the change can be effected 20 business days prior to maturity. . . .

Transfer or sale of Treasury bills

While the Treasury bills are held in a Treasury account, any owner of such bills who wishes to sell them must have the bills transferred through the Federal Reserve communications system to an account maintained by or through a financial institution holding a securities account at a Federal Reserve Bank. A request for withdrawal must be made sufficiently in advance of the maturity date of the bill to permit its timely transfer. The Treasury WILL NOT:

... arrange for conduct of or handle cash transfers involved in transactions after original issue;

... recognize a pledge of book-entry securities for collateral;

... transfer securities among book-entry accounts it maintains, except in case of legal succession.

To effect changes other than ownership transfers, the purchaser's signature must be certified by a notary public. To transfer ownership through a private financial institution, the purchaser's signature must be certified by an officer or employee of a bank or trust company, a Federal savings and loan association, or other organization belonging to the Federal Home Loan Bank System.[5]

The Treasury began in 1986 to offer new note and bond issues in book-entry form only. Bonds and notes that have been issued under offering circulars that authorize both certificate and book-entry form will continue to be available, so long as they are outstanding, in both forms.

When full book entry is implemented, an investor will be able to establish directly with the Treasury a free book-entry account for his notes and bonds just as he may now do for his bills. A new automated system is being developed for the Treasury by the Philadelphia Federal Reserve Bank; this system will permit an investor to have a single account with the Treasury for his bills, notes and bonds.

REGISTERED SECURITIES

It has never been in an investor's interest to take delivery, in registered—rather than book-entry or bearer—form, of Treasury notes and bonds that he might want to sell one day *on the spur of the moment*. An investor who tries to *deregister* (normally, convert to book-entry form) notes or bonds will find that this procedure takes 48 to 72 hours in New York City and that it may take weeks elsewhere. If an investor were to ask a dealer to sell registered notes or bonds for him, the dealer would have to deregister those bonds; doing so would cost the dealer money and time and might expose him to some market risk; consequently, a dealer normally gives an investor wanting to sell such securities a quote well off the market: ⅛ to ¼ of a point off for large amounts, ½ a point off for amounts of $50,000 or less.

THE NEXT CHAPTER

In the next chapter, we turn to the operation of the Fed wire, a key Fed computer facility that money marketeers use to transfer money (of

---

[5]James F. Tucker, *Buying Treasury Securities at Federal Reserve Banks* (Federal Reserve Bank of Richmond, February 1985), pp. 11-16.

the Fed funds variety) and book-entry securities to the tune of hundreds of billions of each, each day.

SOURCES ON BOOK-ENTRY TODAY

Martin, A. E., III. "The Book-Entry System for Treasury Securities." Federal Reserve Bank of Atlanta. *Economic Review,* September, 1985, pp. 15–16.

Sullivan, Mary Sue. "The Treasury Book-Entry System." A Federal Reserve paper reprinted in *Government Securities: Counselling and Regulation.* New York/Washington, D.C.: Law & Business Inc./Harcourt Brace Jovanovich, 1985, pp. 354–62. (Ms. Sullivan is Associate Counsel of the FRBNY.)

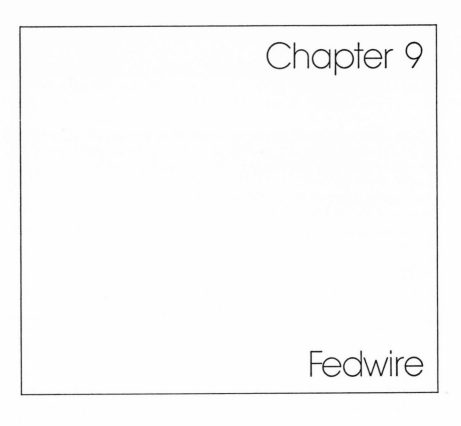

Chapter 9

Fedwire

THIS CHAPTER DESCRIBES FEDWIRE, a key facility in the clearing of money market securities. Specifically, the chapter talks about what Fedwire does, how it works, why it sometimes does not work (computer problems), and what Fedwire hours and fees are.

WHAT FEDWIRE DOES

Fedwire is basically a communications network and settlement system that links Fed banks and offices to any insured depository institution that wants to link up to the Fed. Institutions linked to the Fed use Fedwire both to transfer money (Fed funds) and to transfer book-entry securities to accounts at other depository institutions.

Securities may be transferred over the Fed wire "free," but most often, they are transferred DVP (*delivery versus payment*). For example, a *free delivery* would occur if an investor, who switched from dealer A to dealer B, asked dealer A to transfer securities, which dealer A had been safekeeping for it, to dealer B for safekeeping. Purchases and sales of book-entry securities result almost always in DVP transfers of securities.

Figure 9–1 shows a wire transfer used to settle a DVP trade in Treasury notes. Since parts of the message look as if they were constructed by a cryptographer, we have also included Figure 9–2 which decodes the more mysterious entries on the wire.

While many transfers of funds over Fedwire are generated by securities deliveries, many more are generated by other types of transactions. A *reverse to maturity* may be settled by a *difference check,* that is, a check for the difference between what X owes Y and what Y owes X. An RP may require a wire of accrued interest on a coupon day. Also, a call for margin on an RP may be met by a wire of funds rather than securities.

Besides securities-related transfers of funds, a vast number of funds transfers occur as a result of nonfinancial business transactions. Firm A wires funds to Firm B or some other party.

Trading in the Fed funds market is yet another activity that generates each day tens of thousands of wire transfers of money. As noted earlier, deposit-rich banks make money on their excess reserves, without compromising their liquidity, by selling, in the Fed funds market, these spare dollars, for use overnight, to deposit-poor banks. Deposit-poor banks is a category that includes not only most big U.S. banks, but the U.S. branches of big foreign banks: Japanese banks, British banks, and so on. All sales of Fed funds and returns of such funds are done via wire transfers. Wire transfers are also used to effect the large payments and receipts of Fed funds that big banks, domestic and foreign, experience

FIGURE 9–1
A Fedwire message indicating to a clearing bank, Manny, that $4,630,000 of the 10⅞ of 2/15/87 are being delivered by Ninth CHGO/CUST PVD to ABC Title & Trust. The amount of the payment due is $5,012,166.67.

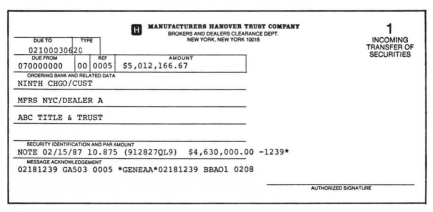

Note: See Figure 9–2 for further explanation of entries and codes.
Source: Manufacturers Hanover Trust.

daily as a result of settlement of *CHIPS* (*the New York Clearing House Interbank Payments System*); most Eurodollar transactions—each day, these amount to a huge sum—are settled through CHIPS.

Figure 9–3 shows a Fedwire used to transfer *money only.* Figure 9–4 deciphers this message. *Note:* None of the cryptographic, numerical-letter

FIGURE 9–2
Wire of incoming securities versus money—explanation of entries and codes

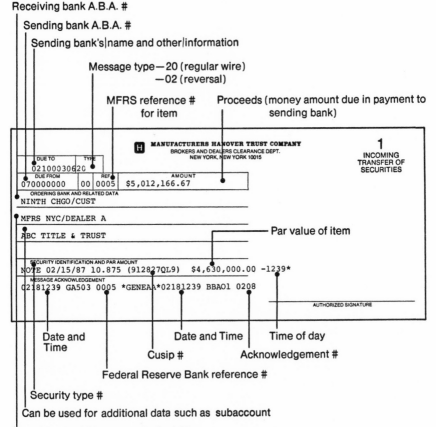

The time/date on the lower left of the wire message states when the message was entered by the sender into its computer; it is called the *input message sequence number* (*IMSN* in Fed jargon).

The time/date on the lower right of the wire message states when the message arrived at the receiving institution; it is the *output message sequence number* (*OMSN* in Fed jargon).

The two times will differ if the sending bank holds the message in pending mode waiting for inventory to come in.

ABA is an acronym for American Bakers Association.

Source: Manufacturers Hanover Trust.

FIGURE 9-3

Copy of a Fed wire requesting a $500,000 transfer of Fed funds from ANYBANK NYC/BROKER to an account at Manny Hanny

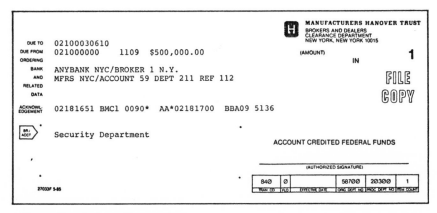

Source: Manufacturers Hanover Trust.

combinations in Figure 9–3 refer to a security, which is as it should be, since they wire transfers money only.

Fedwire may, as we have noted, be used to settle a transfer of funds, a free delivery of securities, or a transfer versus payment of securities. A key feature of Fedwire, whatever the use to which it is put, is that it is a means of settlement in which balances due are paid *transaction by transaction.* CHIPS and several private clearing systems, which are used to clear trades of certain types of securities (corporate stocks and bonds and muni bonds, to name a few), do not work this way. Instead, they call for a *net* settlement at day's end, where the settlement is based on everything that has gone, during the day, both *into* and *out of* a participant's pot or pots (account or accounts with it). For example, Chase is a member of CHIPS. At the end of each business day, CHIPS zips Chase a message: "We settled today this long list of transactions for you. Total transactions resulting in a debit to your account summed to X; total transactions resulting in a credit to your account summed to Y. X exceeds Y by Z; wire us Z dollars." Or alternatively, the message might end: "Y exceeds X by Z; we will wire you, at settlement, Z dollars."

Another difference between payments made over Fedwire and via CHIPS is that a money transfer made over Fedwire is final (irreversible), whereas a money transfer made via CHIPS is not final until CHIPS settles, normally after 6 P.M. New York time.

FIGURE 9-4
Wire transfer of funds—explanation of entries and codes

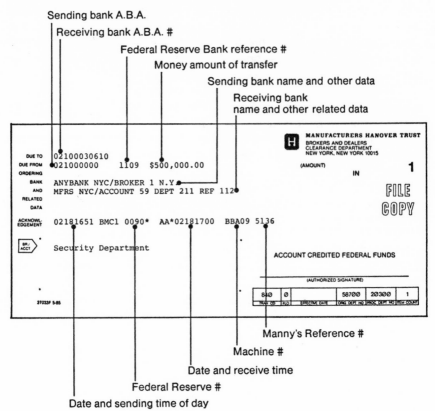

Sending bank A.B.A.
Receiving bank A.B.A. #
Federal Reserve Bank reference #
Money amount of transfer
Sending bank name and other data
Receiving bank
name and other related data

Manny's Reference #
Machine #
Date and receive time
Federal Reserve #
Date and sending time of day

HOW FEDWIRE WORKS

Most, but not quite all, messages sent over the Fed wire are sent by a computer over a leased line and received by a computer at the other end of that line. We could leave our description of the Fed wire at that, but the story of how things tick is interesting. It also explains the delay in converting some securities to book entry.

Goodbye throttle and choke

In the early 1980s, the Fed wire was taxed to its limit with the result that it was subject daily to "throttle," and it tended to "choke." *Throttle*

occurred when traffic on Fedwire was so heavy that the wire, instead of taking messages from banks at its normal rate, three to six per minute, took them at a lower speed. From the user's point of view, throttle at the Fed was like being put on hold for some time every time one called a message into the Fed. Throttling meant that the Fed had to extend daily the hours Fedwire was open just to handle the volume of messages put into the system.

In the early 1980s, Fedwire was also overtaxed in a second way: the automated system then used by the Fed tended to *choke* when it was asked to handle more than 700 issues.

In August of 1983, the Fed finally made a change, one long awaited by the Street, in the automated system it uses to support Fedwire. The Fed replaced its old Sigma system, which was a series of computers developed by Xerox, with an IBM processor; and it totally redesigned its system to maximize *"throughput," the number of transactions the system can handle per unit of time.*

The Fed's new automated system has a throughput of 10 to 15 transactions per minute. Currently, this system has the capacity to handle 38,000 issues; and by making some adjustments in peripheral equipment, the Fed could expand the system's capacity to 100,000 issues, the number of issues that the system was modeled to carry.

Book entry and Fedwire today

Since the Fed introduced its new automated system, the number of issues on book entry and the volume of messages passing through the system daily have grown explosively. Today, Fedwire handles within the N.Y. district 23,000 messages on an average day and as many as 58,000 messages on peak days.

With choking a thing of the past, the Fed's computer currently tracks the interests of banks and other DIs in about 28,000 different issues. The aggregate face value of these issues exceeds a trillion dollars; this number comprises $80 billion of book-entry Treasuries, $80 billion of long-term agencies, $20 billion of agency discount paper, $150 billion of mortgage backs, and securities issued by three international agencies: the World Bank, the Inter-American Development Bank, and the International Bank for Reconstruction and Development.

With its new system in place, the Fed should not again face, for a long time, the problems of either throttle or choke.

A question commonly asked, especially since both Freddie Macs and Fannie Maes have successfully gone book entry, is why GNMAs were never (until a 1986 attempt) converted to book-entry form. Part of the answer is that, until recently, the Fed wasn't soliciting more book-entry

business because it lacked the capacity to handle either more volume or more issues. It has that capacity now, but during the period that it did not, clearing banks and others invested large sums in creating facilities to clear huge volumes of GNMA trades. Naturally, such entities were not going to champion the switching of GNMAs from physical to book-entry form. In 1987, a program was begun to put GNMAs into a depository and to clear trades in them in a book-entry-like environment (Chapter 17).

COMPUTERS: FRONT-END AND BACK-END

A single message over Fedwire to clear a securities trade may generate as many as four changes on the books of the Fed, four changes on the books of the sending and of the receiving banks, several more changes on the books of clients of these banks—and even that is not necessarily the end of the chain. Multiplying the number of changes just enumerated by the number of messages concerning securities trades that pass over Fedwire on an average day produces a mind-boggling number of changes. To communicate information concerning all these changes and to process them, the Street depends on phalanxes of computers that spend their days, sometimes nights as well, talking to each other.

No institution that must process securities transactions gets away with having just one computer. The process of communicating and acting upon messages involves two distinct functions. First, there is a *communications function* that controls the sending and receiving of messages; second, there is an *applications function* that controls the producing of pluses and minuses by the messages—debit this, credit that.

Front-end computers

The communications function is handled by *front-end* computers. A front-end computer is nothing more than a traffic cop or post office; it takes something in and accounts for the fact that it took it in; it then puts something out and accounts for the fact that it has put it out. Finally, at the end of the day, it says, "Everything I took in, I put out." Front-end computers serve several purposes. First, a front-end computer is needed to account, at all times, for the messages an institution receives and sends. Second, an efficiency is derived by separating the traffic-cop function from the applications or accounting function that must also be done. Third, since all banks don't use the same computer language, a front-end computer may have to change the sending bank's computer language into the receiving bank's computer language.

Back-end computers

Once a front-end computer receives a message, it sends that message to a *back-end* or *applications* computer, which processes the message. A message regarding a clearing of a buy might require that a bank increase a client's securities balance, decrease his cash balance, and then notify him that these changes in his balances had been made. This applications function is done by a bank's back-end computer.

The Fed's back-end computers take care of *increases* and *decreases, pluses* and *minuses;* they track how these occur during the day; and at the end of the day, they check that every plus is matched by a minus. If they have done their job properly, the total pluses recorded will equal the total minuses recorded. That's so because every message they handle results in securities and/or money being transferred from the account of one DI to the account of another DI.

The Fed's computers

The Fed has, in its back-end computer, all of the securities positions as well as the cash balances that DIs have in their accounts with it; none of that information is in the Fed's front-end computer. The Fed's front-end computer, a message controller, simply receives and sends messages; it doesn't concern itself with whether the message is for $10 million or $20 million; rather, it concerns itself with identifying that it got a message from Manny and that it gave that message to Irving. It is the Fed's back-end computer, in contrast, that would execute a message from Manny that says: "Dear Fed: Reduce my securities position by $50 million, raise my cash position by a like amount, and make the reverse changes in Irving's accounts."

At day's end, the Fed's back-end computer will say: "Manny, I reduced your securities balance by this amount and gave you that amount of cash through the front end," and "Irving, I increased your securities balance by this amount and reduced your cash by that amount." The Fed's front-end computer will say, "I took in one message from Manny, and I gave out one to Irving." The whole system then proves.

Proving at day's end

Banks linked to Fedwire do not call the Fed at the end of the day to *prove out,* that is, to check that their positions at the Fed are what their in-house calculations show them to be. Instead, at day's end, the Fed's back-end computer produces a *clearing settlement report;* this report summarizes all of the activity that took place in a bank's accounts during the day; for each security, it identifies the bank's opening position,

its ins, its outs, and its closing position. This information is sent by the Fed's front-end computer to the bank. Some banks use automated procedures to compare the Fed's clearing settlement against their own records of their activity for the day; other banks do this job manually.

HOURS AND EXTENSIONS: FEDWIRE

Fedwire opens for *securities transactions* at 9 A.M. E.S.T. and is supposed to close at 2:30 P.M. E.S.T. for regular securities transfers and at 3 P.M. E.S.T. for reversals (Table 9–1). The extra half hour is tacked on to give a bank, which has received a transfer in error and has not caught up with that error, time to reverse the transaction.

Dealer turnaround time.   The second cutoff time described in Table 9–1 refers to *dealer turnaround times.* Starting in the early 1970s, it was recognized that dealers, as market makers, needed flexibility in working with physical securities: time to redeliver out securities delivered late to them. So an agreement, which carried over into the era of book-entry securities, was created among banks, dealers, and their customers. Under this agreement, parties delivering securities agreed to respect the following delivery cutoff times:

Actual delivery by custody and clearing
banks is to occur no later than:

Cutoff time	Type of delivery
2:15 P.M.	Customer-to-dealer
2:30 P.M.	Dealer-to-dealer
2:45 P.M.	Dealer-to-customer

The Fed was never a party to the dealer-turnaround-time agreement. It is a private agreement that the Fed has never policed. Currently, the agreement is applicable in only three Fed districts: New York, San Francisco (which includes Los Angeles), and Chicago. It is in these Fed districts that the traffic of securities into and out of dealer accounts at clearing banks is by far the heaviest.

Hours: Funds transfers

There are three closings on Fedwire for funds transactions: the wire closes at 5 P.M. for interdistrict, third-party transfers; at 6 P.M. for intradistrict, third-party transfers; and at 6:30 P.M. for settlement transfers. *Third-party transfers* are transfers done by banks for individuals or corporations; *settlement transfers* are transactions done between two DIs. If the securities wire were to have to stay open, for some reason, until

TABLE 9-1
Fedwire hours for securities transactions

Federal Reserve Banks of New York

$$\begin{bmatrix} \text{Appendix A to} \\ \text{Operating Circular No. 21A} \\ \text{Effective January 25, 1984} \end{bmatrix}$$

**CLOSING HOURS
FOR ON-LINE TRANSACTIONS
IN BOOK-ENTRY SECURITIES**

*To all Depository Institutions in the Second
Federal Reserve District, and Others Concerned:*

The following schedule contains the closing hours for on-line transactions in book-entry securities under Operating Circular No. 21A. All times listed are Eastern Time.

Origination of On-Line Transactions..	2:30 P.M.
Origination of Turnaround (Redelivery) Transactions to New York, Chicago, Los Angeles, or San Francisco from a dealer to an ultimate customer..	2:45 P.M.
Reversal of On-Line Transactions...	3:00 P.M.

ANTHONY M. SOLOMON,
President

6:30 P.M., then the funds wire would automatically stay open past that time because the Fed must give banks time to settle their reserve positions after the wire for securities transfers has closed.

People involved in securities and funds transfers would work tolerable hours if the Fed wire closed on time. It does so rarely. In 1985 the average closing hour for securities transfers was 5 P.M. to 5:30 P.M. The wire for funds transfers closed later.

Extensions

Throttle used to cause the Fed wire for securities transfers to close late, but it no longer does so. These days, the problem is *extensions*. Thousands of computers are linked up to the Fed wire, and one of these computers is always going down. When this occurs late in the day, the institution whose computer is down will typically ask the Fed to extend the closing of the wire for securities transfers.

The Fed judges each such request on its own merits. What, it asks, would be the impact on the market if it did not grant an extension? The Fed has criteria regarding what it views as minor, moderate, and major

impacts on the market. A computer problem that held up $200 to 500 million of transactions could warrant an extension, but not beyond 6 P.M. The impact on the market of a downed computer would have to be in the billions for the Fed to hold the wire open beyond 6 P.M. Just how long the Fed will keep the wire open depends on how big the problem is. If the computer of a major clearing bank goes down for hours, the wire may be open until midnight or later. Clearing bank personnel have been known to welcome in the new year at their desks thanks to extensions of the Fed wire.

No one is happy with the Fed's policy on extensions. Big banks complain that the Fed grants too many extensions for problems at small banks and that, because of extensions, they must constantly keep personnel late to receive what turn out to be few, if any, late messages. Small banks, on the other hand, complain that the Fed reacts only to problems experienced by the big players. Noted one Fed officer, "Extensions are a phenomenon that takes on different colorations depending on whether one is or is not in trouble. The bank in trouble thinks that it is the most reasonable thing in the world to have an extension."

One certain thing about extensions is that they are not going to go away. Noted the same Fed officer, "Virtually every day someone has a problem with his computer. Computer problems within a major clearing bank happen at least two or three times a week. Of the extensions we grant, about one-third are associated with problems at N.Y. clearing banks; one-third are associated with problems at FRBs throughout the system; and one-third are associated with *market backlog.* In the case of market backlog, no one may have a particular problem, but because of whatever may be happening in the marketplace, a number of transactions are not being processed on a timely basis. We deem there is market backlog when we have three banks saying that they have a significant amount of transactions that haven't yet been processed. We try to grant extensions only when, collectively, it would not be in the best interests of the market to close the system on time."

The above comment was made in the fall of 1985. In early 1986, the Fed was at its wit's end with all the extensions it was being asked to grant. To cut down on extensions, the Fed eliminated market backlog as grounds for an extension. For an extension to occur, the Fed required that some bank or several banks must ask for and be recorded on its board as asking for an extension. Obviously, when there is market backlog, the big clearing banks will be asking for extensions. So the move probably did not reduce extensions to the level the Fed had wanted. Today, the Fed wire closes on average 45 minutes to one hour earlier than it did before the change was made, that is, the wire now closes on average at 4 P.M. rather than at 5 P.M.

Cost of extensions. Whatever the Fed may say about the reasonableness of its policy on extensions, the fact is that extensions tend to be both exasperating and *expensive* for those banks that are not experiencing a problem. In 1985 an operations official at one large New York clearing bank noted, "The biggest problem with the Fed wire, and this is not a new problem, is the absence of a satisfactory extension policy for all or a majority of the users. There are other systems out there, such as CHIPS, that have been able to wrestle with this. We are dealing with a bit different animal, since we are moving cash and securities, but we should be able to resolve this issue.

"Today, whoever asks for an extension seems to get it. One must wonder how much activity is going through some of the districts out in the Midwest (excluding Chicago), in the Southeast, and in the Southwest. To a bank out there, a $100 million trade may be a lot, but it's peanuts to us. Often, we must sit here for hours after the wire is supposed to close while the Fed grants, every half hour, a new extension; and during this period we typically see *no* traffic coming to us. So we have 235 people just sitting at their terminals doing nothing but waiting for the close.

"Extensions are one of the reasons I have a lot of turnover of personnel. Many of our clerks begin work around 9:30 to 10 A.M., and they must stay until the close. In the last three months the system has rarely closed prior to 5 P.M. And once the system closes, our clerks still have one to three hours of work left to process. Consistently, we have 10 to 20 people who work 50 to 55 hours a week because the Fed wire does not close on time.

"Naturally, all this costs us money. My department has about a $35,000-per-month expense for overtime. In addition I pay about $10,000 per month for taxes due to extensions of the Fed wire. Our policy is that anyone who works three hours past their normal quitting time is provided with a taxi home."

The same frustrated clearing banker went on to note, "In the last 15 months, the Fed has met its 2:30 P.M. close only three times: for Hurricane Gloria, for Good Friday, and once in August 84."

Computer snafus

There is a nursery rhyme about the little girl who, when she was good, was very, very good, and when she was bad, was horrid. Something of the same sort could be said about computers. When they are up and working, they are God's gift to those they serve. When they are down, they are hell. Computer glitches produce every now and then a major snafu on the Street.

Irving's snafu. One fine day a clerk set a switch on an Irving Bank computer so that instructions that were supposed to go out over the Fed wire were all written to disk instead. As a result, Irving could accept deliveries of securities, but it could not make them. "We were," said an ex-Irving officer, "acting as a kind of black hole for securities."

"This occurred," he continued, "on a Wednesday. Fortunately, we'd been thinking that funds were going to tighten, so we were long 1½ billion of funds on which we planned to make, when we sold them, some nickels. Around 3:15 P.M., just after the Fed wire closed, we discovered that we had, thanks to our mis-set computer switch, a problem: we had not received $4 billion of funds that we thought we had. When we told our funds trader that, he just walked around holding his head. He could not believe that you could go from 1.5 long to 2.5 short in less than five minutes. We did just that and had to start buying funds.

"We became a black hole for funds. No offer rate [in the funds market] was too high for us. Finally, when we had scrimped something like 800 million out of the funds market, we found that we had bought everything there was; there were no nickels, dimes, or anything left. At that point, we still had about 1.7 billion to go. To get that, we had to go to the Fed. Unfortunately, we had only 350 million of collateral at the Fed—at first, the Fed viewed that as a problem. Finally, however, they graciously decided that, since we were long about 4 billion in securities anyway, we could use those securities as collateral. So we were able to get our 1.7 billion from the Fed."

Computer errors can be costly. Interest on $1.7 billion, even on an overnight borrowing, is bound to amount to a tidy sum.

BONY's snafu. For a time, Irving's borrowing at the Fed was something of a record for a *solvent* bank, but BONY pulled a boner that caused the Irving OD to pale in significance. On a November Thursday in 1985, BONY was preparing to change software in its computer system when trouble hit: BONY could accept deliveries of securities, but it couldn't make them. BONY's technicians took almost 28 hours to clean up that malfunction; during that time, deliveries and payments in the market for Treasuries came to a near standstill. On the Thursday night its snafu began, BONY had to borrow $22½ billion from the FRBNY. That borrowing, said to be the largest ever from the discount window, cost BONY $5 million and a bit of embarrassment.

An amusing sidelight to this story is that rumors of BONY's difficulties caused metal traders to bid up platinum futures. Apparently, metal traders regard a computer snafu at a bank as the economic equivalent of a bank failure, a notion that the Fed, as lender of last resort to banks experiencing computer problems, might find disturbing.

When a computer snafu occurs at one clearing bank, there is *no* glee, *no* gloating at other clearing banks. While every clearing banker swears that so much money and care has gone into the building of his system that it could never go down for long, he also knows that to err is human, and, consequently, he *prays* that the next big computer snafu will not occur at his bank.

FEES FOR USE OF FEDWIRE

The Fed charges fees both for access to and for use of Fedwire. These fees are summarized in Table 9-2.

FEDWIRE: MONEY TRANSFERS

So far, we have focused primarily on Fedwire as a means of transferring wireable securities, typically against payment in Fed funds. Fedwire is also heavily used for pure money transfers, only some of which are related to the trading, owning, and repoing of securities.

Table 9-3 gives the schedule of charges for wire transfers of funds. The fixed monthly and installation fees for on-line connections to Fedwire indicate why most small DIs have not elected to hook up directly to Fedwire; such institutions do not have the volume of wire transactions necessary to justify the paying of such high fees.

Table 9-4 gives the hours for wire transfers of funds in the New York District. Note the wire is open for money transfers longer than it is for securities transfers. The purpose is to permit CHIPS, which clears Eurodollar payments, to settle same-day and to permit banks to make other settlement transactions. Since the money wire cannot close until after the securities wire has closed, the wire for money transfers often closes late.

TABLE 9-2
Fee schedule for transactions in book-entry securities

1. The following schedule contains the fees for transactions in book-entry Treasury and Federal Agency securities under Operating Circular No. 21A. All times listed are Eastern Time.

Origination of On-Line Transactions	*Treasury and Non-Treasury Securities*
9:00 A.M.–12:00 noon	$2.25
12:01 P.M.– 2:00 P.M.	$2.25
2:01 P.M.–closing	$2.25
Origination of Off-Line Transactions	$7.00
Receipt of Off-Line Transactions	$7.00
Monthly Maintenance of Each Account	—
Monthly Maintenance of Each Issue	—

TABLE 9-3
Wire transfers of funds (schedule of charges)

<table>
<tr><td colspan="2" align="center">Wire transfers of funds and other messages</td></tr>
<tr><td>A. Originator:</td><td></td></tr>
<tr><td>Basic charge per message...</td><td>$0.50</td></tr>
<tr><td>Surcharges:</td><td></td></tr>
<tr><td>Off-line origination...</td><td>$6.00</td></tr>
<tr><td>Telephone advice to receiver..</td><td>$3.50</td></tr>
<tr><td>B. Receiver:</td><td></td></tr>
<tr><td>Basic charge per message...</td><td>$0.50</td></tr>
<tr><td>Surcharge:</td><td></td></tr>
<tr><td>Telephone advice requested by receiver
(no surcharge to receiver when originator
requests telephone advice to receiver)....................................</td><td>$3.50</td></tr>
<tr><td colspan="2" align="center">Fixed monthly fees for on-line connections</td></tr>
<tr><td>Dedicated leased line..</td><td>$ 400</td></tr>
<tr><td>Dial-up line..</td><td>$ 60</td></tr>
<tr><td colspan="2" align="center">Installation fees for on-line connections</td></tr>
<tr><td>Basic installation...</td><td>$ 300</td></tr>
<tr><td>Vendor charges..</td><td>Pass-through
actual costs</td></tr>
<tr><td>Hardware compatibility testing..</td><td>$2,500</td></tr>
<tr><td>Software compatibility testing...</td><td>$4,000</td></tr>
<tr><td>Retraining...</td><td>$ 150</td></tr>
</table>

*   *   *   *   *

This Appendix supersedes Appendix B, revised effective September 2, 1986, to Operating Circular No. 8.

Source: FRBNY, Appendix B to Operating Circular No. 8, revised January 1, 1987.

TABLE 9-4
Schedule for wire transfers of funds: FRBNY

Opening hour
1A.   This Bank accepts transfer items and requests (interdistrict and intradistrict) beginning at 8:30 A.M., Eastern Time.

Interdistrict transfers
2.   This Bank accepts interdistrict transfer items (on-line instructions) until 5:00 P.M., Eastern Time, and interdistrict transfer requests (telephonic instructions) until 4:30 P.M., Eastern Time, each business day. In its discretion, this Bank may accept interdistrict transfer items and requests after these times, but the completion of such transfers is also at the discretion of the transferee's Reserve Bank.

Intradistrict transfers
2A.   This Bank accepts intradistrict transfer items (on-line instructions) until 6:00 P.M., Eastern Time, and intradistrict transfer requests (telephonic instructions) until 5:30 P.M., Eastern Time, each business day. In its discretion, this Bank may accept intradistrict transfer items and requests after these times.

Settlement period
3.   This Bank accepts settlement transfer items (on-line instructions) until 6:30 P.M., Eastern Time, and settlement transfer requests (telephonic instructions) until 6:00 P.M., Eastern Time, each business day. A settlement transfer is a transfer between a transferor and a transferee (a) for their own accounts, or (b) for the account on the books of the transferor or the transferee of a respondent that is (i) subject to Federal Reserve reserve requirements (whether or not such respondent actually maintains reserves), or (ii) a participant in the Clearing House Interbank Payments System operated by the New York Clearing House Association. A settlement transfer must be identified with type code 16, and may contain third party information relating only to such respondents or to the transferor or transferee. Settlement transfers may be used to make or to adjust for net settlement transactions. This Bank reserves the right, in its discretion, to refuse to handle a transfer that is received during the settlement period but that does not comply with the requirements for transfers during such period. This Bank also may, in its discretion, accept settlement transfer items and requests after these times, but the completion of interdistrict settlement transfers is also at the discretion of the transferee's Reserve Bank.

Source: FRBNY, Operating Circular No. 8, as revised March 6, 1986.

THE NEXT CHAPTER

In the next chapter, we describe how, thanks to book entry and the Fed wire, the Street clears each day, with relative ease, hundreds of billions of trades in wireable securities.

Clearing wireable securities

IN THIS CHAPTER AND THOSE THAT FOLLOW, we focus on the tasks that must be done to clear money market trades, not on the details of how these tasks are done. The "how" story changes constantly as the Fed, the dealers, the clearing banks, and the custodial banks introduce new computer hardware and software that permit them to interface better with each other and to do their appointed tasks more quickly, with fewer errors, and with less manpower.

THE ESSENCE OF CLEARING

In essence, clearing is a simple operation. A dealer buys and sells securities over the phone. To effect a buy, the dealer must accept delivery of the securities and pay out money; to effect a sell, the dealer must deliver out securities and accept money. A dealer could do these things for himself, and some dealers do self-clear, partially or totally, certain of their trades. However, many dealers do not want to get involved in making and receiving what are likely to amount, over a month, to many thousands of deliveries and receipts of money and securities. Instead, they hire a clearing bank to do all this receiving and delivering of money

and securities for them. Also, in the case of wireable securities, a dealer could not self-clear his trades even if he wanted to because a dealer can neither get direct access to the Fed wire nor have a book-entry account at the Fed as may a bank. Even a dealer who self-clears physical securities must rely on his clearing bank to make and receive payments over the Fed wire for him. Thus, a major function of a dealer's back office is to give to the dealer's clearing bank—each time the dealer does a trade to be cleared, wholly or partially, by that bank—accurate instructions as to what money and securities the clearing bank must receive or deliver on the dealer's behalf to clear that trade.

On a buy by the dealer, the clearing bank is responsible for collecting the securities bought and for paying for these securities. On a sell by the dealer, the clearing bank is responsible for delivering the securities sold and collecting payment for them. For each trade a dealer does, the clearing bank either makes a payment out of or receives a payment into a *money account* that it maintains for the dealer. Simultaneously, it either accepts a delivery into or makes a delivery out of a *securities account* that it also maintains for the dealer. A dealer's money and securities accounts at its clearing bank together comprise that dealer's *clearing account*. Securities in a dealer's clearing account are referred to as its *box position;* this term dates from the days when all securities were in physical form, and a clearing bank literally stored a dealer's securities in a box.

That's clearing in a nutshell. While the essence of clearing can be explained in a few sentences, explaining in detail how clearing is done requires many pages. In the course of a day, a major clearing bank clears 10,000, 15,000, or maybe more trades in different securities, the aggregate value of which may amount to $75 to 100 billion. For the bank to do all this accurately and on a timely basis (not next week), both it and the dealer's operations area must follow many detailed procedures. Running a clearing bank operation resembles staging a Wagnerian opera. For the performance to be a success, a host of people have to be in the right place, at the right time, doing the right thing.

THE CLEARING BANKS

In terms of volume of securities cleared, the biggest clearing banks are Manufacturers Hanover Trust, the Bank of New York, Irving Trust, and a relative newcomer to the business, Security Pacific, a West Coast bank. All of the above institutions are *banks* (a bank subsidiary in the case of Sec Pac). This fact is unsurprising; to act as a clearing agent, an institution must have access to the Fed wire for money and securities transfers. Until recently, the only institutions that had such access were banks.

All the major clearing banks rank among the 20 largest banks in the U.S. This fact, too, is unsurprising on several counts. First, to have a top-notch clearing operation, a bank must invest many millions of dollars in hardware and software. Moreover, that investment is not a one-shot affair. Technology marches ever onward; consequently, clearing banks constantly update their computer hardware, and every now and then, they must do a multimillion-dollar rewrite of their computer software. Only a large bank can afford continuing investments on this scale.

A second reason why only a large bank can hope to become a major clearing bank has to do with access to credit at the Fed. It is common for a large dealer to pay out, *early in the day,* as a result of purchases of securities, millions more dollars than it receives as a result of sales of securities. Whenever this occurs, the dealer runs what's called a *daylight overdraft* with his clearing bank; he has wired out of his clearing account far more money than he has in that account; normally, most or all of this money flows back into the dealer's clearing account later in the day, thereby eliminating his daylight overdraft. To keep the clearing process going, that is, to prevent *gridlock* in the clearing of securities—X can't pay Y until Y pays X and vice versa—clearing banks must honor dealers' payments for securities purchases even if doing so creates big daylight overdrafts in the clearing accounts of many of their large dealer clients.

From a clearing bank's point of view, the main problem with extending such intraday credit to dealers is not any resulting credit risk to the bank; after all, the dealer receives into his clearing account, as payments are made out of that account, securities that collateralize the bank's loan to him. The big problem clearing banks face in meeting dealer's needs for intraday credit is that, by permitting dealers to run big daylight overdrafts with them, major clearing banks as a group are in turn forced to run multibillion-dollar daylight overdrafts with the Fed. The Fed, particularly in recent years, has expressed displeasure over this situation, but it continues, nonetheless, to allow large, well-capitalized banks to run huge daylight overdrafts with it. In effect, this enables such banks to act as clearing banks. Note the Fed would never allow a small DI to run a huge daylight overdraft with it. With respect to the Fed's perception of credit risk, not all DIs are created equal.

Another reason that all major clearing banks are big banks is that a clearing operation contributes a lot of unpredictable variability to a bank's day-to-day reserve balance at the Fed. To live with that variability, a clearing bank needs to know that it can, if need be, borrow large sums overnight or for several days from the Fed at the discount window. For obvious reasons, a top bank can borrow at the discount window vastly greater sums than can a small DI, and that is true no matter how credit-worthy the small DI may be.

With respect to credit availability from the Fed, it is said that BONY, with $847 million of capital and $14.9 billion of assets, is actually too small a bank to clear the volume of trades it does. BONY gets away with its small size because its customers include the largest broker of governments, FBI, and a number of primary dealers as well. Thus, on many of the trades it clears, BONY is able to do the clearing *internally,* that is, simply making offsetting changes in the amounts of money and securities held by several of its clients in their clearing accounts at BONY. Trades that BONY is able to clear via an *internal* (also referred to by some as a *clearing pairoff*) are never seen by the Fed. Sec Pac is in a similar position. It now clears for 18 primary dealers and for RMJ, the second largest broker of governments. If on a given day, Sec Pac clears 20,000 trades in governments, maybe only half of these would have to go through the Fed; for example, if Goldman and E.F. Hutton do a trade via RMJ, then Sec Pac, which clears for all three entities, can clear these transactions internally. If, however, Hutton sells governments to GE which clears through Citi, then to clear the trade, Sec Pac must use the Fed wire. The more trades a clearing bank can clear internally, the less, if any, credit, either intraday or overnight, it will require from the Fed.

All major clearing banks are New York banks or, in the case of Security Pacific, a New York subsidiary of an out-of-town bank. As noted in Chapter 8, the reason for this is grounded in history. It used to be that all securities, including governments, came in physical form. Thus, it made sense to center the bulk of the nation's clearing activity in a single geographic location. That location turned out to be New York City, which was and is the nation's major financial center.

In the above paragraphs, we were speaking of banks that regard clearing as an important profit center and actively solicit clearing business. Many other banks also clear trades for customers who hold securities in custody with them, for correspondent banks, for their dealer operation if they have one, and so on. Thus, for example, every big New York bank does a lot of clearing even though it may not be a major clearing bank as we have used the term.

CLEARING TRADES IN BOOK-ENTRY SECURITIES

The biggest, single job that clearing banks do for dealers is to clear for them trades in securities that are held in book-entry form. The Fed says that, on an average day, it transfers $140 billion of securities over the wire. The clearing banks together clear a much larger volume of securities; well over 10% of all trades cleared by a major clearing bank are between two of its clients. No wire transfer of securities is required to clear such a trade. One clearing banker estimates that the top three

N.Y. clearing banks clear, on average, close to $300 billion of securities a day. That number sounds reasonable, since every $1 billion of securities that moves over the Fed wire requires banks to clear $2 billion of buys and sells.

CLEARING A DEALER-TO-DEALER TRADE

The easiest way to describe what's involved in clearing a trade in a book-entry security, is to walk, step by step, through the clearing procedure. We begin with a dealer-to-dealer trade.

Doing the trade

Suppose that Treasury-note traders at Sali and Merrill agree over the phone to do a $5 million trade in the 2-year note, Merrill sells to Sali.[1] Merrill's trader will write a *trade ticket* saying, "We, Merrill, sold to you, Sali, $5 million of 2-year, U.S. Treasury notes maturing on such and such a date and carrying such and such a coupon. The dollar price on the trade is 99–26 ($99 plus $^{26}/_{32}$) per $100 of face value. The trade date is . . . (today's date), the settlement date is . . . (usually date of the next business day)." Sali's trader will also write a ticket containing precisely the same information, only the Sali ticket will begin "We, Sali, bought from you, Merrill, ..."

If, on a trade, the trade date and the settlement date are identical, that is, if a trade settles the same day it is done, the trade is said to be a *cash trade*. Cash trades are common in the bill market. If the settlement date on a trade is the next business day following the trade date, the trade is said to be done for *regular settlement.* Bond trades are usually done for regular settlement.

Clearing procedures: Dealer operations

Once the traders at Merrill and Sali have completed their trade tickets describing Merrill's sale to Sali, each will give his ticket to someone in his *operations area*—also dubbed "cage" or "back office." A dealer's operations people have several responsibilities. First, operations must *clean up* the information on the trader's ticket, check that the information the trader has scribbled in haste is accurate, and add any other information its clearing bank will need to clear the trade. Second, operations must

---

[1] Actually, two primary dealers are more likely to trade through a broker than direct. At the end of our example, we discuss how introduction of a broker changes the example. Note that a trade between a primary dealer and a secondary dealer would typically be done direct, not brokered. A secondary dealer with small positions often buys from a big dealer many of the securities he sells to his retail clients.

send to the counterparty a written *confirmation slip* (*confirm*) that states the details of the trade agreed to orally. Third, operations must send to the dealer's clearing bank accurate instructions as to how to clear the trade. Finally, operations must, once the trade is cleared, prove the trade: check that the clearing bank's record of what it did jibes with the dealer's record of what it was supposed to do.

To clear a trade in the 2-year note, the first thing operations people at Sali and Merrill do is an *extension:* calculate how many dollars and cents $5 million of the 2-year note is worth at 99–26 when accrued interest is added to principal. Typically, two shops (be they two dealers or a dealer and a broker) who have done a trade will at some point do a recap—compare figures to check that they have both come up with the same *money.* In the government-securities, primary-dealer environment, a shop doing a trade (almost always through a broker) may not bother to compare the money on that trade with his counterparty. The dealer figures, "Calculating the money on a trade is now automated, so errors are few and usually involve price. Say I'm mistaken about price on a trade for regular settlement—I've got 98 ¼, the other guy has ½; when we try to settle that trade next day, we'll find that error and resolve our difference in 10 minutes."

Once a shop has figured the money on a trade, this number is written on the trade ticket. To execute the trade, a clerk in operations first cleans up, if necessary, the information on the trade ticket. (Has the trader written, for the face amount of the trade, just 5 instead of 5MM? The letter, M, is the Street's shorthand for thousand.) Next, the clerk types into a computer all the information on the trade ticket. He also inputs to the computer any other information that the dealer or its clearing bank will need to execute the trade: the CUSIP number of the security traded and the counterparty's proper name, address, and in-house ID number, if it has one.[2] On a sell (an RP), in which the securities bought (the collateral received) by the investor are not to be safekept by the dealer or its clearing bank ("Tri-Party RPs," Chapter 14), the file on the trade must also include the counterparty's standing *delivery instructions,* where it wants its securities delivered—to account X at bank Y in city Z (usually N.Y.C.). Once the dealer's clerk has input into the dealer's computer all this information (data on the customer was probably already stored in an easily accessed computer file), he directs the latter to produce a confirm for

---

[2]*CUSIP* is an acronym for the *Committee on Uniform Securities Identification Procedures.* Treasury securities, most federal credit agency securities (including mortgage backs), municipal bonds, corporate stocks, and corporate bonds all have identifying CUSIP numbers. These numbers are assigned, for a fee, by Standard & Poor's.

the customer, duplicates of that confirm for the dealer, and clearing instructions for the dealer's clearing bank.

Suppose that Merrill clears through Manufacturers Hanover Trust, Sali through the Bank of New York. Merrill's clearing instructions will tell Manny to clear its trade with Sali. Meanwhile, Sali's clearing instructions will tell BONY to clear its trade with Merrill.

Clearing procedures: The clearing banks

Different dealers transmit instructions to their clearing banks in different ways. Some big N.Y. dealers have a computer-to-computer link with their clearing banks. Small Newport Beach, California, dealers use the phone to call in instructions for clearing cash trades and Express Mail to send confirms for trades that settle the next day. Dealers falling in between in size and volume of trades may use a dedicated Telex machine to get messages to their clearing bank. However a dealer communicates with his clearing bank, the information communicated is always the same: this is what I bought or sold; I did the trade with X; the money was Y; and so on.

Many dealers get information to their clearing banks on the trades they have done for regular (next-day) settlement during the night following the trade. For trades scheduled to settle the next day, Merrill, for instance, waits to send instructions to Manny until early morning, 3 A.M., of the day these trades are to settle. Merrill's early-bird instructions are processed by Manny's night crew before the day crew arrives. Clearing banks never sleep.

Back to Merrill and Manny. Manny's computer reads Merrill's message (clearing instructions) and says, "Ah ha, Merrill has sold 2-year notes to Sali. We must get ready to deliver those securities and to receive payment for them." To do this, Manny's computer creates what is called a *pending mode;* it commits to memory Merrill's instructions; then it spits out a ticket describing Merrill's note trade with Sali and tickets describing all of Merrill's other trades as well; and it's set for action.[3]

The tickets, produced by Manny's computer, are sorted by issue and then go to Merrill's account manager at Manny. He notes what trades Merrill has done and checks on a CRT whether Merrill has in its *box position* (clearing account at Manny) the various securities it has sold, including the notes it has sold to Sali. Suppose Merrill does not have any 2-year notes to deliver to Sali. No problem. The Merrill account

---

[3]The march of technology: for big accounts, tickets created by a clearing bank's computer are being replaced at some clearing banks by information displayed on CRTs.

manager sets the Merrill ticket aside and waits for some 2-year notes to be delivered into Merrill's account.

Merrill, having sold 2-year notes to Sali, must get these securities into its account either by buying them or, if Merrill has shorted the 2-year note, by reversing them in. Otherwise Merrill will *fail* on its promised delivery to Sali. A fail to deliver would cost Merrill money: the 2-year note keeps accruing interest; consequently, the amount of accrued interest Merrill would have to pay to buy these notes goes up each day the fail continues; meanwhile, the amount of accrued interest Sali has agreed to pay Merrill stays constant.

Back to our example. Time passes, and $29 million of 2-year notes come into Merrill's account at Manny. The Merrill account manager checks to see whether he can now make Merrill's delivery to Sali. He can't. Merrill, after it sold $5 million of 2-year notes to Sali, sold another $25 million of this issue to Goldman.

Like most dealers, Merrill does not want its sell tickets cleared on a first-in, first-out basis. It wants its biggest sells in an issue delivered first, its smallest sells delivered last. There's a good reason. Suppose Manny delivered first the $5 million of 2-year notes Merrill has sold to Sali. This would leave $24 million of the 2-year note in Merrill's box position, $1 million too few for Merrill to make delivery to Goldman. If nothing else happened in Merrill's account during the day, say, due to the failure by some customer to deliver $1 million of 2-year notes to Merrill, Merrill would be stuck with $24 million of undelivered 2-year notes. When it became inevitable that Merrill would fail to Goldman, Merrill would have to finance these notes overnight at Manny's dealer loan rate. Fails that have to be financed by a dealer's clearing bank are expensive, since the dealer ends up in effect being *double financed;* so dealers try mightily to avoid such fails.

Suppose that Merrill gets enough 2-year notes in the box to make delivery to Goldman and to cover any other large sells it has in this issue. It may now say to its account manager at Manny, "We've got $8 million of 2-year notes in the box, our big deliveries are done, so shoot those $5 million of the 2-year note that we owe Sali over to them."

The post-2 P.M. rush

The effort we have just described, made by every dealer to make sure he does not fail on big deliveries, leads to a huge peaking problem on the Fed wire just before the latter closes. Said one clearing banker, "There's a peaking problem on the Fed wire because every bank tries to maximize the deliveries it makes for each of its dealer clients. Our bank, for example, builds an inventory in a dealer's position in an issue until the largest sale that that dealer has made in that issue can be

satisfied; we don't want to make a small delivery, then fail on a big one. We build and build inventory; everyone does this. As a result, the traffic put on the wire gets delayed later and later.

"This building up of inventory creates built-in bottlenecks in the system: One dealer is waiting for X amount from another dealer who is waiting for Y amount from another dealer, and so on. Until the beginning dealer in the chain has sufficient inventory to release his delivery, every trade in the chain will be held back. Also, not until dealers have a good indication that the Fed is going to close, will they release positions that they'd rather not release and deliver whatever they can. The upshot is that today, over 50% of the activity over the wire is cleared after 2 P.M.. To put this in perspective, recall that the wire opens early A.M. and that it is supposed to close at 2:30 P.M.

"The Fed does not have the throughput (speed in seconds that it can get a message from Bank A to Bank B) to clear 50% of the activity that passes over the wire in a mere half hour. Consequently, the Fed won't guarantee deliveries sent out during the last five minutes before the wire closes. If we try to bombard the Fed wire with a big chunk of our activity during the last five minutes that the wire is open, chances are we won't get all those deliveries out and fails will occur. When that happens, either we, the clearing bank, or the dealer must eat the fails; the Fed won't."

With no congestion, throughput might take seconds; with congestion, it might take minutes. To understand the problem, it helps to count the computers that get into the act of processing a Fed wire. When a bank releases a message (a transaction) from its back-end computer to its front-end computer, the latter sends that message on to the Fed's front-end computer which in turn transmits the message to the Fed's back-end computer for processing; that computer, once it has done its work, sends an appropriate message to the Fed's front-end (communications) computer, which in turn transmits that message to the receiving bank. When the receiving bank's front-end computer gets the message, it relays it to its own back-end computer. The process of a wire delivery entails sending a message through at least six computers.

When the Fed wire is closing and there is congestion, it might take a message minutes to get through all those computers. When that occurs, either the Fed may reject the sending bank's message because it did not acknowledge receipt of the message before its cutoff time *or* the receiving bank may reject the delivery, which it has the right to do, because it received the delivery after the cutoff time.

As a clearing banker said, "At the end of the day, trying to deliver securities over the wire is like trying to put your hand through a window that someone is about to shut: You either get your hand in with the securities *or* you don't and, if you don't, you've got fails."

The Fed wire and book-entry settlement

Back to our Merrill-delivers-to-Sali example. Finally, Merrill's account manager says, "OK, we're ready to deliver to Sali," and he types a message into a terminal to tell Manny's computer to send $5 million of 2-year notes taken out of Merrill's box position to the account of Sali at BONY. Manny's still-in-the-pending-mode, back-end computer gets the message it has been waiting for, and zips a message to Manny's front-end computer. The latter directs Manny's outgoing traffic in computer messages and not only happens to speak a language comprehensible to the Fed's computer, but happens to have a direct line to that lady.

Message and format. To execute Merrill's trade with Sali, Manny's front-end computer need only send a true KISS (keep it short and simple) message to the Fed's computer. The reason: Just as dealers have two accounts at their clearing bank, Manny and all other large banks have two sorts of accounts at the Fed, a money (reserve) account and at least one account in which they hold book-entry securities.

Manny's message to the Fed goes, "This is Manny calling. Transfer, *DVP* [delivery versus payment], from our account, X, with you, $5 million of securities with CUSIP number, Y, to Sali care of BONY account, Z." The last part of this message is referred to as the receiving bank's *format*.[4] A deliver message will fly on the wire only if the delivery instructions, included by the dealer's operations area in its instructions to its clearing bank, were correct, or if they were not, have been put in correct form by the clearing bank. (Recall that at Manny, cleaning up dealers' delivery instructions on sell trades and entering the corrected instructions into Manny's computer is part of what must be done to get the latter into a pending mode.)

Delivery instructions cannot read, "Chase Manhattan Bank, 1 Chase Plaza, Custodial Department, 43rd floor, attention Lou Smith." That may be OK for a messenger delivering CDs, but it reads like garbage to the Fed's computer, which will kick it back. The Fed's computer can act only on delivery instructions that state the destination of the money or securities transferred in a system-recognizable mnemonic. Every week the Fed publishes a "bible," a long computer printout that lists alphabetically the proper address format to be used in transferring securities to every book-entry account that banks and other DIs maintain with it. The proper format for the send instruction, in the above example, would be *CHASE NYC/CUST*. The proper format for Merrill's delivery to Sali would probably be BK OF NYC/SALI if Sali cleared 2-year

---

[4] Recall Figures 9-1 and 9-2 on pp. 106 and 107.

notes at BONY. Sali, it so happens, doesn't, but in our example we are only supposing.

The Fed in action. All the Fed's computer wants to know is who (spelled correctly) is sending what (amount and proper CUSIP number) to whom (also spelled correctly, please). Messages over the Fed wire are less tightly formatted than are messages through CHIPS, the New York clearing house for checks and wire transfers of money not traditionally made in Fed funds. Consequently, it is possible to write more than who, what, and to whom in a Fed wire that flies. Any information in a Fed wire beyond who, what, and to whom—it's a nice day, this trade is an RP—is disregarded by the Fed's computer.

Knowing who, what—$5 million of securities with CUSIP number X worth Y dollars—and to whom allows the Fed's computer to get into action to clear Merrill's sell to Sali. The Fed's computer debits Manny's appropriate account for the amount of the issue to be transferred and credits those securities to the appropriate account at BONY. Simultaneously, since this is a delivery-versus-payment transfer, the Fed's computer debits, without asking if it's OK, BONY's reserve account with it for Y dollars and credits Manny's reserve account for the same amount.

Back at BONY. BONY has not been sleeping while Manny and Merrill were preparing, by getting Manny's computer into a pending mode, to shower it with securities and to whisk away precious reserve dollars. Sali's back office, like Merrill's, has also sent instructions to its clearing bank saying, "We, Sali, bought from Merrill securities X for Y dollars. Please take them in against payment." That instruction got BONY's computer into its equivalent of a pending mode, so it was not surprised when the Fed's computer summarily credited one of its accounts for $5 million of securities for the account of Sali and debited its reserve account for Y dollars. It recognized the delivery as something it was supposed to receive.

In many cases, a clearing bank's computer is programmed either to kick back ("DK" for don't know) any Fed wire that it gets but does not anticipate, or at least to signal to someone at the bank to call the receiving dealer and to ask whether it should accept an unanticipated trade or a trade on which the money is off. However, some big dealers who do a lot of trading build a tolerance level into their instructions to their clearing bank; they will accept a trade even if the money is slightly off; on incoming securities, they would rather straighten out the money later than DK a trade and risk a fail to deliver.

If BONY, for some reason, were to DK the delivery from Manny, then the Fed's computer would credit to BONY's reserve account the dollars

it has just debited this account, thus putting the account back where it started; the Fed would get the money to do this by debiting Manny's reserve account for a like amount. Simultaneously, the Fed would transfer the $5 million of securities that it had transferred from a Manny account to a BONY account back from the BONY account to the Manny account. For obvious reasons, this procedure is called a *reversal*.

BONY might DK a delivery from Merrill to Sali if some piece of information in the transfer wire—CUSIP number, money, or whatever—did not agree with the information on the trade transmitted to it by Sali. Provided the Fed wire is not congested, DKs occur within seconds after a message, which must pass through at least six computers, is sent by a clearing bank's back-end computer over the Fed wire. If a delivery that a clearing bank is trying to make is DK'd by the receiving bank, the sending bank, if it's made a mistake, will try again; if it has made a mistake and now gets the message right, the transfer will go through.

Crediting and debiting money and securities

Once BONY takes in securities for Sali, BONY's computer will automatically credit Sali's clearing account for the $5 million of securities received and debit Sali's money account for the Y dollars paid out for these securities. At the same time, Manny's computer would debit Merrill's clearing account with it for the $5 million in 2-year notes delivered to Sali and credit Merrill's account with it for the Y dollars received in payment for those securities.

All of the above credits and debits to various securities and money accounts are easy to follow because the money and securities sides of the transaction always lead, for each party, to a pair or to several pairs of offsetting debits and credits. For example, Sali's clearing account at BONY will show two offsetting changes in assets: *minus Y dollars in its money account and plus $5 million of 2-year notes worth Y dollars in its security account. Meanwhile, BONY's accounts at the Fed, will undergo the same offsetting changes that occurred in Sali's accounts at BONY. At the same time, BONY will experience two offsetting changes in its liabilities: plus $5 million of 2-year notes worth Y dollars in Sali's securities account with it and minus Y dollars in Sali's money account with it.*

No Fed wire

Actually, Sali clears 2-year notes through Manny, not BONY. That changes the clearing story, but just two steps of it, one near the beginning and one at the end. Assume again that Merrill sells $5 million of 2-year notes to Sali. That trade sets in motion precisely the same clear-

ing procedures described above. Only this time Sali, like Merrill, sends its instructions to clear the trade to Manny. When Merrill's account manager at Manny decides he can finally deliver securities to Sali, he will recognize that Sali is a customer of Manny and that the trade can therefore be cleared *without using the Fed wire,* which he in fact could not use, even if he wanted to, because the securities are not, from the Fed's vantage point going anywhere; to clear the trade, Merrill's and Sali's account managers at Manny simply direct Manny's computer, which is in its usual pending mode, to make appropriate changes that it was waiting to make in both Sali's and Merrill's money and securities accounts at Manny. Manny's reserve and securities accounts at the Fed undergo *no* change.

Paper and real trades.   Lawyers and prosecutors are wont to describe trades that they want to discredit for one reason or another as *paper trades. Real trades,* which are always understood to be fine and upstanding, have various characteristics (*indicia*) not shared by paper trades; of these—the list is not always the same—the most commonly mentioned is that real trades are trades that clear over the Fed wire. By this definition of "real," well over 10% of the trades made between primary dealers, operating under the Fed's ever-watchful eye, are unreal.

Clearing pairoffs.   Trades that can be cleared without a transfer over the Fed wire, depending on who is speaking, are referred to as *pairoffs* or *internals.* A pairoff may occur in the course of a clearing bank's operations not only when it clears a trade done by two dealers, but when it clears a trade done between an interdealer broker and a dealer (Chapter 6).

EXAMPLE OF A MERRILL BUY FROM AND SELL TO SALI: TRADE TICKETS, CONFIRMS, CLEARING INSTRUCTIONS, OPPORTUNITY FOR PAIROFF

We've described in general terms how the clearing of an interdealer trade in wireable securities is done and what trade tickets and other documents are generated along the way. To end this discussion, we present an example of two interdealer trades that could be cleared by a pairoff. Also, we present key documents generated as these trades are made and cleared.

Merrill salls T Notes to Sali

Suppose that Merrill Lynch Government Securities, Inc. (Merrill Lynch *GSI*) sells, on 7/29/86, to Salomon Brothers $5 million (5MM) of Treasury

notes, the 7s of 6/30/88. The agreed-upon price is 100 35/64. Aside: In Chapter 4, we noted that government notes and bonds are priced on quote sheets in 32nds; often, however, the pricing of governments in the interdealer market is finer: a *plus sign* may be added to a price indicating that the price is the stated price *plus one half of ⅟₃₂,* that is, ⅟₆₄. Thus, the trade price we have assumed, 100 35/64, corresponds to a price of 100 17+.

The trade ticket. As the Merrill trader sells notes to Sali, he writes the trade ticket illustrated in Figure 10-1. Note the trade is done for regular settlement, so the settlement date on the trade ticket is 7/30/86. The other information on the trade ticket is sparse; to begin the clearing process, all that Merrill's back office need know is that the trade is with Sali, whose account number is X, and that the trade is for $5 million face value of a particular note at a particular price.

Figuring the money. The next step that someone or some computer at Merrill must take to clear the trade is to *figure the money* on the trade: how much Sali must pay Merrill. Table 10-1 shows this calculation. Step one is to convert the price in 64s to a decimal equivalent. Step two is to calculate the dollar amount to be paid for principal; it is $5 million

FIGURE 10-1
Merrill trade ticket: Sale of T notes to Sali

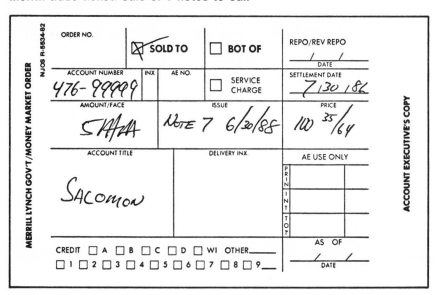

times the decimal calculated in step one. Step three is to calculate accrued interest (a_i). This step requires that a clerk determine, using a computer or a periodically updated book that gives the required infor- mation, the number of days that will have elapsed from the last coupon date to the settlement date. On the security in question, this number is 30. The clerk must also determine the number of days in the current coupon period (6/30/86 to 12/30/86). For the security in question, this number is 184. Using these two numbers and the coupon on the securi- ty, it's easy to calculate accrued interest on the notes. As the formula for a_i in Table 10-1 shows, the amount of interest accrued on the notes as of the settlement date is the face amount of the notes *times* one-half the coupon rate (recall that a note pays interest twice a year) *times* the fraction of the current coupon period that will have elapsed as of settle- ment day. The fourth and final step in figuring the money on the trade is to add principal and accrued interest to get the total money due.

Clearing instructions. At this point, a clerk in Merrill's back office uses (1) the information on the trade ticket, (2) the money figures, if they are not calculated automatically by Merrill's computer, and (3) informa- tion in Sali's account file, accessed by its unique account number, to generate a confirm to be sent to Sali (Figure 10-2). Merrill also adds to the tape of instructions—that it will send to Manny during the wee hours of the 7/30/86—instructions as to how Manny is to clear this trade: deliver to Sali $5 million of the 7s of 6/30/88 against payment in Fed funds of $5,055,876.36.

Later the same day, 7/30/86, Manny will, following Merrill's instructions to it, prepare (actually, it is Manny's computer reading Merrill's tape that

TABLE 10-1
Calculating the money on the trade described in Figure 10-1: Mer- rill sells to Sali $5 million of 7% T notes maturing on 6/30/88

Step 1: Calculate dollar price in decimal form:
Par + $^{35}\!/_{64}$ = 1.00546875

Step 2: Calculate dollars due for principal:
$5,000,000 × 1.00546875 = $5,027,343.75

Step 3: Calculate accrued interest (a_i) through 7/30/86:

Days since last coupon: 30
Days in current coupon period: 184
Coupon rate: 0.07
$$a_i = (\$5,000,000) \left(\frac{.07}{2} \right) \left(\frac{30}{184} \right) = \$28,532.61$$

Step 4: Sum principal and accrued interest:
Total money on the trade = $5,055,876.36

FIGURE 10-2
Merrill confirmation to Sali of a sale of notes to Sali

```
                                        CONFIRMATION
Merrill Lynch
Government Securities Inc.                           PAGE        OF

One Liberty Plaza 165 Broadway New York New York 10080 (212) 766-3000


  Salomon Bros.
  1 New York Plaza
  New York, NY 10004
  Attn:  P & S Dept.                     RECEIVE FROM
                                         MANUFACTURERS HANOVER TRUST


AS PRINCIPAL WE CONFIRM THE FOLLOWING TRADE.
  TRADE DATE      SETTLEMENT DATE         ACCOUNT              REFERENCE NO.
                                            NO.
  7-29-86          7-30-86              476-99999          G6210027805

                                                           TKT NO. 0002

WE SOLD TO YOU

           SECURITY                RATE                DUE
UNITED STATES TREASURY NOTES       7.00               6-30-88

PAR VALUE        5,000,000.00      PRICE   100.546875  PRINCIPAL  $5,027,343.75

INTEREST DAYS          30       INTEREST   $28,532.61

TOTAL          $5,055,876.36

PAYMENT IN FED FUNDS



                                                       CUSTOMER'S COPY
```

does the work) a ticket that instructs the Manny account manager on the Merrill desk to clear Merrill's trade. This ticket is shown in Figure 10-3.

As noted, it so happens that Merrill and Sali both clear their trades in T notes at Manny. Thus, Sali too will have sent instructions to Manny to clear its buy from Merrill, and Manny would thus be able to clear this trade simply by adjusting appropriately the amounts of *both* money and securities in the clearing accounts with it of *both* Merrill and Sali. To clear the trade, *no* Fed wire would be required.

Merrill buys T notes from Sali

Now let's add a wrinkle to our example, one designed to illustrate one way in which a *pairoff* might occur. Suppose that, on 7/28/86, Merrill happened to have bought $5 million of the 7s of 6/30/88 and that this trade, too, was to settle on 7/30/86. Finally, suppose that this second trade was priced not at 100 $\frac{35}{64}$—as was the Merrill sell to Sali—but at 100 $\frac{15}{32}$.

FIGURE 10-3
Ticket instructing manager of Merrill desk at Manny to clear Merrill's sale of notes to Sali

Merrill Lynch GSI
One Liberty Plaza
New York, N.Y. 10080

Cleared By
MANUFACTURERS HANOVER
TRUST COMPANY
BROKERS & DEALERS CLEARANCE DEPT.
40 WALL STREET, 3RD FLR., NEW YORK, N.Y. 10015

REFERENCE NUMBER	TRADE TYPE	TRADE DATE	SETTLE DATE	DELIVERY DATE
G6210027805	Deliver	7/29/86	7/30/86	

ACCOUNT NAME	SPECIAL INSTRUCTIONS
	MFRS NYC/SALOMON

CUSTOMER NO. 476-99999
ABA NO. 021000306

QUANTITY	CUSIP NUMBER	SECURITY DESCRIPTION
5,000,000.00	912000BG	Note 06/30/88 7.00

PRICE	NET AMOUNT
100.546875	5,055,876.36

209135

PRINCIPAL 5,027,343.75
INTEREST   28,532.61
FEE

Wire

TAPE SEQ. NO. 199

TRAN NO. 1493

TICKET SEQ. NO. 0002

TIME   09:48

10/84

Upon delivery of the securities described hereon, which are attached hereto, to the purchaser or his designee, the purchaser shall acquire all rights in such securities which we had or had actual authority to convey, and the risk of loss shall pass to the purchaser, provided however, that if full payment for such securities has not been received at or by the time of delivery thereof; it is agreed that a purchase money security interest in favor of the above mentioned Broker/Dealer shall attach to such securities, which interest shall not terminate until such time as full payment therefor has been received by us.

FIGURE 10-4
Merrill trade ticket—buy of T notes from Sali

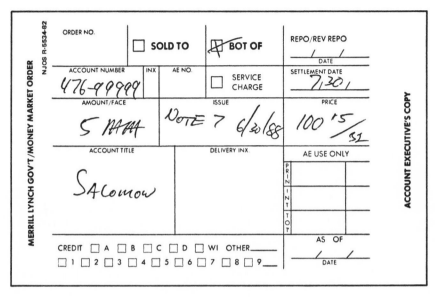

The trade ticket for this second trade (Merrill buys from Sali) is given in Figure 10-4. This trade yields the money calculation given in Table 10-2. The confirm sent by Merrill to Sali is shown in Figure 10-5. The ticket prepared by Manny's computer for the manager of the Merrill desk at Manny is shown in Figure 10-6.

Pairoff by difference check

Both of the trades we've described could be cleared one at a time by Manny, but this would cost Manny effort and time; and it would cost Merrill and Sali fees. To save the paying of needless fees to their clearing banks both Merrill and Sali (and other dealers as well) have back-office procedures for spotting buys and sells that offset each other. The above two trades do precisely that: Merrill has sold to Sali the same amount of the same securities it bought from Sali a day earlier, and the two trades are to settle on the same day. To clear both trades on a *net* basis, *no* securities at all need move between Merrill's clearing account and Sali's clearing account. What must move is a *difference check* in the amount of $3,906.25 from Sali to Merrill; the check equals the money Merrill made (Sali lost) on the two trades because the price at which Merrill sold notes to Sale exceeded by %₆₄ the price at which Merrill bought those same

TABLE 10–2
Figuring the money on the trade described in Figure 10–4: Merrill buys from Sali $5 million of 7% T notes maturing on 6/30/88

Step 1: Calculate dollar price in decimal form:
Par + $^{15}\!/_{32}$ = 1.0046875

Step 2: Calculate dollars due for principal:
$5,000,000 × 1.0046875 = $5,023,437.50

Step 3: Calculate accrued interest (a_i) through 7/30/86:

Days since last coupon: 30
Days in current coupon period: 184
Coupon rate: 0.07
$$a_i = (\$5,000,000)\left(\frac{.07}{2}\right)\left(\frac{30}{184}\right) = \$28,532.61$$

Step 4: Sum principal and accrued interest:
Total money on the trade = $5,051,970.11

notes from Sali. Once the difference check is sent—actually, it's a payment of Fed funds—Merrill and Sali are square with respect to settlement of the two trades. Naturally, when two dealers decide to clear two or more trades via a pairoff, they must *kill* any instructions previously sent to their respective clearing banks directing the latter to clear the trades to be paired off on a one-at-a-time basis.

Automation

To our description of how a dealer-to-dealer trade is cleared, we should add several points. First, clearing is becoming more and more *automated* wherever automation pays. For big accounts such as Merrill, Manny no longer has its computer spit out paper tickets for each Merrill trade it is to clear. Instead, all information on pending receives and delivers into Merrill's clearing account are displayed on a CRT on the Merrill desk at Manny; also, in Merrill's operations area, there is a CRT that displays the same information. Manny's automated system gives Merrill options: Early in the day, Merrill can put its deliveries on hold while it builds inventory to make big deliveries first; later, when it has sufficient inventory, it can put the system on auto-settle, and its pending deliveries will go out automatically—bang, bang, bang. Automating the handling of a big clearing account probably cuts the operating costs of both the clearing bank and the dealer. In addition, it has a second advantage: The less a human must intervene in the clearing process, the less opportunity there is for error. What Manny is doing today in the way automating the Merrill account and its other big accounts probably differs little from what other clearing banks are doing for their big accounts.

Even with an automated system, some human judgment may be called for as the wire is closing. For example, if Merrill has in the box $24 million

FIGURE 10-5
Merrill confirmation to Sali of a buy of notes from Sali

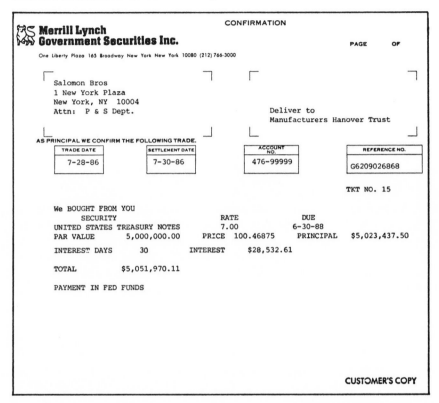

of an issue and is building inventory to make a $25 million delivery of that issue, at some point someone at Manny or at Merrill has got to say, "Hey, the wire is closing—that extra $1 million we were waiting for is not coming in. We had better shoot out two pending deliveries of 10 each. Otherwise, Manny is going to have to finance Merrill's full $24 million position overnight."

The brokers

There is a second important point we must make about our example of the clearing of a dealer-to-dealer trade. In that example, we assumed that Merrill and Sali traded T notes *directly* with each other. Occasionally, a dealer will trade governments directly with another dealer, but most times they will do such trades through a *blind broker*. If Merrill sells

FIGURE 10-6
Ticket instructing manager of Merrill desk at Manny to clear Merrill's buy of notes from Sali

Merrill Lynch GSI
One Liberty Plaza
New York, N.Y. 10080

Cleared By
**MANUFACTURERS HANOVER
TRUST COMPANY**
BROKERS & DEALERS CLEARANCE DEPT.
40 WALL STREET, 3RD FLR., NEW YORK, N.Y. 10015

REFERENCE NUMBER	TRADE TYPE	TRADE DATE	SETTLE DATE	DELIVERY DATE
G6209026868	Receive	7/28/86	7/30/86	

ACCOUNT NAME	SPECIAL INSTRUCTIONS
	MFRS NYC/SALOMON

CUSTOMER NO. 476-99999
ABA NO. 021000306

QUANTITY	CUSIP NUMBER	SECURITY DESCRIPTION
5,000,000.00	912000BG	Note 06/30/88 7.00

PRICE		NET AMOUNT
100.46875		5,051,970.11

PRINCIPAL 5,023,437.50
INTEREST   28,532.61
FEE

Wire

TAPE SEQ. NO. 211

TRAN NO. 1670

TICKET SEQ. NO. 0015

TIME 12:59

20913F

10/04

Upon delivery of the securities described hereon, which are attached hereto, to the purchaser or his designee, the purchaser shall acquire all rights in such securities which we had or had actual authority to convey, and the risk of loss shall pass to the purchaser, provided however, that if full payment for such securities has not been received at or by the time of delivery thereof; it is agreed that a purchase money security interest in favor of the above mentioned Broker/Dealer shall attach to such securities, which interest shall not terminate until such time as full payment therefor has been received by us.

through a broker, it has *no* idea of who the buyer on the other side of the trade is; it might be any one of 53 other primary and aspiring-to-be-primary dealers.

Our example of a Merrill sell to Sali can easily be expanded and made more realistic by the insertion of a broker, say RMJ, between Sali and Merrill. In that case, Merrill sells to RMJ which in turn sells to Sali. Clearing of these trades follows the identical pattern we described above except that now Manny must clear Merrill's sale to RMJ, which clears at Security Pacific (Sec Pac), *and* Sec Pac must clear RMJ's sale to Sali.

A DEALER-TO-CUSTOMER TRADE: NO DEALER SAFEKEEPING

The above scenario illustrates how a dealer-to-dealer trade is cleared. A dealer-to-customer trade is cleared in much the same way, except that a large institutional investor typically uses as agent the custodial area of a bank, often a N.Y.C. bank.

To illustrate, suppose now that Merrill sells $10 million of 3-month bills to the Ford portfolio. Ford cannot hold book-entry securities itself; it must have some financial institution hold them for it. It could have a selling dealer safekeep for it securities it bought from that dealer, but suppose that, like many big accounts, it does not want to expose itself to the credit risk it feels it would incur if it left securities with a dealer for safekeeping.[5]

To avoid incurring this perceived credit risk, large portfolio managers typically have a bank hold for them all securities they own; they also have that bank clear for them whatever buys and sells they do, both of book-entry and physical securities. Accounts in which a bank holds securities for a customer are called custodial, safekeeping, or segregated accounts. There is no consistency in jargon. We will use the term *custodial account* to indicate an investor's account at a bank.

A custodial bank may perform various levels of service for a customer. The minimum it will do is hold a customer's securities and clear its buys and sells. For additional fees—custody is a big fee area for banks—a custodial bank may do bookkeeping for the customer, that is, prepare reports saying: this is the income, coupon and other, you received on

---

[5] Big investors are wont to ask, "Where would I stand if a dealer with whom I had left millions of dollars of my valuable securities for safekeeping went bankrupt?" Banks who make money on custody accounts naturally encourage an investor to think that his securities are safer if he leaves them in custody with a bank than if he safekeeps them with a dealer or does in-house RP with a dealer. Some top-of-the-pile dealers resent this attitude. Such a dealer reasons, "We've got as much or more capital than some custody banks, and we haven't got loans to LDCs. So how can someone say that an institution that is a bank is necessarily a better credit than us just because that institution is a bank?"

your securities; these are the capital gains (losses) you earned (incurred) in buying and selling securities; and so on. A custodial bank may also prepare for a customer reports analyzing the customer's portfolio: this is the average maturity of the securities you own, the breakdown by type of security—CDs, BAs, Treasuries, and so on. Generally, the larger the portfolio, the more elaborate the custodial services the customer's bank will provide, and the higher the fees it will charge.

Getting back to our example, we assume that Ford uses Morgan, N.Y., for custody. Most, but not all, managers of large portfolios choose a N.Y.C. custody agent because a bank with direct access to the New York Fed can provide more rapid and efficient clearing services than can a regional bank. This reflects the fact that the New York Fed has, until recently, provided faster and more efficient services to local banks on line with it than have any of the other eleven regional Fed banks. Also, clearing of *physical* securities is expensive and difficult for out-of-town banks to do; New York City is the national center for the clearing of physical securities, the one town in which the large majority of the transfers of physical securities that a clearing or custodial bank might need to make can be done by a messenger on foot. For both of these reasons, a number of regional banks have set up a subsidiary in New York City; doing so enables them to compete on a level playing field with New York City banks in providing custodial services to investors and, in the case of some banks, clearing services to dealers.

Doing the trade

The first steps that occur in a dealer-to-customer trade resemble closely those that occur in a dealer-to-dealer trade. To continue our Merrill-Ford example, Ford's and Merrill's traders strike their deal on the phone—Ford's trader agrees to buy $10 million of 3-month bills at a discount of 7.95. Each trader writes a trade ticket detailing the essentials of the trade; Ford's ticket, for example, might say, "We bought, today, at a discount of 7.95 for same-day settlement on 12/5/85, from Merrill $10 million of 3-month bills maturing on 2/13/86." In each trader's shop, someone will be responsible for figuring the money on a trade of $10 million of bills, at a discount of 7.95, X days from maturity. As in a dealer-to-dealer trade, the two shops will compare money to ensure that Ford is preparing to pay Merrill the amount of money Merrill figures the securities it is selling to Ford are worth.

Getting out clearing instructions

The Merrill trader will send its ticket to its back office, as it would for a trade with Sali, and its back office will go through the same procedures

described above: clean up the information that the trader has given it and add any further information needed to clear the trade. The latter would include the CUSIP number of the bill issue and Ford's standing delivery instructions to Merrill. Once Merrill has prepared a file in its computer containing all relevant information on the trade, it will prepare a computer-generated confirm for Ford as well as instructions to its clearing bank, Manny, directing it to clear the trade.

Ford, meanwhile, will also have an operations person preparing a complete record of all details of its trade with Merrill; using that information, its operations people will prepare instructions for its custodial bank, Morgan, to clear its trade with Merrill. Ford's instructions to Morgan would say, "We have bought from Merrill $10 million of bills, CUSIP number Y, maturing in X days. Please accept delivery of these securities, and pay out, versus delivery, the money due, which is Z dollars. Settlement is today."

The clearing banks at work

Once Morgan receives Ford's instructions, it will feed this information into its computer and it will be on the lookout for Merrill's delivery to Ford. Poised on the opposite side of the street, Manny's computer will, when it receives Merrill's delivery instructions, go into a pending mode and shoot out a ticket of instructions to the manager of the Merrill account.

From there on in, delivery will proceed as in our earlier example of a Merrill-to-Sali delivery. Once Merrill's account manager at Manny determines that Merrill has sufficient bills in its box position to make delivery to Ford, it will then direct that the bills be sent, from Merrill's account at Manny, over the Fed wire versus payment to Ford's account at Morgan. The address format on the wire that Manny sends might read *MORGAN/CUST/FORD*. Note, the only part of this address that the Fed need read is *MORGAN/CUST*. The last word in the address, *FORD*, is there simply to tell Morgan what to do with the securities once it gets them: deliver these securities against payment to Ford's custody account with it.

If Manny delivers to Ford's account at Morgan the securities Morgan has been instructed by Ford to accept, the trade will clear smoothly; and as it does, the following changes will occur in the balance sheets of the parties to the clearing. Merrill's holding of bills will fall, but its cash balance in its clearing account will rise. Identical changes will occur in Manny's reserve and securities accounts at the Fed. Meanwhile, across the street, precisely the *opposite* balance-sheet changes will be occurring. The cash balance in Ford's account at Morgan will fall while its holdings of bills will rise. Simultaneously, changes identical to those that

occur in Ford's accounts at Morgan will occur in Morgan's reserve and securities accounts at the Fed.

EXAMPLE OF A MERRILL SALE TO AMOCO: TRADE TICKET, CONFIRM, AND CLEARING INSTRUCTIONS

We've described in general terms how a dealer-to-customer trade in wireable securities is cleared if the customer uses a custodial bank to hold his securities and to clear his trades. To end our discussion, we present an example of a dealer-to-customer trade and of key documents generated as this trade is made and cleared.

Suppose that Merrill sells, on 1/31/86, to Amoco for cash (same-day) settlement $10 million (10MM) of Treasury bills maturing on 2/13/86. Recall from Chapter 3 that bills are quoted at a rate of discount, not at a dollar price. Suppose that the agreed-upon rate of discount in the Merrill-Amoco trade is 7.95. Suppose also that Amoco directs that Merrill deliver its bills to its custody account at Morgan, N.Y.C.

As the Merrill trader sells bills to Amoco, he writes the trade ticket illustrated in Figure 10-7. Merrill's back office next figures the money on the trade (recall that we illustrated this calculation in Chapter 3), and

FIGURE 10-7
Merrill trade ticket—sale of $10 million of T bills to Amoco

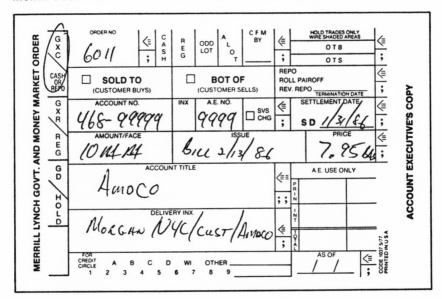

it prepares on the Merrill computer a confirm to be sent to Amoco (Figure 10–8). At the same time, Amoco instructs Morgan to expect delivery, to its account at Morgan, of the bills it has purchased from Merrill. Amoco also instructs Morgan to make payment versus delivery for these securities.

Merrill's back office also instructs Manny to clear its trade with Amoco. When these instructions are received at Manny, Manny's computer generates a ticket for the manager of the Merrill desk at Manny directing him to clear the trade. This ticket is shown in Figure 10–9. Note that the trade and settlement dates coincide. Note also that delivery is to *MORGAN NYC/CUST/AMOCO.*

PAIROFFS AGAIN

We noted earlier that every dealer on the Street seeks to simplify the settling of his trades with other dealers by arranging as many pairoffs as

FIGURE 10–8
Merrill confirmation to Amoco of a sale of T bills to Amoco

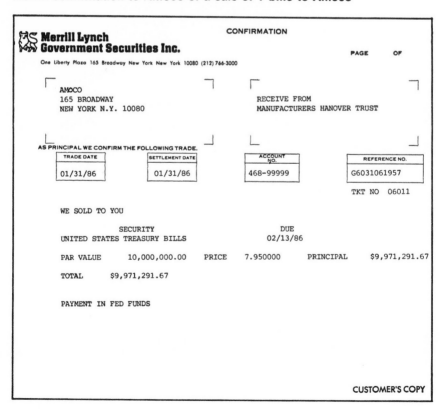

FIGURE 10-9
Ticket instructing manager of the Merrill desk at Manny to clear Merrill's sale of T bills to Amoco (*delivery is to be made at Morgan, N.Y.C.*)

Merrill Lynch GSI
One Liberty Plaza
New York, N.Y. 10015

Cleared By
**MANUFACTURERS HANOVER
TRUST COMPANY**
BROKERS & DEALERS CLEARANCE DEPT.
40 WALL STREET, 3RD FLR., NEW YORK, N.Y. 10015

REFERENCE NUMBER	TRADE TYPE	TRADE DATE	SETTLE DATE	DELIVERY DATE
G6031061957	Deliver	01/31/86	01/31/86	

ACCOUNT NAME		SPECIAL INSTRUCTIONS
		MORGAN NYC/CUST/AMOCO

CUSTOMER NO.   468-99999
ABA NO.   021000238

QUANTITY	CUSIP NUMBER	SECURITY DESCRIPTION
10,000,000	912999BKE	Bill 02/13/86

PRICE		NET AMOUNT
.000		9,971,291.67

PRINCIPAL .00
INTEREST .00

FEE

Wire

TAPE SEQ. NO. 0199   TRAN NO.   0391

TICKET SEQ. NO. 06011   TIME 01:26

20913F

10/84

possible. Each such pairoff calls for a bilateral netting of the dealer's trades with some important counterparty. All of the trades settled by a particular pairoff must be in the same issue and must settle on the same day. In a pairoff, it is the settlement date, not the trade date, that counts. For example, if Sali sells 10MM of security X to DLJ for settlement five days hence, and DLJ then sells, on settlement day, those same securities back to Sali, the two trades can be settled by a pairoff. Since *wi* (when issued) trades in Treasuries cannot be settled until the wi period trading ends and the new Treasury issue being traded is settled, many of the *wi* buys and sells made by active traders in new Treasury issues end up being settled by pairoffs.

Dealers commonly pairoff not only trades with other dealers, but trades with active customers. For a customer, as for a dealer, pairoffs reduce the cost of and simplify clearing. An obvious opportunity for a pairoff between a dealer and a customer would be a situation in which a customer both buys from a dealer and sells to the same dealer identical amounts of a given security for settlement on the same day. A pairoff would also be possible if a dealer sold securities to a customer and then immediately reversed in those securities from the customer. It is not uncommon, particularly in Ginnie Maes, for a buyer of securities to finance his purchase with the selling dealer. Still another opportunity for a pairoff, dealer-to-customer, occurs when a dealer sells securities to a customer and then immediately borrows those securities from the customer.

To maximize the number of trades settled by pairoff, a big dealer typically programs a back-office computer to produce a potential-pairoffs file. Working from that file *blotter,* the dealer contacts each counterparty with whom he might do a pairoff to see whether that party wants to pairoff several trades.

One might, with some justice, characterize the system currently used by dealers in governments for pairing off trades as primitive. This system permits only *bilateral* pairoffs in a *single* issue. There is no logical reason why a dealer's system could not be set up to search out opportunities for *multi-issue* netting. For example, if Morgan sells Sali one issue and buys from Sali another issue, securities must move both ways to settle these trades, but only one difference check, as opposed to two wire transfers of money, would be required to settle both trades. One roadblock to multi-issue netting is that it would create a credit risk: If each delivery is not to be made against payment, then who delivers first?

Dealers in governments, eyeing the DTC-NSCC system for settling trades in corporate securities, would all like, eventually, to have a system for settling trades in governments that would permit both *multi-issue* and *multilateral* settlement of such trades (end of Chapter 16). Unfortunately,

it's far easier for dealers to say that they'd like such a settlement system than it is for them to agree on the precise design of the system.

THE NEXT CHAPTER

We've talked in this chapter about how the Street clears trades in wireable securities. In the next chapter, we focus on how the Street clears trades in *physical* securities, such as BAs and CDs. Clearing trades in physicals is a lot trickier than clearing trades in wireables because, most times when a physical money market security is traded, *paper must move.*

Chapter 11

Clearing trades in physical securities

ALL TREASURY AND MANY FEDERAL AGENCY SECURITIES either may be, or can only be, held in book-entry form. Once all parties who play a role in the clearing of a trade in book-entry securities have done their preparatory work, a trade in such securities can, as we've seen, be cleared by the sending of a single message over the Fed wire. That is the magic of book entry, and without that magic, the government market, in which the primary dealers alone trade, on an average day, $100 billion of securities, would collapse, trapped in a mire of DKs, fails, unfinished paper work, and undelivered securities.

A number of important money market instruments have not yet been converted to book entry. The principal reason is that such securities are too heterogeneous—with respect to the name of the issuer, the dates of issue and maturity, the face amount, and the coupon or discount rate paid—to be converted with ease to book entry. Money market securities still in *physical* form include CDs, BAs, commercial paper, muni notes, and certain types of mortgage-backed securities.

GOOD DELIVERY: BEARER AND REGISTERED SECURITIES

A physical security may be in either bearer or registered form. In the money market, it is common for borrowers to issue bearer paper and for that paper to be traded in bearer form only, even if the issuer would permit registration of the paper. Physical T bills used to be held and traded on the Street in bearer form. BAs and CDs are typically, if not always, in bearer form. In contrast, many non-money market securities come in registered form; these include certain pass-throughs, muni bonds, corporate bonds, and corporate stocks.

Trades in physical securities are, at the wholesale level of which we are speaking, done *delivery versus payment (DVP)*.[1] When a dealer sells an investor (or vice versa) a physical security (certificate), he must, to get his money, make *good delivery* of the security he has sold. One aspect of good delivery is that the seller must deliver, to the buyer, the security in a form (1) such that the buyer may obtain and enjoy all rights and privileges (e.g., receipt of coupon interest) associated with ownership of the security and (2) such that the buyer may, if he chooses, register that security in his own name.

In the case of a bearer security, the above aspect of good delivery creates no problems. The seller's name appears nowhere on the security; and, once the seller delivers, versus payment, the security to the buyer, the security is assumed to be owned by the buyer. After delivery, the buyer bears the security; he is, thus, legally free to do whatever he pleases with the security: to resell it in bearer form, to hold it in bearer form, or to register it in his name.

Good delivery: Registered securities

To comply with the aspect of good delivery we have just discussed, the seller must, in the case of registered securities, do some paper work. This paper work is akin to something individuals do routinely. When an individual sells a car, he must, depending on the state, sign some sort of title or assignment form so that the buyer can prove, when he goes to register his car and get new plates, that he owns the car.

---

[1] Sometimes, trades are done *payment versus delivery (PVD)*. If a retail account buys securities from a dealer or broker, that account must pay for his securities before the latter will deliver those securities to him. If, for example, Merrill sells $50,000 of muni bonds to Joe Smith, Smith is required to pay Merrill money by settlement day; only if Smith does so, will he get his bonds on settlement day. That's the opposite of the way things work on a *DVP* trade of CDs or other physical securities between dealers or between a dealer and a big institutional account.

Back to registered securities. To make good delivery of a registered security, a seller must do one of two things: (1) he must execute the assignment form on the back of the security—it is printed there by the issuer specifically for that purpose—or (2) he must execute a separate assignment form (*bond or stock power*) that he then attaches to the security.

The alternative the seller uses is a matter of convenience. If a dealer or custodial agent is executing a sale for an out-of-town customer whose securities he holds, it is simpler and cheaper for that dealer or agent to send the customer a form that the customer is to sign on line X than to send the customer securities that bear an assignment form that the customer must execute. A danger with sending securities to the customer is that he will, in haste or confusion, end up signing the wrong name, signing in the wrong place, or making some other mistake.

Even when the owner is not a small, out-of-town investor but, say, a New York dealer, the method of attaching bond powers may still be used to make securities negotiable. Merrill may instruct Manny to register 1,000 GNMAs in its name and then, the next week, decide to sell 100 of these certificates. Manny will look at Merrill's certificates; see that they are not endorsed; and know that Sali won't take them, nor will Chemical, nor will some private party. To be used to effect a good delivery, Merrill's certificates must be put into negotiable form. Consequently, Manny will say, "Hey, Merrill, get someone down here authorized to sign, on behalf of Merrill GSI, the certificates you want to sell." Merrill may respond, "Gee, that's sort of a problem; I can't send my people down there just now. Why don't you send up some 1832 forms, and I'll have my people sign them up here. Then you can attach one to each certificate." Said a clearing banker, "Hearing that, you might think that there are people on the Street with piles of pre-signed 1832s. I am not going to tell you that I have such a pile, but some people on the Street probably do."

Once the assignment form on the back of a registered security has been properly executed or a properly executed bond power has been attacted to that security, the security becomes, in effect, a *bearer security* and can be used to effect a good delivery.[2] If the buyer of the security wants to put that security into his name, it is normally his problem and responsibility to take the steps necessary to do so: to submit the security, together with appropriately executed forms, to the issuer's transfer agent and to pay a nominal, if any, fee.

Assignment forms and bond powers normally have a line on which the name of the buyer may be inscribed. This line is rarely filled out;

---

[2]Sometimes, but not frequently, a clearing bank, if it can't get a properly executed bond power, will slap an absence of endorsement guarantee onto a registered security so that the latter can be delivered out.

instead, *the securities are assigned in blank.* There are several reasons for this practice. First, the seller may be concerned about credit risk: he may not want to record the buyer's name on any form until the buyer actually gets money to him. In the clearing of physical securities, this creates a problem, because, as noted below, the delivery of certificates to the buyer or his agent preceeds, typically, the wiring of monies in payment for those certificates. A second reason for assigning securities in blank is that a dealer buying securities from another dealer may want bearer paper that it can redeliver to a customer to whom it has sold that paper.

Securities in street name

That would probably be the end of this part of the story if all registered securities were owned by individuals and unincorporated entities. However, in the world in which we live, most large investors are corporations of one sort or another, and they have boards of directors. Existing law provides for the sale of registered securities by a corporation in a quaint and cumbersome way. A corporation, wanting to sell such securities, is supposed to pass a board resolution OKing the sale and to attach a copy of the board's resolution to the certificates to be sold. Corporate boards do not meet every day; also, OKing a particular sale of securities might be, at a given meeting, item 35 on the board's agenda. The board may not get to item 35 on a given day.

Corporations that want to participate actively in securities markets need to find a legal way to sell registered securities the moment they decide to. Two approaches are used. Some corporations, like Metropolitan Life, require that all physical securities that they buy be registered in their name; to permit rapid sale of such securities, such entities pass a general board resolution authorizing some officer of the corporation to sell securities owned by the corporation at his discretion. For example, some big corporations that invest in GNMAs pass such a board resolution for GNMAs and file it with Chemical, the transfer agent. A second, and far more common, approach is for a corporation to have all registered securities it buys put into *street name. A security is said to be in a street name when it is registered in the name of a nominee* (also when it is registered in the name of a dealer). Nominees are, typically, shell partnerships whose sole function is to act as nominee and to perform whatever attendant duties that entails, for instance, passing through payments of interest and dividends.

Dealers regularly use nominees. So, too, do banks. Manny, for example, registers securities that it buys for its portfolio in the name of a nominee, Frankel & Associates. Morgan Bank registers certain securities

that it holds in custody for customers in the name of Ince & Co. Street names aren't exactly household words. A security owned by a dealer is said to be in street name whether the dealer registers that security in the name of his nominee or in his own name. A given dealer may do either depending on the circumstances.

CLEARING A DEALER-TO-DEALER TRADE

In the money market, dealers, investors, and clearing banks are involved in trading and clearing both bearer and registered securities. Clearing trades in such securities usually requires some movement of certificates or other paper, from one bank's vault to another's or, at least, from one place in a given bank's vault to another.

The easiest way to describe what's involved in clearing a trade in physical securities is to walk, step by step, through the clearing procedure. We begin with a dealer-to-dealer trade.

Assume that Merrill's CD trader buys $10 million of Chase CDs from Sali's trader, and assume that both dealers use clearing banks to clear their CD trades. Each trader will write a trade ticket. From these tickets, operations people at both shops will produce confirms. Sali's confirm to Merrill will say, "Dear Merrill: We sold you today, for settlement tomorrow, $10 million of Chase CDs maturing on day X and carrying a coupon of Y; the yield on the CDs is 8.15%; the dollar value of the principal plus accrued interest is Z dollars." Merrill will produce a "We bought . . ." confirm for Sali containing the same information. At some point, operations people in the two shops will compare their calculations of the money on the trade to ensure that their numbers agree. Sali may even send over a three-part confirm to Merrill and tell Merrill, "Keep the first part; stamp the second part if it agrees with your numbers; then send the stamped confirm back to me."

Once this step is done, Sali will send a ticket, a delivery instruction or the actual receipted confirm, to its clearing bank to instruct the latter to deliver the securities in question to Merrill against payment. At the same time, Merrill will instruct its clearing bank to take in the securities to be delivered to it by Sali against payment of funds.

The clearing banks at work

For a clearing bank, the first step in clearing a securities trade is the same whether the securities are book-entry or physical. The instructions as to what the bank must do must be input to its computer so that the latter gets into a pending or equivalent mode. On digesting its instructions from Merrill, the computer at Merrill's clearing bank (assume again

it is Manny) will say, "Ah ha, Merrill has done a trade and, to clear it, I must do X, Y, and Z."

Manny's computer will spit out an instruction that goes to the Merrill desk at Manny. Meanwhile, Sali will instruct its clearing bank, say it's Irving Trust, to prepare to deliver, against payment, $10 million of Chase CDs to Merrill at Manny. Assume that the trade is made for next-day settlement and that Sali has the Chase CDs, to be delivered to Merrill, in its box position. Then, on receipt of Sali's instructions, Irving will instruct its vault personnel to *pull* $10 million of the correct Chase CDs (right coupon and right maturity date) out of the vault in which it stores physical securities for Sali; an Irving clerk will carefully count and verify— Is everything OK?—the securities pulled from the vault to check that no mistake has been made and that the securities pulled are in good order.

Irving will then send, via messenger, to Manny the CDs Sali has instructed it to deliver there for the account of Merrill. These securities will come in "over the window" at 40 Wall Street. The clerical worker at Manny, who takes the securities in, will give Irving's messenger a stamped receipt saying that Manny has accepted the securities on behalf of Merrill (Fig. 11-1). The stamped receipt Manny gives the Irving messenger is actually a stamped copy of a *delivery bill* that the Irving messenger presents to the Manny clerk when he delivers the securities. A delivery bill is precisely what its name indicates, a bill that accompanies a delivery.

FIGURE 11-1
Sample of timed stamp that appears on a copy of delivering institution's form (delivery bill) accompanying physical securities

RECEIVED SUBJECT
TO COUNT & EXAMINATION

1986 AUG — 1 P 2: 13

MANUFACTURERS HANOVER
TRUST COMPANY
BROKERS, DEALERS
CLEARANCE

Note: This is an acknowledgment of receipt of an item pending examination. After examination, item will either be rejected or paid for.

Manny retains a copy, time-stamped by it, of the delivery bill that Irving's messenger gave it. This delivery bill tells Manny what securities have been delivered to it, for whose account those securities were delivered, and the amount that Manny will be expected to pay out, in this case, to Irving for the account of Sali.

On the Street, deliveries of physical securities are always accepted *subject to count and examination.* The receiver of the securities promises to pay, by wiring Fed funds, for the securities received as soon as it has examined these securities to verify that they are in good order: that the correct securities have been delivered in the correct amount, that the securities are properly signed, if necessary, and so on.

One item that must be checked on CD deliveries is the size (face amounts) of the securities delivered. In the wholesale CD market, it is normally understood that, while $5 million is a round lot for trading purposes, any paper that changes hands must be in $1 million pieces. Delivery by Sali of two $5 million Chase CDs, as opposed to ten $1 million Chase CDs, would not constitute good delivery.

The reason that CD dealers normally want delivery of $1 million pieces is to prevent fails. Merrill, which has bought $10 million of Chase CDs, may have contracted to sell $4 million to another dealer, $3 million to a money market mutual fund, $2 million to Ford, and $1 million to GM. If for some reason—perhaps a new back-office clerk—Sali had asked Chase to write it two $5 million CDs, and it had delivered that paper to Merrill, Merrill would, if Manny accepted the paper, be in trouble. There is no way that Merrill could use two $5 million pieces to make the four CD deliveries it was scheduled to make. Consequently, Merrill would have to fail on all those deliveries for at least a day, maybe two, while it put the two $5 million CDs into Chase for a *denominational exchange.*

While savvy Street traders never accept delivery of CDs in pieces larger than $1 million, they sometimes ask banks to write them new CDs in smaller pieces. For example, Merrill might buy $5 million of new CDs from Morgan and ask Morgan to issue those CDs in 3-by-1 and 20-by-100 pieces. In this case, Merrill is asking for three $1 million CDs (good delivery any time) and 20 $100,000 CDs, which it might be planning to sell through its branches to smaller institutions, people with pension funds, and so on. Every type of physical security has its own little quirks that a receiving bank must know in order to determine whether delivery is in good form.

Back to our example: Sali sells to Merrill and delivers, at Manny, Chase CDs. The CDs that Manny had taken in over the window from Sali would go to Merrill's desk at Manny. There, an account manager would check the delivery against instructions received by Manny from Merrill: Have the correct securities been delivered? Are they in good order? Is the money correct? If the securities delivered were *not* in good order—the

size was wrong or the coupon or maturity date was incorrect—Manny would notify Irving to pick up these securities along with a form showing Manny's reason for rejecting the delivery; naturally, Manny would make *no* payment to Irving for the rejected delivery. In the more likely event that the securities delivered were in good order, Manny would instruct its money transfer department to wire the appropriate money to Irving for the account of Sali.

Once the Chase CDs delivered to Merrill by Sali were on the Merrill desk at Manny, Merrill's account manager would check Merrill's pending instructions to see whether any of these securities had been sold by Merrill and should be delivered out by Manny on behalf of Merrill.

CLEARING A CUSTOMER-TO-DEALER TRADE

Merrill might well have sold $2 million of the Chase CDs to the GE portfolio, whose custodial agent, we'll assume, is Citibank. If so, Manny will send, by messenger to Citi for the account of GE, $2 million of the Chase CDs that Sali has delivered into the Merrill account.

Manny and other clearing banks that handle billions of dollars a day of physical securities naturally want to ensure that none of these securities fall between the cracks, get lost, or get stolen. So clearing banks move securities around according to a choreographed dance that generates time-stamped receipts each time securities are moved from one place to another and, thus, from the custody of one person to another. The clearing bank clerk who takes in securities over the window generates one receipt. Another receipt is generated when the securities delivered are deposited on the "desk" maintained by a clearing bank for the dealer to whom the securities are delivered.

In our example, when the Merrill account manager at Manny sends $2 million of Chase CDs down to Manny's delivery room to be delivered to Citi, yet another receipt will be generated. Then, when Manny's messenger is given these securities, he will sign a receipt for them and walk off carrying both the securities and a delivery bill to be handed to the receiving bank. That bank must time stamp the delivery bill to indicate that it has received delivery at the proper location.

When Manny delivers its Chase CDs for Merrill to Citi, the stamped delivery bill it receives will state that the securities have been accepted *subject to counting and examination* and that, if all is in order, payment for these securities will be made later in the business day.

FREE DELIVERIES

Infrequently, a clearing bank will be instructed to make a *free delivery,* that is, a delivery against *no* payment. When a clearing bank makes a

free delivery of a physical security, it wants more than a clocked receipt from the receiver's window. Instead, the delivering bank will normally ask for an official signature—after the securities have been examined and counted—from whoever at the receiving bank is authorized to accept such deliveries. On the delivery bill accompanying a free delivery, the space where the money due would normally appear is blank. What the delivering bank asks for is an official receipt on that same form.

CLEARING: PHYSICAL VERSUS BOOK-ENTRY SECURITIES

In both of our examples—a delivery of CDs, Sali to Merrill, and a redelivery of those CDs, Merrill to GE—the clearing process described resembles, especially through the initial steps, the steps that the contracting parties and their clearing agents would have taken if the trade had been in book-entry securities. There are three main differences between the clearing of physical and book-entry securities. First, physical securities must be verified and counted by both the delivering bank and the receiving bank. Second, a number of time-stamped receipts must be generated by both banks as the securities are moved around, either within the bank or on the street; these receipts generate a paper trail that tells where the securities were at what time—useful information should the securities go astray.

Third, whereas payment and delivery are really simultaneous in the case of book-entry securities, there is, in the delivery of physical securities, always a *lag* between the moment securities are delivered and the moment payment is made. No practical way exists to eliminate this lag because no clearing bank, or agent bank, is going to pay out millions of dollars for securities without first verifying that they have received the precise securities that their customer bought and that these securities are in good order.

On deliveries of physical securities, there are lots of opportunities for a bank to make a delivery that is not in good order, and such deliveries occur often. A delivery of muni notes may require that a stack of certificates, carefully counted, be delivered. On deliveries of registered securities, such as some pass-throughs, a properly executed bond power must be attached to each certificate, so that all of the certificates delivered are in negotiable form.

When delivery consists of a stack of registered securities, one mistake sometimes made is that some of those securities lack a properly executed, attached bond power, maybe the bond powers are all there, but the signer missed signing one or two of them. Some out-of-town customers will authorize their clearing agent in New York to sign securities that they have mistakenly failed to endorse properly. For ex-

ample, a Seattle bank might authorize its New York clearing bank to sign for it securities that the bank had sold and sent, without a proper signature, to New York for clearing. This makes sense since sending the securities back to Seattle to be signed would force the Seattle bank selling the securities into a multiday fail on which it would be the party losing money.

EXAMPLE OF A PURCHASE OF A CD: CONFIRM AND CLEARING INSTRUCTIONS

We've described in general terms how a trade in *physical* securities is cleared. To end our discussion, we present an example of a dealer-customer trade in a CD, and we show key documents generated as this trade is cleared.

Suppose that Merrill buys, on 7/23/86, from Romero & Brothers, Inc., for cash (same-day) settlement $4 million (4MM) of Acme Bank and Trust CDs that pay a rate of 6 17/32 that were issued on 7/21/86 and that mature on 10/22/87.

After the trade is agreed upon, Merrill's operations area will generate for Romero the confirm shown in Figure 11-2. Note this confirm describes precisely (1) what securities Merrill has bought and (2) the principal value of and the interest accrued on these securities. The confirmation also instructs Romero to deliver the securities to Merrill at Manny ("Receive at Manufacturers"), and it specifies that payment for the securities will be made by Merrill in "FED Funds."

Merrill also generates instructions to Manny, its clearing bank, directing the latter to clear this trade. When Manny gets Merrill's instructions, it will generate, for the manager of the Merrill desk at Manny, the ticket shown in Figure 11-3. This ticket instructs this individual to clear the trade, once good delivery of the securities is made, by paying $4,001,451.33 in Fed funds to Romero Brothers' account at Marine N.Y.C.

When a messenger from Romero's agent, Marine N.Y.C., delivers the Acme CDs to Manny, a delivery bill will accompany these CDs. Manny will put its time-stamped receipt (Figure 11-1) on the copy of that bill that is retained by the delivery messenger. Manny will then pass the securities to the manager of the Merrill desk. The latter has been alerted by the arrival of a ticket (Figure 11-3) to anticipate receipt of these securities. If count and examination of the securities received indicate that Romero has made good delivery on the trade, the Merrill account manager will order that appropriate payment in Fed funds be made out of Merrill's clearing account to Romero's account at Marine. Should the securities delivered fail in any way the tests of good delivery, Manny would request that Romero's bank, Marine, send a messenger to Manny to pick up the rejected delivery.

FIGURE 11-2
Merrill confirmation to Romero & Brothers, Inc., of a purchase of CDs from Romero

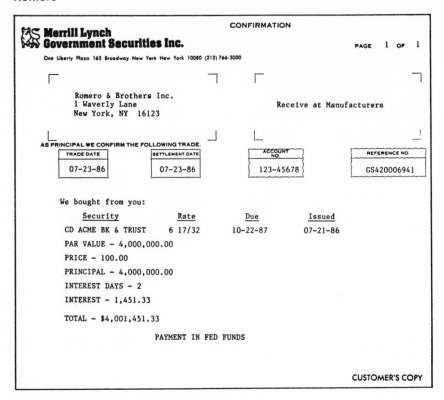

CONTROLLING SECURITIES MISHANDLING AND THEFT

Many headaches arise in the clearing of physical securities because such clearing requires the shunting of valuable pieces of paper from point A to point B and perhaps the storing of those pieces of paper at point C (the vault). This shunting of valuable paper creates opportunities for theft and, on a more mundane level, for the misplacement, loss, and mutilation of securities.

Mishandling of securities

To properly clear physical securities, a clearing bank's personnel must keep track of the securities being cleared and ensure that they are handled in a proper and orderly way. Since the clearing of physical

FIGURE 11-3

Ticket instructing manager of Merrill desk at Manny to clear Merrill's purchase of CDs from Romero

| Merrill Lynch MMI
One Liberty Plaza
New York, N.Y. 10080 | Cleared By
MANUFACTURERS HANOVER
TRUST COMPANY
BROKERS & DEALERS CLEARANCE DEPT.
40 WALL STREET, 3RD FLR., NEW YORK, N.Y. 10015 | H |

REFERENCE NUMBER	TRADE TYPE	TRADE DATE	SETTLE DATE	DELIVERY DATE
GS420006941	Receive	7/23/86	7/23/86	

ACCOUNT NAME	SPECIAL INSTRUCTIONS
	MARINE NYC/ROMERO N.Y.

CUSTOMER NO. 12345678

ABA NO. 021001088

QUANTITY	CUSIP NUMBER	SECURITY DESCRIPTION
4,000,000.00		CD ACME BK.TRUST 6 17/32 Dated 7/21/86 Due 10/22/87

PRICE		NET AMOUNT
100.		4,001,451.33

PRINCIPAL 4,000,000.00

INTEREST   1,451.33

FEE

TAPE SEQ. NO. C0500   TRAN NO. 200-0500

TICKET SEQ. NO. 00400   TIME 13:14

20913F

10/84

Upon delivery of the securities described hereon, which are attached hereto, to the purchaser or his designee, the purchaser shall acquire all rights in such securities which we had or had actual authority to convey, and the risk of loss shall pass to the purchaser, provided however, that if full payment for such securities has not been received at or by the time of delivery thereof; it is agreed that a purchase money security interest in favor of the above mentioned Broker/Dealer shall attach to such securities, which interest shall not terminate until such time as full payment therefor has been received by us.

securities at a major clearing bank requires that a mini-army of people handle, daily, thousands of paper securities, the above is easier said than done.

One source of difficulty is that it's tough for a clearing bank to get all of its personnel to regard physical securities as valuable pieces of paper in the same way they would regard $100 bills as valuable pieces of paper. To the average person, a $100 bill is *real* money, whereas a $5 million BA seems akin to monopoly money. A clearing banker made this point with a story: "One day, a vault custodian remarked that she was upset; it was pay day, and she had lost, after cashing her check, $20. I said, 'Your loss of $20 points up the importance, since you work in a vault containing $150 billion of securities, of your being doubly careful not to misplace securities.' She turned and said, 'Yes, but my lost money was *real* money.' "

The unreality of the value of physical securities must also explain how it could dawn on a clearing-bank clerk, as in fact it did, to take a $1 million security home for her mother to see and to then forget, for several days, to return that security to the bank.

Besides the unreality factor, there is also a gremlin factor that must operate at every clearing bank. Surely, it is the house gremlin who causes people to toss million-dollar securities into a drawer. And who but the house gremlin could lead a clerk to use a GNMA certificate as copying paper in a Xerox machine? That caper caused a Treasury Department investigator to descend on one clearing bank, an officer of which had to explain, "No, our personnel are not trying to forge GNMAs; it was all an innocent mistake; and, by the way, we need a new, clean certificate."

At times, the risks associated with handling and storing physical securities can overwhelm even a normally unflappable clearing banker. "We used to clear," said one such banker, "stripped physical Treasuries; and, at one time, we had, in our vault, hundreds of millions of dollars of stripped coupons, each the size of a big postage stamp. One day I walked into the vault, looked at those coupons, and asked, 'What if a thief got in here? What if someone drops a match? What if a disgruntled employee flushes some coupons down the toilet?' We could not replace stripped coupons—the Treasury won't do it—so, we quit clearing them."

Despite the unreality and gremlin factors, every clearing bank has its hero, the guy whose alertness made an important contribution. Some years ago, a clever engraver, working in cahoots with the Mafia, was printing up some superbly forged municipal bonds, all of which had the same certificate number. His forgery might have gone undetected until the issue's next coupon date, but, thanks to an alert vault custodian, it didn't. "Hey," said he, "something funny is going on. I've been asked to file and store in the vault two certificates from a single issue, and they've both got the same serial number." The forger's business was halted fast.

Theft of securities

As noted, thefts, which seemed large at the time, of physical Treasury securities forced acceleration of the introduction of the book-entry system for Treasuries. Today, over 90% of Treasury securities, and a lot of agencies too, are in book-entry form, but there are still plenty of physical securities—commercial paper, BAs, CDs, many GNMAs, and many muni notes and bonds—kicking around Wall Street.

Any larcenous soul who decides to swipe a physical money market instrument and then sell it is probably making one of the big mistakes of his life. The problem is lack of credibility at the point of sale. A person who walks into a broker/dealer trying to peddle a $1 million piece of bearer paper is probably going to arouse suspicion.

A case in point. One bright day, a messenger from a clearing bank set out to deliver a GNMA in bearer form (bond power attached) to the buyer's custodian bank. The messenger got the right bank, the right floor but the wrong door. As he stood puzzled in an empty office, a well-dressed guy came up and said that, yes, he'd accept delivery of the GNMA. By afternoon's end, when the clearing bank making the delivery discovered, because it hadn't been paid, that the delivery had gone awry, the gentleman who had taken the certificate was plotting to sell it. Next day, he showed up at a broker/dealer and said, "I've got a $1 million GNMA that I want to sell. Since I'll be doing a lot of trading of stocks, put $600,000 of the proceeds in an account for me with you and give me a check for the balance." Fortunately, the broker's rep with whom he spoke thought to dig a bit into the provenance of the proffered GNMA. He discovered that it was stolen. The seller got his check, but it was delivered by an FBI agent. The latter, disguised as a messenger, carried and used a pair of handcuffs.

For years, clever crooks who stole bearer securities knew better than to try to sell them. A far safer ploy was to use stolen securities as collateral for a loan from a bank in the hinterland. Today, however, even this ploy has become risky because there is now in place an efficient system for tracking all stolen bearer securities (physical securities, not wireables) that have CUSIP numbers: Treasuries, agencies, many municipal issues, and corporate stocks and bonds.

The organization that does the tracking is the *Securities Information Center* (SIC) in Massachusetts. Clearing banks and brokers who are members of the NYSE are required to run a check on securities delivered to them by institutions that do not participate in the SIC. For example, if a small out-of-town bank delivered, say, bearer muni bonds to a N.Y.C. clearing bank for a retail customer for whom it had been holding those bonds in custody, the bank would have to check that those bonds had not been stolen before it accepted them.

A clearing banker described the procedure he goes through to check bearer securities as follows:

I have a certain phone number I call, and there is a certain format I must go through. The whole call is programmed. I identify who is calling by giving the number assigned to our institution. The girl who answers does not even say hello. She says, "Is this an inquiry or a *referral* [*notice of stolen securities*]?" If I am checking to see whether a particular security was stolen, I will say, "Inquiry." She will say, "What is your FINs [Financial Institutions] number?" I give her my number. She will say, "What is your access code?" That is all she says. And I give her that number. Then she says, "CUSIP number?" I give her that, and she next asks, "Certificate numbers?" And I give her them. Then she will come back and say, "No referral, validation number X," and I record that number. That puts it on the record that, at the time I inquired, there was no referral against the securities.

Naturally, the story ends a little differently if a bank checks on securities against which there is a referral.

The Securities Information Center encompasses even foreign bank offices located outside the U.S. This was discovered a touch late by several culprits who attempted to peddle, at a Swiss bank, bearer securities stolen the day before in the United States and then flown directly across the Atlantic to Switzerland.

PUTTING A STOP ON AND GETTING A REPLACEMENT FOR MUTILATED, MISPLACED, OR STOLEN SECURITIES

Most times, if a security is lost, mutilated, or stolen, it's possible to put what's called a *stop* (stop transfer) on the security by notifying some power that be and to obtain a replacement certificate. The procedure used depends on the type of security in question.

Securities tracked by SIC

The Securities Information Center tracks only *physical* securities that are in *bearer form* and have a *CUSIP number.* If such a security is lost or stolen, the loss is supposed to be reported to the SIC; a *referral* is supposed to be put on the lost security. Then application may be made to the issuer for a replacement certificate. Obtaining the latter is likely to take some time, and the owner of the lost security may be required to post a surety bond and meet other requirements before he can obtain a replacement certificate.

Registered securities

The SIC does not track *registered* securities. If such a security is lost, stolen, or mutilated, the loss must be reported to the transfer agent. For example, a loss of a GNMA certificate would be reported to Chemical Bank, the GNMA transfer agent. If the institution losing a security has a full description of the lost security (issuer, issue date, coupon, face amount, maturity date, pool number, certificate number, or whatever—what's required varies from one type of security to another), the transfer agent can delve into its computer files; determine, hopefully, that the lost security is still registered in the name that appeared on it; and say, "OK, we will put a stop on that security." To get a replacement certificate, the party that has lost the security must first obtain a *surety* bond from its insurance company; the purpose of this bond is to protect the issuing agent in case the request for a stop and replacement is mistaken or fraudulent, and the security later shows up. Once the transfer agent receives the surety bond and a nominal fee, it will issue a replacement certificate.

Know thy certificate number

When a physical security goes astray, the first thing that some power that be will want to know is the number on the lost certificate. Thus, a clearing bank or any other party that handles physical securities must be careful, whenever they receive such securities, to record the certificate numbers of these securities. However, when activity at a clearing bank gets frantic, people sometimes forget to do so. They just count the securities received; and, if these securities are going out on a sale right away, they match them up to the sale ticket and ship them out. Noted one clearing banker, "We had one guy who took the easy way out on recording certificate numbers. If securities came in that were to be delivered out immediately on a sale, he would write on the sale ticket 'See buy ticket' and vice versa. He never recorded the numbers."

If a clearing bank loses a physical security and does not have a record of its certificate number, all is not necessarily lost; the number can be obtained one way or another, but sometimes doing so takes real digging. The first, obvious, and easiest approach to obtaining the number of a certificate that has been delivered in and then lost is to ask the party that delivered the certificate what number was on it. It's standard practice at clearing banks to record certificate numbers not only when securities are delivered in but when they are delivered out.

Sometimes, however, a situation arises in which no such simple approach will suffice to dig up missing certificate numbers. Recalled one clearing banker, "Years ago, when governments were physical, one of our

accounts was missing some securities when he went to prove his box position. In reporting the loss to our protection department, we found that we had no certificate numbers. The issue, brand new, had been actively traded during the day. To determine the unknown certificate numbers, what we had to do was to get, from the Fed, the certificate numbers of all of the securities they had allotted us; then we checked all of the numbers on all of our deliveries and on all of our receipts of the issue during the day. By a long process of elimination, we finally figured out the certificate numbers of the missing securities and distributed them to the industry."

Needless to say, a clearing-bank clerk had best not be caught failing to record certificate numbers when he is supposed to, at least not if he wants his job long-term.

Treasury securities

Physical Treasuries, like other securities in certificate form, can be replaced if they are lost, stolen, or mutilated. To obtain a replacement certificate, the owner of the lost security must first report the loss of the security to the Treasury in Washington and request that a stop be put on that security. He must then fill out various legal documents sent to him by the Treasury and post a security bond. Normally, the various steps in this procedure require several months to complete. The owner of a registered security that is lost will lose no coupon interest since the Treasury will automatically send him payments of coupon interest as long as he is the registered owner of the security. However, the owner of a bearer security must, if he wants the Treasury to replace any coupons on his lost security, pay the Treasury a price equal to the discounted value of those coupons unless he can, for example, prove that the coupons were destroyed by presenting a half-burned or mutilated certificate with coupons still attached to it.

Maturing physical securities

When a physical security, registered or bearer, matures, the owner normally must return the security to the issuer to receive repayment of principal. The purpose of this exercise is to enable the issuer to cancel those securities that have matured and been paid off.

FAILS TO DELIVER

Every dealer and investor loves to be "failed to," provided that the fail does *not* cause him to fail on the other side. If a seller of securities fails to deliver the securities he has sold on the agreed settlement date, *the*

party failed to (i.e., the buyer) *earns accrued interest as if he owned the securities, but he need put up no money until the securities are actually delivered.* This is *important* because an investor who is failed to is given, in effect, the opportunity to be *double invested,* that is, to own $2 of assets for every $1 he was supposed to pay, but did not have to pay, for the securities he failed to receive. Being double invested is such an attractive state that investors sometimes exercise various ploys to achieve it.

For example, one astute Wall Streeter is said to have always bought lots of 13 Treasury bonds for his family trust. His reason was not faith that the number 13 was lucky; rather, experience had taught him that the bank that sold bonds to the trust would always fail for days on a delivery of 13 off-the-run bonds.

Every dealer assigns to some person responsibility for seeing to it that the dealer earns rather than loses money on fails. Every dealer knows that he will experience some fails on deliveries to him. Playing the *fails game* calls for the dealer to ensure that he makes no unnecessary fails and that, if he's forced into a fail by, say, a late delivery or a fail to deliver to him, he makes the smallest possible fail on the opposite side: Perhaps by reducing his box position, he can match a $5 million fail to deliver to him with just a $1 million fail to deliver on his part.

From a dealer's point of view, one attractive feature of dealer safekeeping is that it is the dealer, not the investor, who profits when securities that the investor has purchased from the dealer (and paid for) fail temporarily to come in. Seen from the opposite point of view, one advantage to an institutional investor of taking delivery of all securities he purchases is that, by doing so, he puts himself in a position to offset some of his clearing and custody costs with earnings on fails. More about fails and the fails game in Chapter 12.

THE NEXT CHAPTER

In Chapter 12, we describe the clearing of RPs and reverses. This is a mega-buck business even by Street standards; an RP for 1/4 of $1 billion raises no eyebrows. Chapter 12 also explores the many ways in which dealers finance their operations—including tenacious tries to win at the fails game. Finally, Chapter 12 describes something akin to elaborate checkbook-balancing that dealers and banks manage to do daily.

Chapter 12

RPs, proving, and dealer financing

THIS CHAPTER DISCUSSES SEVERAL IMPORTANT ASPECTS OF CLEARING that were not covered in Chapters 10 and 11. We focus first on the clearing of RPs and reverse, then on dealer financing, and, finally, on proving: the cross-checking by banks and dealers of their records to ensure that everyone's (a dealer's, his bank's, and the Fed's) records jibe.

CLEARING RPS AND REVERSES

A substantial portion of the securities trades cleared each day by clearing banks are one leg, front or back, of either an RP or a reverse. When a dealer does an RP he writes *two* tickets, a *sell* ticket that initiates the transaction and a *buy* ticket that ends the transaction (or just one ticket if he's so automated that his system will produce the second ticket from the first). The sell side of the transaction typically settles on the trade date or on the following business day; the buy side settles a day or more later. When a dealer does a reverse, there are also two sides to the transaction, but, in this case, the buy side settles before the sell side. RPs and reverses are done in both book-entry and physical securities.

Whenever a dealer does an RP or a reverse with a customer or with another dealer, its operations area makes up and sends out (1) instructions to its clearing bank to clear the trade and (2) appropriate confirms to its counterparty.

A buy or a sell confirm that describes the terms of one leg of either an RP or a reverse may, but need not, contain *trailer information,* that is, information indicating some or all of the following: that the trade being confirmed is an RP or a reverse; that the term of the transaction is X days; that the trade is being done at a rate of Y%; and that the collateral, if the trade is an RP, is to be safekept by the dealer. See Figures 12-1 and 12-2 for examples of RP and reverse confirms.

So far as a dealer's clearing bank is concerned, buys and sells generated by RPs and reverses differ in no significant way from outright buys and sells; both are cleared in precisely the same way.[1] To a dealer's clearing bank, all trailer information that may appear on either an RP or a reverse confirm or other clearing instruction, including identification of the trade as either an RP or a reverse, is information to be ignored because it is *totally irrelevant* with respect to anything the clearing bank must or must not do.

In particular, if a dealer indicates on a sell confirm, which is leg one of an RP, that he will safekeep the securities for the customer, this indication is not taken by the clearing bank as an instruction to move

FIGURE 12-1

Carroll McEntee & McGinley confirmation to an RP customer of leg one of the transaction—the customer buys FHLB notes from CM&M

FILE COPY

CARROLL MC ENTEE & MC GINLEY
INCORPORATED
40 WALL STREET, NEW YORK, N.Y. 10005
TELEPHONE: 825-9467

DEALERS IN U.S. TREASURY AND FEDERAL AGENCY SECURITIES.

WE CONFIRM SALE TO YOU:

AMOUNT	SECURITY	PRICE	TRADE DATE	SETTLEMENT DATE	ACCOUNT NUMBER	TRADE NO.
7,000,000	FED HOME LOAN BK 9.75 DUE 7-25-90	100	1/10/86	1/10/86	4975790	209686

PRINCIPAL	INTEREST	SERVICE	WIRE FEE	CLEARANCE	RATE	NET AMOUNT
7,000,000.00	.00				7.625	7,000,000.00

CN# 313388NH7

DELIVERY INSTRUCTIONS:

Name of client
Address of client

6390

CARROLL MC ENTEE & MC GINLEY
INCORPORATED

REPURCHASE AGREEMENT
*** TIME OF TRADE AVAILABLE UPON REQUEST *** BY__________

DELIVERY BY MARINE MIDLAND 140 BROADWAY, NEW YORK, N.Y.-BROKERS CLEAR DEPT.

[1]Exception: an entity that repoed registered, physical securities would not want the "buyer" (lender of money) to register those securities in his name. (Chapter 17).

FIGURE 12–2
Carroll McEntee & McGinley confirmation to a reverse RP customer of leg one of the transaction—the customer sells T bonds to CM&M

FILE COPY

CARROLL MC ENTEE & MC GINLEY
INCORPORATED
40 WALL STREET, NEW YORK, N.Y. 10005
TELEPHONE: 825-9467

DEALERS IN U.S. TREASURY AND FEDERAL AGENCY SECURITIES.

WE CONFIRM PURCHASE FROM YOU:

AMOUNT	SECURITY	PRICE	TRADE DATE	SETTLEMENT DATE	ACCOUNT NUMBER	TRADE NO.
500,000	U.S. TREAS. BONDS 12.625 DUE 5-15-95	120.8	1/10/86	1/10/86	4975790	209696

PRINCIPAL	INTEREST	SERVICE	WIRE FEE	CLEARANCE	RATE	NET AMOUNT
601,250.00	.00				6.000	601,250.00

CN# 912810CN6

DELIVERY INSTRUCTIONS:

Name of client
Address of client

CARROLL MC ENTEE & MC GINLEY
INCORPORATED

REVERSE REPURCHASE AGREEMENT

*** TIME OF TRADE AVAILABLE UPON REQUEST *** BY__________

DELIVER TO MARINE MIDLAND 140 BROADWAY, NEW YORK, N.Y.-BROKERS CLEAR DEPT.

securities from the dealer's clearing account to his safekeeping account if he has one. A dealer who desires that such a transfer be made must issue a separate instruction to its clearing bank directing the latter to effect, for a fee, the desired transfer of securities from the dealer's clearing account to some other account maintained by the dealer.

The exception that proves the rule: There is one situation in which a clearing bank really cares whether a given transaction is an RP because in that case the clearing bank has extra responsibilities to assume, namely, acting as custodian of the RP collateral. This unique case involves *tri-party RPs,* which are discussed in Chapter 14.

DEALER FINANCING

Since, as market makers, dealers trade off their own positions and also seek to profit by carrying speculative positions and doing arbitrages, every dealer ends up holding securities equal to a large multiple of its net worth; in other words, it runs a *highly leveraged balance sheet.* It is hard to translate "highly leveraged" into a number because the big dealers in governments are a mixed bag: money market banks, dealers in governments and agencies only, diversified firms that also deal in corporate stocks and bonds and offer investment banking services, GSI subs of such firms (these strictly limit their activities to governments and other exempt securities), and finally Japanese and other foreign dealers. Big banks are required by the Fed to maintain capital/asset ratios of 25 to 1 or better, and that limits the amount of leverage these banks want to

create in their government dealing operations and discourages them, in particular, from running big matched books. Diversified firms with a mix of business tend to maintain capital/asset ratios in the range to 30 or 40 to 1. Finally, GSI's with rich parents, such as Merrill Lynch, may have capital/asset ratios of 80 to 90 or even 100 to 1. Clearly, to finance the bulk of their positions, dealers, whatever their ilk, must regularly acquire, one way or another, a lot of *other people's money.*

Fed RPs

The Fed, through frequent open market operations (buys, RPs, and reverses of government securities in which the Fed's counterparty is a bank or nonbank dealer), seeks to hold aggregate, nonborrowed bank reserves at a level consistent with its current macroeconomic targets. On a day to day basis, bank reserves are constantly being jogged up and down by changes in variables exogenous to the Fed's management of monetary policy. Such exogenous factors, dubbed "operating factors" by the Fed, include changes in Treasury balances at the Fed, changes in float, and seasonal changes in currency in circulation. Because changes in operating factors are unpredictable and often short-lived, the Fed does easy-to-implement, short-term RPs and reverses to offset them: RPs to add to bank reserves, reverses to drain bank reserves. When the Fed does RP with dealers, it is, in effect, lending to them. Such lending, while it is used by dealers to fund their positions, is not a source on which dealers can rely regularly for large amounts of funds. Fed RPs are an unpredictable, intermittent affair done always at the volition of the Fed, never at the volition of the dealers.

Dealer-initiated RPs

Dealers, using securities they own as collateral, have always been able to borrow from banks to finance their positions. However, from a dealer's point of view, the problem with using such funding is that banks, in setting their dealer loan rates, naturally add a spread for themselves to their cost of funds.

During the 1950s, dealers, eyeing the low, regulated rates banks paid their depositors, corporate and other, and the much higher rates banks charged dealers for loans, wondered if there were not some way they could borrow directly from funds-surplus units—eliminate the bank as middleman—and thereby cut their cost of funds. Dealers did exactly that when they revived, at that time, all-private RPs. The RPs dealers began doing with private lenders were modeled after the RPs they were doing with the Fed. Specifically, a dealer would sell to a private supplier of funds, corporate or other, securities he wanted to finance; at the same time,

he would agree to repurchase those same securities at a later date at a fixed price. The deal was always structured so that the lender of funds ended up with an investment on which he had *no* market risk and on which he earned an agreed interest rate, the repo rate.

While RPs have always been, and still are, structured as *paired sells and buys* of securities—as securities transactions—the economic substance of such a transaction resembles closely that of a *collateralized loan*. Certainly, the Street has always thought of the RPs dealers do as collateralized borrowings, and it has always used the term *collateral* to describe securities "sold" by a dealer doing an RP.

Dealer-initiated RPs, which began with a few innovative deals between major dealers, such as Discount Corporation, and big investors, such as GM, were attractive to all dealers, to banks wanting to finance their portfolios, and to other borrowers as well. RPs also proved tremendously attractive to a wide range of investors, including municipalities. By doing an RP, an investor was able to invest an amount of his choosing to a date of his choosing while assuming *no* market risk. The RP market was a natural; and reflecting this, it grew from meager beginnings in the 1950s to become what is probably the largest private, short-term debt market in the United States. While precise statistics are lacking, the amount of private RPs done today must amount to well over $200 billion at any time.

Currently, dealers in governments and other money market instruments use RPs to finance well over 90% of their positions. Today's RP market has two major attractions to dealers. First, the RP market is a *deep* market in which dealers are able to borrow huge sums of money on a highly flexible basis. Second, RP money is *cheap;* typically, the overnight RP rate is a spread below the Fed funds rate; that is, RP money is cheaper than the next cheapest funds a bank can buy. Not surprisingly, the rates that banks charge dealers on overnight loans against securities are substantially higher than the overnight RP rate.

Secured bank loans to dealers

Before the RP market mushroomed to its present size, secured bank loans were the principal means by which dealers financed their positions in securities of all types. Today, in contrast, money market dealers, because of cost considerations, rely primarily on RP financing; nonetheless, even for such dealers, secured bank loans represent a key form of residual funding.

Dealer loan rates.   Rates on bank loans to dealers have always varied depending on the liquidity and quality of the collateral financed. For decades, banks have been willing to finance government and other money market collateral at a rate that's a small spread, ¼% or ½%, above the

Fed funds rate. In contrast, banks once were willing to finance other securities only at their prime lending rate or at prime plus a spread.

As interest rates climbed after World War II, the spread between the funds rate and the prime rate widened. Eventually, this led dealers to protest the structure of dealer loan rates. Said Merrill and other dealers to their respective clearing banks, "Fed funds are at 8%, prime is at 11%. On government collateral, you are giving me an 8½% rate, but on IBM, GM, and AT&T you are charging me 11%. That's nonsense; blue chip stocks are just as good collateral as governments."

Banks got the message and invented a new rate, *the call loan rate.* Banks set their call loan rate at a level above their rate on overnight loans against government collateral, but below their prime rate (Figure 12-3). Initially, banks would lend at their call loan rate only against NYSE collateral, but, during the 1970s, competition among lenders changed that. Competition forced banks to finance, for dealers, most corporate and muni bonds at the call loan rate or at a spread to it.

The tiering that exists today of bank rates for dealer loans is pretty much what we've described. Dealers are able to finance governments, agencies, and other money market securities at a spread off funds. To finance any other collateral with a bank, they must pay the broker call loan rate or that rate plus a spread. Today, few dealers pay prime-based rates for bank loans except on lower-quality muni paper and, sometimes, on corporate bonds.

That said, note the rate a dealer must pay to finance a given piece of paper will depend partly on what the paper is, ofttimes much more on who the dealer is. Currently, there are hundreds—no one has counted just how many—of dealers in governments; most are small to middling in size; only a few are well-capitalized, high-volume, professionally run operations. Besides dealers in governments and other money market paper, there are also other dealers who specialize in a narrower niche of the market, such as municipal securities. All of these dealers need a clearing bank to clear some, if not all, of their trades. Naturally, in extending credit to smaller dealers, clearing banks distinguish with great care between dealers who are top, middling, and weaker credits; and they adjust the rates they charge different clients for clearing loans accordingly.

A Merrill or a Sali that has good access to credit from many sources will be able to bargain with its clearing bank for a rate that is a narrow spread above that bank's cost of funds, whereas a smaller, weaker credit will have no choice but to pay up to get money—at least to finance nongovernment paper. Thus, a small, out-of-town muni dealer might be happy to get credit from a New York clearing bank at prime plus a quarter, whereas Merrill would be shocked to be asked to pay such a rate and would not do so.

FIGURE 12-3
Money Market rates

MONEY RATES

Monday, March 9, 1987
The key U.S. and foreign annual interest rates below are a guide to general levels but don't always represent actual transactions.

PRIME RATE: 7½%. The base rate on corporate loans at large U.S. money center commercial banks.

FEDERAL FUNDS: 6 5/16% high, 6 1/16% low, 6⅛% near closing bid, 6¼% offered. Reserves traded among commercial banks for overnight use in amounts of $1 million or more. Source: Prebon Money Brokers Inc., N.Y.

DISCOUNT RATE: 5½%. The charge on loans to depository institutions by the New York Federal Reserve Bank.

✓ **CALL MONEY:** 7% to 7½%. The charge on loans to brokers on stock exchange collateral.

COMMERCIAL PAPER placed directly by General Motors Acceptance Corp.: 6.15% 30 to 44 days; 6⅛% 45 to 89 days; 6% 90 to 119 days; 5.95% 120 to 149 days; 5.90% 150 to 179 days; 5.85% 180 to 270 days.

COMMERCIAL PAPER: High-grade unsecured notes sold through dealers by major corporations in multiples of $1,000: 6.15% 30 days; 6⅛% 60 days; 6% 90 days.

CERTIFICATES OF DEPOSIT: 6.17% one month; 6.17% two months; 6.17% three months; 6.17% six months; 6.35% one year. Typical rates paid by major banks on new issues of negotiable C.D.s, usually on amounts of $1 million and more. The minimum unit is $100,000.

BANKERS ACCEPTANCES: 6.07% 30 days; 6.06% 60 days; 6.01% 90 days; 6% 120 days; 5.98% 150 days; 5.98% 180 days. Negotiable, bank-backed business credit instruments typically financing an import order.

LONDON LATE EURODOLLARS: 6½% to 6⅜% one month; 6½% to 6⅜% two months; 6½% to 6⅜% three months; 6½% to 6⅜% four months; 6½% to 6⅜% five months; 6½% to 6⅜% six months.

LONDON INTERBANK OFFERED RATES (LIBOR): 6½% three months; 6½% six months; 6 9/16% one year. The average of interbank offered rates for dollar deposits in the London market based on quotations at five major banks.

FOREIGN PRIME RATES: Canada 9.25%; Germany 6.75%; Japan 4.42%; Switzerland 5.75%; Britain 11%. These rate indications aren't directly comparable; lending practices vary widely by location. Source: Morgan Guaranty Trust Co.

TREASURY BILLS: Results of the Monday, March 9, 1987, auction of short-term U.S. government bills, sold at a discount from face value in units of $10,000 to $1 million: 5.63%, 13 weeks; 5.59%, 26 weeks.

FEDERAL HOME LOAN MORTGAGE CORP. (Freddie Mac): Posted yields on 30-year mortgage commitments for delivery within 30 days. 8.91%, standard conventional fixed-rate mortgages; 6.875%, 2% rate capped one-year adjustable rate mortgages.

FEDERAL NATIONAL MORTGAGE ASSOCIATION (Fannie Mae): Posted yields on 30 year mortgage commitments for delivery within 30 days (priced at par). 8.71%, standard conventional fixed rate-mortgages; 8.35%, 6/2 rate capped one-year adjustable rate mortgages.

MERRILL LYNCH READY ASSETS TRUST: 5.30%. Annualized average rate of return after expenses for the past 30 days; not a forecast of future returns.

Source: *The Wall Street Journal.*

The way a clearing bank earns a profit, at least on some of its accounts, is as follows: Ticket costs about cover or cover by a small margin the bank's operating expenses—the real money the bank makes on the account derives from its lending to the account at a tidy spread above its cost of funds. To the extent that a clearing bank earns its profit this way, it is rather like a credit card company: The profit a credit card company earns derives not from the 4% or whatever it extracts from retailers, but from the financing charges it imposes on cardholders who do not pay off each month the full debit balances in their accounts.

The spread between the rates that a clearing bank will charge a top credit and a lesser credit to finance a given type of paper varies with the level of interest rates; this spread is narrow when interest rates are low, wide when interest rates are high. Occasionally, the rates a clearing bank charges become downright usurious. For example, at the end of December 1985, when funds were at 15% and bouncing around, some clearing banks were asking certain clients to pay a 30% annual rate for overnight financing. The primary objective of a bank that did that was not to maximize profits, but, rather, to drive temporarily some of its clients to alternative sources of funding—the bank was seeking to windowdress its balance sheet by cutting down both its overnight loans to dealers and its overnight borrowings of funds. Another factor operating at that time was that dealers were awash in new muni issues that they had to finance; these issues were rushed to market to beat an anticipated change in the tax code, one that did not in fact occur until a year later.

While money market dealers use RPs to finance the bulk of their positions, the dealer loans that they receive from their clearing banks and from other banks remain an important element in their financing. Dealers use bank loans to finance odd-lot pieces that are too small or too expensive, given transactions costs, to RP. Dealers also rely on loans from their clearing bank to meet daily any unexpected financing needs that arise due to fails by them to deliver. *A dealer's clearing bank is his lender of last resort.*

Clearing banks are content to provide only residual financing to dealers. These banks view the rate they get on dealer loans as none too attractive. Also, if clearing banks were to finance the total positions in governments and other money market instruments held by their dealer clients, that would destroy, as they well know, their capital/asset ratios.

While dealers, typically, rely only sparingly on their clearing banks for financing, the total dealer loans that a major clearing bank makes amount to a sizable and, over time, highly variable sum. On a given day, a major clearing bank's total dealer loans might, depending on the cost and availability of RP money, run from $0.5 billion to $1.5 billion. Of that sum, a single big dealer might be borrowing as much as $400 million. In the world of dealer loans, all borrowers are not created equal.

Types of dealer loans

Position loans.   Clearing banks basically make two sorts of loans to dealers. First, there are position loans. A dealer has a piece of inventory to finance; he calls his clearing bank, gets a rate quote, and, if he decides to take it, books a loan. Clearing banks make position loans in competition with RPs and with loans from other clearing banks. Whether a bank quotes an aggressive rate on position loans to dealers varies from day to day depending on how flush with funds it is. A dealer, on hearing the rate that a bank quotes him, will know immediately whether that bank wants his business.

On a given day, a dealer may find that the bank quoting the best rate on position loans is not his clearing bank, but some other New York City bank. If so, it is a simple matter for the dealer to borrow from this second bank using as collateral securities at his clearing bank. If, for example, a dealer who clears through Manny finds, on a given day, that Citi is offering the best dealer loan rate, he can borrow from Citi against collateral left at Manny; the dealer does this by asking Manny to do two things: (1) set aside, as collateral for Citi, securities in his box position and (2) sent to Citi a receipt for that collateral. This arrangement, designed to reduce costly movements of collateral, is done according to an agreement among N.Y.C. banks.

Box loans.   The second sort of loans that clearing banks make to dealers is to finance, "clean up," whatever is left in the dealer's box position at day's end: the odds and ends the dealer has not financed as well as any securities he has failed to deliver. Clearing banks always ask dealers to estimate the amount of end of day financing they will need. Clearing banks do not want big surprises, but they often get them anyway; dealers are notoriously poor at forecasting their residual financing needs.

It is understood between a dealer and his clearing bank that the dealer will always hold in his box position sufficient securities to collateralize any loan that his clearing bank must extend to him. However, dealers sometimes slip up, perhaps due to an error, and run an uncollateralized overdraft with their clearing bank. Clearing banks don't like this to occur, and when it does, they charge the dealer a penalty loan rate. Clearing banks seem to feel that some dealers need an occasional slap on the wrist to keep them from getting sloppy about their operations area, an orphan child at too many shops. This remark applies to smaller dealers who do not always have a highly professional operations area.

Free box.   All dealers have net worth (capital), sometimes very substantial amounts of it. Thus, it stands to reason that, at times, a dealer, who may have—depending on the number of markets in which he operates—a quite varied collection of assets, will have some of his capital invested in his positions in those securities that his clearing bank clears.

In that case, the dealer will own, free and clear, some portion of the securities in his clearing account. A dealer refers to such securities as his *free box,* and it represents to him his current ability to further leverage his position.

Once the market has closed, it is easy to measure a dealer's free box. It is whatever securities the dealer owns that he has not pledged as collateral either for a clearing bank loan or for RPs. Sometimes, a dealer who does a lot of RP and who holds the collateral for that RP in a segregated safekeeping account for his customers, will, when a new trading day starts, place all of the securities that he has used to collateralize maturing RPs back into his free box; he often does so, moreover, before he returns to his RP customers any monies due them on such RPs (Chapter 14 on *letter repos*). In this case, a dealer's free box will, during the early part of the day, include significant amounts of collateral that the dealer must, unless he sells it, put out on repo or otherwise finance before the end of the day.

Credit risk.   When a clearing bank agrees to clear securities trades for a dealer, it requires the dealer to sign an agreement spelling out the nature of the arrangement between the two parties. A key provision of this agreement is that securities in the dealer's box position will serve as collateral for the dealer's loan and that the clearing bank will have an *absolute lien* on these securities. This provision of the clearing agreement is designed to reduce the clearing bank's credit risk vis-à-vis the dealer.

A second provision that has the same intent requires that the dealer fully collateralize, at all times, his loan from the clearing bank; in other words, the dealer must ensure that the aggregate loan he requires from his clearing bank does not exceed the market value of the securities in his box position minus whatever *margin* (*haircut*) his clearing bank demands. *A haircut is the difference between the current market value of securities and the amount a clearing bank or other lender will lend to a dealer against these securities.* Parties who lend money against securities haircut these securities to protect against a possible fall in the market value of their collateral: they seek, in other words, to reduce the credit risk to which their loans to dealers expose them. Lenders of money to money market dealers take haircuts that average 2% on governments, slightly more if the collateral is less liquid.

While a well-run clearing bank demands adequate collateral to back dealer loans, it also takes many other steps to protect itself against credit risk vis-à-vis its dealer clients. First, it will take on a new dealer client only if the latter has decent financials and passes whatever other tests

the bank's credit committee may impose. Second, in assigning a dealer a line of credit, the clearing bank's credit department will set a limit on the size of the clearing loan that the bank will extend to the dealer. Third, a clearing bank will, once it takes on a dealer, monitor that dealer closely to ensure that it would be in a position to notice, early on, any deterioration in the dealer's situation.

Noted one clearing banker, "There is not a dealer that we don't know. I personally know who is good and who is bad—who you want to avoid like the plague and who you want to go after. We have an extensive credit review once a week for all of our accounts. Also, we review, from a credit perspective, every day throughout the day, what is going on in each of our clients' accounts.

"We usually get monthly and quarterly financials for all our accounts. Most dealers are required by the SEC or NASD to file a quarterly Focus Report, which outlines their financial position. We receive a copy of that report, and we can tell if the numbers on it are for real."

For a clearing bank, monitoring dealers involves more than looking at what financials dealers send in. Noted the same clearing banker, "We know all our customers. We make it a practice to go out and visit them. We can tell a lot about a shop just by being there for an hour or so. We also learn about a shop by who they are hiring and who they are losing. If a shop loses a key trader, we know that may cut their profits substantially; a single trader may bring into a shop a million or more of profit a year. By monitoring our accounts, we try to stop trouble before it happens." The above comments surely overstate a clearing bank omniscient knowledge of its clients; still, these comments correctly describe things that such a bank does seek to track in assessing the creditworthiness of each of its clients, especially smaller ones.

Intraday credit risk.   It's easy to fall into the trap of thinking that the credit that a clearing bank extends to a dealer is somehow more secure overnight, after the amounts of both collateral in the dealer's box and of his loan are fixed, than it is during the trading day when securities and money are, in the heat of the clearing process, moving rapid fire into and out of the dealer's clearing account. Actually, the securities in a dealer's clearing account provide collateral for its OD from the clearing bank regardless of the time of day. The reason that a clearing bank, at a certain time of day, fixes a dealer's clearing loan and records and prices the dealer's collateral, is not principally to secure its loan, but rather to give the bank a basis on which to charge the dealer interest daily for funds it provides to him. The natural time of day for the clearing bank to pick to fix the dealer's loan is when business for the day is over.

Dealer bankruptcies and risk creditor suits.   Probably, clearing banks were never sleepy in monitoring their credit exposure vis-à-vis their accounts. Today, however, clearing banks are highly alert in doing so.

In recent years, two events have occurred that no clearing bank can have failed to notice: First, a continuing parade of government securities dealers has gone bankrupt; second, a number of these bankruptcies, Lion and Comark to name two, resulted in suits being filed by the dealer's creditors against the failed dealer's clearing bank.

Clearing banks feel that, if they run their operations carefully, they are well protected against possible loss due to the bankruptcy of one of their accounts. The clearing agreement that a dealer signs with his clearing bank gives the latter not only an absolute lien against the securities in the dealer's clearing account, but the right to sell the dealer's collateral should the dealer fail, for any reason, to meet his commitments under the agreement. Clearing banks try to ensure that all of the dealer loans they make are always fully collateralized. To this end, they forbid a dealer to transfer securities out of his clearing account if that transfer would cause the dealer's loan from the clearing bank to be undercollateralized.

In their suits against the banks who cleared for dealers that failed, some creditors of these dealers have argued that the clearing bank was a party to the dealer's fraud. Other creditors have argued that the clearing bank, in the course of its daily contact with the dealer, should have observed that the dealer was defrauding customers—specifically customers who left, in safekeeping with the dealer, securities and RP collateral that the dealer was supposed to deposit, but did not always do so, in a safekeeping account that he maintained for the sole benefit of his customers at his clearing bank.

Clearing banks make an attractive target for suits by a failed dealer's creditors because they are supposed to be sophisticated and, as a practical matter, they have *deep pockets.* Money spent suing an indigent culprit, however guilty, is money wasted.

The suits that have been filed against clearing banks by creditors of bankrupt dealers shock clearing bankers who view themselves as *a species of hear no evil, see no evil monkey. In their view, a clearing banker's job is to execute clearing instructions, period.* If it were to happen that a set of clearing instructions from a dealer stated that the dealer swore on a stack of bibles that he would put the securities being cleared into a safekeeping account for the sole benefit of the customer who had purchased those securities, that information would, note clearing bankers, be irrelevant to their clearing of the trade. Moreover, because this is so, it would be unreasonable, argue clearing bankers, for anyone to expect a clearing bank either to notice such information or to act in any way on it.

To anyone familiar with the mechanics of clearing and with the handling of dealer loans, the case made by clearing bankers seems strong. Nonetheless, clearing bankers worry that, one day, one of them may lose a suit brought by a creditor of a failed dealer because the judge or jury feels more sympathy toward the creditor, perhaps a small, unsophisticated municipality, than they do toward the "rich" and powerful defendant. So far, the litigation brought by dealer creditors against clearing banks has all been settled out of court. This litigation has, thus, resulted in no court decision that either sustains or conflicts with the clearing bankers' view that a clearing bank's responsibilities are solely to execute promptly and accurately instructions received.

Obviously, it is in the economic self-interest of every clearing bank to carefully monitor its credit risk vis-à-vis its accounts. To conclude from this that a clearing bank also has some enlarged responsibility to monitor the credit risk of the customers of its accounts relative to these accounts is a big leap—one that it would be difficult to support either by fact or logic.

Fails and dealer financing costs

On a given day, if a dealer is failed to in an amount that exceeds his fails to deliver, he is said to have a *positive fail ratio;* conversely, if a dealer has, on a given day, fails to deliver that exceed the amount by which he is failed to, he is said to have a *negative fail ratio.* Whenever a dealer runs a *negative fail ratio,* he *increases,* by the amount of his *net* fails (fails to deliver *minus* fails to receive), the total borrowing he must do to finance his position. Conversely, whenever a dealer runs a *positive fail ratio,* he *decreases,* by the absolute amount of his *net* fails, the total borrowing he must do to finance his position.

A negative fail ratio unnecessarily increases a dealer's financing costs, whereas a positive fail ratio decreases a dealer's financing costs. For a dealer, being failed to is a substitute for obtaining bank financing or doing RP—a quite attractive substitute because it costs the dealer not the high bank loan rate, nor the lower RP rate, but rather 0%: Net fails to a dealer are a source of *free financing* for that dealer.

Obviously, every alert dealer seeks to run a positive fail ratio. If a dealer succeeds in doing so, his success can, by lowering the firm's costs, contribute significantly to the firm's profitability. How important a positive fail ratio can be to a firm's profitability is suggested by a few numbers: One top dealer says that, on an average night, its fails to deliver run $200 million, its fails to receive about $225 million; another top dealer says that its fails to receive run about $200 million and that most of its fails

are on the receive side. Positive fail ratios bring in big bucks to many of the big dealers on the Street.

Avoiding fails. Creating a positive fail ratio requires a lot of effort on the part of a dealer, and in particular, it requires that he maintain an efficient back office. Having a consistently positive fail ratio is one of the benefits that's likely to accrue to a shop that makes the effort and spends the money necessary to run a top-notch back office.

In his effort to avoid fails, a dealer can expect some help from his clearing bank. A dealer's clearing bank understands how important it is to each of its accounts, big and small, to minimize fails. Thus, all day long a clearing bank patiently answers dealer queries as to whether this came in or that went out. Big clients whose computers are hooked up to their clearing bank's computer get a memo printout in their shop each time their clearing bank executes a transaction for their account; thus, they have the information necessary to keep abreast of their positions throughout the day. Smaller accounts lack such ready information on their positions. Noted one clearing banker, "On the smaller accounts, we give them a rundown at 1 P.M.: 'These came in, these didn't come in . . . ,' and so on. We call those items in so that the dealer can be aware of all larger items that haven't come in. Say the dealer has a sale of $7 million, and he has 2 in the box. At 1 P.M., we tell him that the 5 hasn't come in yet to make the 7. If he doesn't do anything about it, he is going to have to finance the $2 million he has in the box. He then gets on the phone to the party that owes him the 5 and pressures him to get the 5 in so that he can turn the 7 around."

Why fails occur. In the world of pure governments, fails—at least for dealers with efficient back offices—tend to be centered around the six or eight hot issues which typically are either new issues or the cheapest-to-deliver issues for futures contracts. In such issues, big shorts may create a situation in which, temporarily for the most part, there are too few securities in the system for everyone to meet their obligations. The latter occurred in May 1986 when U.S. dealers shorted a Treasury bond issue in which Japanese dealers held big positions; contrary to the expectation of U.S. dealers, the Japanese chose, for a time, not to sell that issue when the Treasury auctioned a new long bond. This left the U.S. dealers scrambling without success to cover their shorts. The upshot was some huge fails.

When a dealer sees that his fails to receive threaten his ability to make certain deliveries, he will, if he has a good back office, either borrow or reverse in the securities he needs to make his deliveries. All big dealers do this; governments can be borrowed or reversed in easily and quickly;

and it's much cheaper for a dealer to deliver securities obtained via one of these routes than it is for him to fail. We discuss at the end of Chapter 13 the advantages of reversing in securities versus borrowing them.

Our remarks in the preceding paragraph notwithstanding, dealers often do fail on deliveries of governments not to speak of on deliveries of other types of securities. When a dealer with a good back office fails on a delivery of governments, it is usually the result of some sort of screw up—a clerical error or whatever.

The fails game.   For a dealer to win at the fails game—have a position fail ratio—his back office must be on top of a lot of details. It must get out clean instructions to the dealer's clearing bank, manage its inventory throughout the day (make big deliveries first), borrow or reverse in securities to cover shorts and fails to receive, and so on.

A dealer probably won't limit his strategy for winning the fails game to just being efficient. In addition, he's likely to make some *gambles* when he thinks the odds are in his favor. Here's one sort of gamble a dealer might make to profit from fails. Suppose that a dealer has bought for his own position four blocks of $5 million of a particular bill issue. Perhaps because the issue is tight, he finances only three of these blocks and *plays* the final block *for fail.* If that block doesn't come in, he earns the whole bill rate at zero cost. If the block does come in too late for him to RP it, he will have to finance the block at the bank loan rate.

To illustrate, suppose that the repo rate is 6, the bill rate 5½, and the bank loan rate 7. In playing one block out of four for fail, the dealer is making a bet. He is saying, "I am pretty sure that one of those four blocks of 5 is going to fail. If it does, I'll win 550 basis points. If it does not, my financing cost for that block will be up 100 basis points because if the block comes in, it's likely to come in after the repo market has closed." A big dealer who plays deliveries for fail and loses ends up into his bank credit line—he has stuff coming in that he has not financed. That's OK because that is a lot of what his bank loan line is all about.

Customer DKs.   As noted in the previous chapter, investors like to be failed to because it permits them to be double invested. They get the same effect when they DK a delivery from a dealer too late for the dealer to clear up whatever error has occurred. Customer DKs of deliveries are a big problem for dealers because they cost dealers a lot of money.

Some customer DKs are the result of errors by the dealer: The money on the trade is wrong or whatever. Still other customer DKs result from the customer not getting the right information to his bank or from that bank not transmitting the information received to the right area. Any one of a number of slip-ups might occur. DKs on trades with foreign accounts,

which are proliferating, are getting more and more common. Foreign accounts seem to have a hard time getting information on a trade to their bank on time, especially if the trade is for next day settlement.

There's also the possibility that a customer DK is the result of a customer deciding to create a fail so that he can be double invested. Said one dealer, "When a customer DKs on a Friday afternoon before a three-day weekend, you always have a suspicion that maybe he is playing the game of DKing so that he can have the use of the funds over the weekend. Often, it is difficult to chase after these people and collect interest due. [The dealer can claim interest due if the DK was illegitimate.] However, if the amount due is only interest on $20,000 over the weekend, you may be talking about only $80 bucks, in which case it is not worth it to go after the client for interest due. The Europeans are much more diligent than the Americans on collecting interest on fails to deliver; the Europeans will collect every penny due them. Perhaps volume has not overwhelmed them as much as it has us. Still, we do go after a lot of clients and other dealers as well for interest due us."

One sporting way customers seek to generate fails to them is by taking all of their deliveries, at least of wireables, at some out-of-town bank—maybe a Detroit bank if it's Chrysler—and then DKing any security that comes in as much as a second late. As we've noted, Fedwires take time which creates the possibility that a delivery that goes out on time (before the cutoff time) will arrive late (after the cutoff time).[2]

Fails and extensions.   How well a dealer does, on a given day, in achieving his goal of having a positive fail ratio depends always on the particular circumstances of the day (did someone push the wrong button?) and partly, too, on luck (on whom are the gods smiling today?). Said one dealer, "We love it when the Fed wire closes on time because that puts us an extra $200 or $300 million on the plus side. Our customers have failed to deliver to us whereas we have borrowed securities and made our deliveries. In straight governments, I am talking about our fails to receive going, when the wire closes on time, from maybe $200 million to half a billion."

Unsecured bank loans.   We have described two ways in which dealers obtain financing: doing RPs and obtaining loans from their clearing bank or banks. For dealers who are *Cadillac credits,* there is a third alternative. Often, such a dealer has established with a foreign bank a line against which it can borrow overnight on an *uncollateralized basis.* A dealer that has such a line might, late in a given day, experience an unanticipated demand for financing, perhaps because it received late delivery of

---

[2]For cutoff times on deliveries of securities over the Fed wire, see Table 9–1, p. 114.

securities it had played for fail. If so, the dealer can obtain the financing it needs simply with a phone call—no delivery of collateral necessary.

To illustrate, suppose Fed funds are at 6, the bank loan rate at 7¼. A class A credit, say, a Sali, or a Merrill, receives in a lot of securities, and it's too late to RP them because the Fed wire is closing. The firm puts in a call to Diachi N.Y.C., Paribas N.Y.C., or some other foreign bank and asks that bank's funds trader to obtain for it $50 or even $400 million of overnight financing. The bank's trader replies, maybe in broken English that that's doable, and he writes the ticket. He then buys, in the Fed funds market, the money that he's agreed to lend. Probably, his bank will, as a foreign bank—albeit one with a good name—have to pay ⅛ up for funds. To that ⅛, the bank's trader adds ⅛ for the bank's spread, so his rate to the dealer is approximately ¼ over the funds rate; in our example, that works out to 6¼. That rate is a full point less than the 7¼ loan rate offered by clearing banks. Thus, the foreign bank's loan rate looks, at 3 P.M., mighty attractive to our dealer in need of funds. Earlier in the day, however, when our dealer still could have financed at the RP rate, which was likely *below* the funds rate, the foreign bank's quote, set at a spread *above* the funds rate, would have been unattractive.

We should add that a really big dealer could not safely rely just on his clearing bank for *all* of his bank loan needs. Such a dealer must have lines with many, perhaps virtually every, major bank in the world. Cost may not be the only factor that leads such a dealer to borrow from a bank other than his clearing bank. Said one major dealer, "We have lines with virtually every major bank in the world. At any time of day, if we have miscalculated our fail positions or had some inefficiency in operations whereby we end up with a funding requirement in excess of what our clearing bank is able to give us, we must have the ability [provided by lines at other banks] to get funds somewhere. Such loans are not just a matter of saving money; it might be, on a given day, that our funding needs exceed what we can ask for from our clearing bank. We can get secured loans from our clearing bank for just about any amount, but if we go into them at 3 P.M. for $500 million, maybe they are going to charge us some astronomical rate or maybe they just do not have that kind of money. In either case, we'd probably go overseas to borrow.

PROVING AT DAY'S END

Most people toil once a month to get their checkbook reconciled with their bank statement. The last penny is, somehow, always off. With respect to clearing, dealers and clearing banks go through a similar procedure, only they do it every business day. When a dealer's back office checks to see that its records of what has occurred, during a given day,

in its clearing account jibe with the clearing bank's records of what has occurred, the dealer is said to be *proving* his account.

Activity and position reports

At the close of business each day, a clearing bank generates on its computer an activity report for each dealer client. For purchases, that report records total items received, identifies each item, gives the total par value of receipts of each issue, and, finally, records the total money that will be charged to the account as payment for all securities received. For sells, the clearing bank's activity report records a similar set of data. The clearing bank also generates, for the cash account, a *position report* that shows the account's final position at the end of the day.

It's easy for the clearing bank to generate activity and position reports for each of its clients because, as it clears trades during the day, its computer captures and holds in abeyance data on each trade it clears. Thus, by the close of business each day, the clearing bank's computer has stored within it, all of the data the clearing bank needs to generate such reports for each client.

How a clearing bank gets a dealer's position report to him will depend on the dealer's size and degree of automation. Noted one clearing bank, "We are obligated to send to each client a position report every day. For computerized accounts, we print out a position report in their shop. For out-of-town customers, we use Express Mail mostly, but we have some clients to whom we can send a report via Teletype. Some small local accounts prove with us over the phone; then early the next morning, they send a man down for their report. We have a package *bundle* waiting for them at our window."

Fee report

After the clearing bank's computer generates activity and position reports, it produces, for each account, a third report. That report says, "On behalf of account X, we did these trades in book-entry securities; these trades in physical securities; our rates per transaction are . . . ; and this is the total amount of fees we are charging account X for our services."

Proving in the dealer's back office

Each day, in proving his position, a dealer will cross check his in-house records of his position against the position report his clearing bank gives him.

The objective in the dealer's back office, when it proves its clearing account, is to come up with the same numbers that its clearing bank has for each of the dealer's holdings of various securities in the dealer's clearing account and for the money, if any, or the overdraft that is in that clearing account. The amount of the dealer's overdraft in his clearing account equals the amount of his day's-end clearing loan. Note, the latter is always a residual variable.

To prove its clearing account, a dealer's back office starts with yesterday's position in money and securities and adjusts its money position for the interest due on yesterday's clearing loan. It then backs out from these figures all of its buys and sells that cleared during the day; to obtain these figures, the dealer's back office starts with all of its trades that were supposed to settle during the day and then adjusts them for both its fails to receive and its fails to deliver. The new settlement-date position that the dealer's back office comes up with should prove with the bank's figures: what securities the bank says are in the dealer's box position and to what amount it says his clearing loan nets.

On an average day, a dealer's operations people will have no trouble proving the dealer's clearing account, but on a busy day, they may uncover a few errors either on their part or on that of the clearing bank.

Proving: Banks vis-à-vis the Fed

As noted in Chapter 9, clearing banks and other banks linked to Fedwire do not call the Fed at the end of the day to prove out. Instead, at day's end, the Fed's back-end computer produces, for each bank that has cleared securities trades over the Fed wire, a *clearing settlement report;* this report summarizes all of the activity that took place in the bank's accounts during the day; for each security, it identifies the bank's opening position, its ins, its outs, and its closing position. This information is sent, automatically, by the Fed's computer to the bank. Clearing banks use automated procedures to compare the Fed's clearing settlement against their in-house records of their activity for the day.

Proving at the clearing bank

Each morning, the loan that the clearing bank made the previous day to a dealer is taken off, and the dealer is free to deliver out, as a result of sales or RPs, the securities that served as collateral for that loan. During the day, securities will flow into and out of the dealer's account; and each time this occurs, there will be an offsetting money flow: A sale of securities will produce a money inflow, a purchase of securities a money outflow.

Technically, the dealer runs a daylight overdraft in his account with his clearing bank during the day, but the resulting credit risk to the clearing bank is minimal; as noted, the clearing bank can always rest assured that, because of the way money and securities flows work in a delivery-versus-payment market, any rise in the dealer's intraday overdraft at his clearing bank will be matched by a like rise in the value of the securities in his clearing account.

The "clean-up" loan that a clearing bank extends to a dealer at the end of each business day is a residual variable. That loan amounts to whatever it must amount to given (1) the size of the bank's previous-day loan to the dealer; (2) the interest and clearing fees charged to his account; and (3) the inflows and outflows of money and securities that occurred during the day into and from his account as a result of buys, sells, and financing transactions.

THE NEXT CHAPTER

So far, we have made only cursory mention of clearing fees, of self-clearing, and of covering shorts. In the next chapter, we turn to these important topics.

Chapter 13

Clearing fees, self-clearing, and covering shorts

IN THIS CHAPTER, WE DISCUSS CLEARING FEES, the services for which these fees pay, remote settlement, and self-clearing. Also, at the end of the chapter, we take a look at spec accounts and the mechanics of borrowing securities.

CLEARING FEES

Thanks to the efficiency of operation made possible by the book-entry system, clearing banks are able to clear a trade in book-entry securities with one-third to one-half the labor they need to clear a trade in physical securities. Clearing bank fees reflect this differential. Currently, clearing banks charge around $6 a trade for clearing trades in book-entry securities. To this basic fee, they add $2.25 to cover the fee they must pay the Fed for each Fed wire message they send. Clearing fees on physical securities are much higher than those on book-entry securities. To clear a trade in physical securities, clearing banks charge from $15 to $25, depending on the security cleared.

Not all dealers are charged precisely the same fee by their clearing bank. A dealer who has a highly automated, high-volume system that

puts out "clean" instructions pays the basic fee. In contrast, a dealer who sends in instructions that the clearing bank must "clean up" (i.e., correct) pays a higher fee. Lower clearing fees are a secondary, but significant, payoff that accrues to dealers who maintain an efficient back office.

Consistent with their philosophy—the more work, the higher the fee—clearing banks charge, for transfers of securities between a dealer's clearing and safekeeping accounts, a fee that is about two-thirds the fee they charge to clear a straight trade in book-entry securities.

Clearing bank fees cover several different services that a clearing bank provides its customers. These services are: execution, the assumption of risk of loss due to errors in execution, the provision of access to daylight overdraft to dealer clients, and the assumption of some credit risk vis-à-vis each such client.

Execution

What dealers want most from their clearing banks, besides accurate execution, is speedy execution. Speed becomes crucial on trades that are cleared just prior to the closing of the Fed wire. The desire of dealers to minimize fails gives dealers an incentive to stall clearing many trades until late in the day; no dealer wants to deliver out small batches of securities early in the day and, as a result, fail on a large delivery later. To meet the demands of dealers for speedy execution, major clearing banks have honed their operations to the point where they advertise, for book-entry securities, a guaranteed two-minute turnaround: the clearing bank promises that, if it receives clearing instructions from a dealer two minutes or more before the Fed wire closes, it will clear that trade before the wire closes. This guarantee puts the clearing bank at *risk:* if it fails to meet its promised turnaround time and, as a result, forces a dealer into a costly fail, it, not the dealer, must bear the cost of that fail.

To make good on its guaranteed two-minute turnaround, a clearing bank that has many dealer clients must invest millions in computer software and hardware, and it must have a large, well-trained staff. Both requirements are extremely costly, which is one reason why only a handful of banks have chosen to be big players in the clearing business.

Note clearing and custody are two separate businesses. Ford and other portfolio accounts get no guaranteed two-minute turnaround time on their custody accounts with Morgan and other banks. To obtain that level of service, a big investor would have to open an account in the clearance area of a clearing bank. Currently, banks that are not top clearing banks clear, for corporations and financial institutions, many trades in a fashion that is more leisurely and less people-and-capital-intensive than that in which top clearing banks clear trades for dealers.

The clearing banks' guarantee of a turnaround time leads, noted one clearing banker, "to an incredibly gray area. What is timeliness of instruction so that I can get an instruction into my system and honor my turnaround commitment? What is a good delivery instruction? If we get an instruction that says, Chase custodian department, 16th floor, we may interpret that to be CHASE/CUST whereas the format should be CHASE/TRUST. Problems arise with respect to deliveries when a dealer gets a new salesperson who sends something to operations which sends us God knows what. Sometimes a dealer must take a fail for us to make our point. At a lot of shops, the operations side tends to be ignored until things start not to go so well. Fortunately, our operation makes a lot of money for our bank, so we get the resources we need to fulfill our side of the clearing bargain."

Risk of error

Clearing banks end up financing a certain amount of dealer fails not only because they must shoot a lot of messages through the Fed wire at the last minute, but because they sometimes make mistakes. The same clearing banker went on to say, "On a 12,000-trade day, we might make half a dozen mistakes. Since we must eat the cost of a fail that results from our mistake, we hope that our mistakes occur on $1 million, not $20 million, trades. Naturally, $100 million problems always arise on Fridays or before a long weekend. On the day before Labor Day weekend, we found a $65 million problem. With rates at 11%, that would have been a big hit for four days. We saved about $40 million of the trade, which was an outright sale going to seven or eight different places. On the rest of the trade, we ended up giving someone a free dealer loan."

One problem that can cause a clearing bank to take a big hit is a computer snafu. As noted below, a computer snafu that halted its deliveries of securities forced Irving Trust to borrow, one night, $1.7 billion from the Fed; and a similar problem forced BONY, at a later date, to borrow $20 billion from the Fed!

On trades involving physical securities, another source of clearing-bank error that crops up now and then is that such securities have a way, despite the elaborate precautions that clearing banks take, of getting lost for a time between the cracks. For example, one clearing-bank clerk mistakenly put $400 million of commercial paper into a drawer; as a result, it was sent out late for redemption.

Access to daylight overdraft

On Wall Street the term *daylight overdraft* refers to a negative balance that an entity runs in a deposit, clearing, or settlement account for some number of hours between the opening and closing of business.

Daylight overdraft is a natural and inevitable phenomenon that arises in large amounts as a result of the functioning of the payments mechanism and as a result of the clearing of securities. Daylight overdraft arises, for instance, in all of the following situations. Big Japanese banks that have accounts with N.Y.C. banks return early in the day billions of Fed funds that they purchased the preceding day; as a result, these foreign banks run daylight overdrafts at the N.Y.C. banks, which in turn run daylight overdrafts at the Fed. These overdrafts end when the Japanese banks buy, later in the day, new Fed funds to replace those that they returned to previous-day sellers of funds. N.Y.C. banks and their customers, corporate and financial, engage everyday in a wide variety of Eurodollar and foreign exchange transactions that are settled through CHIPS. Since CHIPS settles at day's end, some N.Y.C. banks end up running, each day, big daylight overdrafts with CHIPS whereas other N.Y.C. banks end up running big intraday credits.

Securities transactions are another major source of daylight overdraft at banks. At the clearing level, Merrill may be, early in the day, a big *net* buyer of securities that it does not RP until late in the day. This will cause Merrill to go *OD (overdrawn)*, temporarily, in its clearing account at Manny and Manny to go OD, temporarily, at the Fed. At the custody level, Ford may sell securities in the morning and immediately buy other securities. If Ford pays for its new securities before it is paid for the securities it sold, that will cause Ford to go OD with its custodian, Morgan, and that will enlarge Morgan's OD with the Fed.

Dealers, like Merrill, could not possibly operate as they do if they did not receive access, via their clearing bank, to large daylight overdrafts. Access to such intraday credit is an important service that major clearing banks provide their customers. Moreover, this fact is one reason why only a big bank can be a clearing bank. The Fed permits Manny, with its big capital base, to run daily with its multibillion-dollar daylight overdrafts; the Fed would not let just any bank do that. Even a bank as big as BONY is able to clear the huge daily volume of trades it does only because the activities of its largest customer, FBI (a governments broker that acts as principal in trades it brokers) generate relatively little daylight overdraft.

FED POLICY ON DAYLIGHT OVERDRAFT

For many years, sizable amounts of daylight overdraft have been a feature of the U.S. banking system at various levels—customers with their banks and banks with the Fed and with CHIPS. While daylight overdraft would probably have been a feature of the U.S. banking system no matter how that system were organized and regulated, it is surely also true that

two factors, peculiar to the American scene, have contributed enormously to the growth of daylight overdrafts in the United States. These factors are (1) restrictions on intrastate and interstate banking that precluded major banks from branching and (2) pernicious Reg Q that created a situation in which rational bank depositors, small and large, got into a habit, gradually over the years, of keeping the smallest possible deposit balances at their banks. As a result of these factors, we have in the United States a fragmented banking system (15,000 banks) striving to process huge volumes of pure money transfers and money transfers associated with securities transactions. Had bank regulation been more sensible, the U.S. banking system would not have been constrained by such a relatively modest deposit base.

Not so many years ago, the size of daylight overdraft was not exactly a burning issue. People who realized it was there and who were in a position to gauge its magnitude regarded it pretty much as an inevitable daily, transitory by-product of the functioning of a huge banking system that processed each day a vast number of money transfers and securities transactions.

Then the Fed began to look closely at daylight overdraft. For what it's worth, the unofficial story of how this came to pass is that during the Continental Illinois Bank crisis, Federal Reserve Chairman Paul Volcker, when called to testify before Congress, was asked, "If Continental Illinois goes down today, what losses might the Fed sustain?" Volcker had no clue whether the number might be $500 million or $5 billion. Presumably, the only reason he thought it might be greater than zero—the Fed being other than the FDIC—had something to do with daylight overdraft. In any case, the notion took hold—at least in Washington—that, when a bank ran a daylight OD with the Fed, that OD exposed the Fed to credit risk.

The idea that the Fed's credit risk vis-à-vis a bank is a function, simple or complex, of the size of that bank's daylight overdraft is nigh impossible to defend. Banks do not transfer either money alone or money against securities willy-nilly for a customer, be that customer John Jones, a major corporation, or a world class foreign bank. A bank that lends to or does any business with a customer that, in its view, exposes it, even on an intraday basis, to credit risk evaluates carefully the creditworthiness of that customer; then, on the basis of that evaluation, the bank establishes a line—a carefully monitored limit—on the total risk that it will assume vis-à-vis that customer. Since a bank's daylight overdraft reflects largely transfers done by a bank for its customers, the correct measure of the risk associated with that daylight overdraft ought, one would think, to be a function of the credit not of the bank, but of its customers. That, however, is not how the Fed thinks.

Caps on daylight overdraft caused by money transfers

The Fed observed that banks were running daylight overdrafts with it that ran into the tens of billions of dollars; Fed officials perceived credit risk and they decided to reduce their exposure by compressing daylight overdraft in the system. To do so, the Fed began by imposing caps on the daylight overdrafts that individual banks may run as a result of their pure money transfers. There is a two-week average cap and a maximum per day. The caps for a bank of exceptional creditworthiness are that its average overdrafts at the Fed may not exceed two times its capital and that its maximum overdraft per day may not exceed three times its capital.

A payments system with zero daylight overdraft would be a payments system in *gridlock,* since some bank or banks must make the first payments to get the ball rolling. Recognizing this, an officer of CHIPS once noted, "If we squeeze daylight overdraft out of CHIPS, one of two events will occur: we will have gridlock or the daylight overdraft necessary for the system to function will pop out in Zurich or elsewhere." If this is indeed true, then shrinking daylight overdraft through regulation would seem to be a sure formula for degrading the payments mechanism, a point that the central bank ought to appreciate.

So far, that seems to be the case. Many banks have felt it necessary to meter, in effect, outgoing wire transfers to stay within their Fed caps. As a result, they have been forced to try to change in certain ways how their customers do business. One result is that certain big direct issuers of commercial paper, such as Ford Motor Credit, now issue their commercial paper not at one, but at every major N.Y.C. bank. This change permits such issuers to make and receive payments from a host of big investors via intrabank, rather than interbank, transfer of funds. The effect of this change is to permit daylight overdraft to appear only at the level of the bank vis-à-vis its customer, not at the level of the bank vis-à-vis the Fed. The impact of such rearrangements of payments practices on economic efficiency is dubious at best. Still more dubious is how such rearrangements will materially lower risk credit risk at any level of the system. With or without daylight overdraft, the Fed is and remains the *de facto* guarantor of every major money market bank.

Caps on daylight overdraft arising from securities transactions

The Fed is also proposing to place caps on daylight overdraft arising from securities transactions. It is hard to find any rational argument for why this is necessary. Bank overdrafts with the Fed that arise out of securities transactions are almost all, in effect, collateralized, either

directly by highly liquid, high-quality securities (e.g., Treasuries) or by collateralized loans on which the collateral involves again highly liquid, high-quality securities. For example, intraday Merrill borrows, after putting down margin, from Manny which, in turn, borrows from the Fed; Merrill uses the money to pay for securities that Manny holds. Where is the big credit risk to anyone? Merrill has market risk, but then part of the job of Manny's credit department is to ensure that there is some reasonable relationship between Merrill's capital, Merrill's general creditworthiness, and the amount of credit that Manny extends to Merrill.

The Fed's efforts to control the daylight overdrafts that major U.S. banks run with it is having an impact on clearing. To reduce their daylight overdrafts vis-à-vis the Fed, clearing banks are taking steps to reduce the daylight overdrafts that their dealer clients run with them. There are several problems with this. First, just about any step that one dealer takes to reduce its daylight overdraft with its clearing bank will—absent a major restructuring of the clearing mechanism—raises some other dealer's daylight overdraft with its clearing bank. Thus, it is hard to see how the daylight overdrafts that result from clearing can be arbitrarily reduced without reducing the efficiency with which securities are currently cleared. Second, forcing clearing banks to reduce the daylight overdrafts that their dealer clients run with them is bound to have an anticompetitive effect. Clearing banks are going to end up saying to prospective clients, "We can't clear for you because we've already allocated, to established firms—Sali, Merrill, Lehman—that slice of our permitted daylight overdraft that we reserve for clearing. Sorry, but we're fresh out of daylight overdraft."

A final question with respect to the regulation of daylight overdraft, however it arises, is this: How, in a *growing economy,* can the payments mechanism and the clearing mechanism cope with an increasing volume of transactions, pure money and money versus securities, if daylight overdraft, at all levels of the banking system, is to be constricted? The Fed's policy on daylight overdraft makes no sense to anyone on Wall street.

SELF-CLEARING

Most large dealers who trade a variety of instruments—governments, BAs, CDs, GNMAs, and so on—do not rely on a single clearing bank to clear all their trades. Large dealers routinely use more than one clearing bank for several reasons. First, different clearing banks have different areas of strength; also, some banks won't clear certain types of paper: Manny clears physical GNMAs, but not BAs. Security Pacific, in contrast, is happy to clear BAs. Second, a dealer who uses more than one clearing bank is able to engage in what amounts to continuous comparison

shopping; every month, such a dealer can ask, "How did bank A compare with bank B in terms of speed of execution, accuracy of execution, fees charged, and so on? Has A produced some innovation that B does not yet offer?" Third, a dealer who clears all of his trades in all types of paper with a single bank is putting all his eggs in one basket, a risky thing to do. A dealer pondering this might well ask, "Where would my firm be in the unlikely event that something happened to threaten the solvency of my sole clearing bank? Also, where would my firm be if, say, a massive computer problem at my sole clearing bank forced it to halt operations, not for one day, as BONY did in November 1985, but for several days?" It's easy for a thoughtful dealer to conclude, "One never knows what unlikely event might occur; so I'll sleep better if I spread my clearing business around."

Some large dealers opt not only to use several clearing banks, but to self-clear, partially or wholly, their trades in certain types of securities.

Remote settlement

Major clearing banks all offer big dealers the option of doing in-house some of the clerical work involved in clearing trades in book-entry securities. The bank gives the dealer some PCs or consoles, and the dealer has his own people use that equipment to arrange his deliveries and receipts of wireable securities through the Fed. Goldman, which uses remote settlement for governments, may have as many as 10 clerical employees doing work that its clearing bank would otherwise do.

When a dealer uses remote settlement, each message (instruction) he generates goes to his clearing bank. The latter has an administrator who checks the message to see that it is in proper form and who also does a quick credit review to see that any funds needed are there. Once the clearing bank is satisfied that a message is OK, it shoots that message over the Fed wire; this can be done without clerical people at the clearing bank having to touch the message.

Remote clearing appeals to clearing bankers. It reduces the number of people they must employ and, thus, their cost of doing business. Another big plus from the point of a clearing bank is that a dealer who uses remote settlement assumes responsibility for any errors he makes. If a dealer directs Manny to send securities to Columbus, and Manny sends them to Cleveland, that's Manny's problem. If, alternatively, Goldman, makes such a mistake in-house, any resulting problems and costs are its to bear.

Since the use by a clearing bank's accounts of remote settlement reduces the bank's costs, clearing banks charge lower fees on trades that a dealer clears via remote settlement. Thus, one advantage to a dealer

of doing remote settlement is that, he may, if he operates efficiently, be able to reduce his all-in clearing costs. A second advantage is that, by doing remote settlement, a dealer becomes master of his own destiny. If he wants to do a $2 million transaction before he does a $10 million transaction, he can execute that decision on the spot without having to call his clearing bank and say, "Hey, please do A before B." Despite its obvious advantages, many sophisticated firms choose not to use remote settlement; they prefer to have their clearing bank do the *full job* of clearing and shoulder the *full risk* of possible loss due to inadvertent errors.

Self-clearing physicals

Remote settlement permits a dealer to do as much of the clearing of trades in book-entry securities as he can do for himself. Sending or receiving a Fed wire that moves *book-entry* securities is something only the dealer's clearing bank, not he, can do.

Physical securities are a different animal. A dealer can, and some dealers do, have their own in-house vault for storing physical securities. Such a dealer can establish a cage to accept deliveries of physical securities to it; and it can, just as clearing banks do, deliver out such securities by messenger. However, in clearing trades in physical securities, a dealer must still rely on his clearing bank to make and receive payments in Fed funds.

Financing self-clearing.   A big problem that dealers who self-clear face is getting credit to pay for securities delivered to them. Clearing banks are happy to extend credit to a dealer, up to the dealer's credit line with them, against securities that are delivered to the dealer's account at the clearing bank and against which the clearing bank has an absolute lien. Getting credit becomes a problem for a dealer who self-clears because such a dealer directs that securities being delivered to him be sent not to his clearing bank, but rather directly to him. Thus, when such a dealer requests bank financing of his positions, he is asking his bank for the risk equivalent of an unsecured loan.

Dealers who self-clear and who happen to be Cadillac credits can obtain from their bank a line of credit and day loans. A day loan, for which the dealer pays a 1% fee, covers the dealer's intraday exposure between the time he receives securities and the time at which he redelivers those securities to some third party. Suppose a dealer who self-clears gets, early in the day, securities for which he must pay; he might call his bank and say, "I've just gotten in $100 million of securities. I need you to wire $100 million out of my account. [No dealer in his right mind would leave

$100 million of cash in his account.] I have to redeliver those securities to someone else [on a sale or an RP]; I'll have money to wash against my loan [from you] tonight."

A clearing bank that agrees to make the sort of loan we've just described will do so reluctantly and only for topcredits. How does the bank know whether the dealer does or does not have in his shop the $100 million of securities he says he does? Also, the bank has no control over what the dealer, if he has actually received the securities, might do with them. This is in sharp contrast to what goes on when a bank extends credit to a dealer to add securities to his box position at the bank; recall that a clearing bank normally won't execute a dealer's instruction to move securities out of its box position if doing so would cause the bank's loan to that dealer to become undercollateralized. All this gives the clearing bank lots of protection when it is the clearing bank that clears—start to finish—the dealer's trades.

Dealers who self-clear try every tack possible to reduce their intraday financing needs. One such tack is for a dealer to wait to make payments for securities delivered to him until late in the day after he has received monies for securities he has delivered to others. A problem with this approach is that it risks shifting one firm's financing problem onto another firm, since no firm can benefit from paying late in the day if every other firm also does so.

Dealers who self-clear need access not only to intraday credit, but to overnight financing at their clearing bank. An operations officer at a Cadillac credit explained how his firm obtains such financing, "We get *AP (agreement to pledge)* loans from our bank. We call the bank and say, 'We want $200 million, and we will send you a list of the collateral, which is in *our* vault.' AP loans, which started out being corporate and equity loans, have been around since 1970. They were always restricted in the sense that only top dealers could borrow using this vehicle. For years, we insisted that the bank come in once a month and count our collateral. They don't do that anymore; maybe, they're in once a year, but they have the right to come in *any time* they want."

Many people on the Street are uncomfortable about the way payments are made against *physical* securities regardless of how the trade is cleared. Whether a dealer clears himself or has his clearing bank clear his trades in physical securities, it is always true that *payment for such securities is made some time after delivery.* Many on the Street view this untidy arrangement as creating large and unacceptable credit risks.

Motives for self-clearing.   Not for nothing do clearing banks clear; they do it to earn a profit. By self-clearing efficiently, a dealer ought to be able to capture for himself the clearing bank's profit. Thus, one motive of dealers who self-clear is to increase their profits by decreasing one im-

portant element of their costs. Dealers have, however, other even more compelling motives for self-clearing.

One such motive is to speed up the clearing process. Noted one dealer's operations person, "When you use a clearing bank, you put a middleman and a time delay between information and the processing of that information. When a delivery is made, the bank makes the delivery. They have to notify their computer, which turns around and starts a chain [of events] to get the delivery done. Then they tell us what they have done. All this takes extra time. Why not just have our people make the deliveries?"

Yet another motive for self-clearing is to cut the opportunities for error, usually human. Said the same operations guy, "Problems occur in operations every time you get a human being involved. A clearing bank—with its complement of human beings—is just a middleman, and you do not have to use them for physical securities as you do for wireables."

A related motive for self-clearing is phrased by some operations people as "getting control over our own destiny." In the case of Ginnies in particular, the complexities of delivery and the size of the fails that prevail on the Street—sometimes, over a billion on each side for a big dealer—create problems at which a dealer may want to throw more money and resources than his clearing bank is willing to do. Typical of this attitude is the following comment by a dealer's operations person who describes his firm's decision to go to self-clearing of Ginnies, "It was gridlock on the Street [in Ginnies]. We were carrying a heavy negative fail ratio too. We were not getting good information from the bank on time. We wanted them to hire more people, but we could not force them to do so. They were totally out of control. Finally, we said, 'If we are going to go down the tubes, we might as well be doing it ourselves.' We decided we had to be in better control. We could not just keep saying, 'The bank screwed up.' "

Mechanics of self-clearing. The mechanics of clearing a physical security are definitely simpler when a dealer self-clears than when he uses a clearing bank. A back office person described the process as follows: "Say, we sell a CD to Sali. Money market trades cut off early, around 11 A.M. The trade goes to our back office. In a self-clearing mode, we will get an instruction down to our cage, which, to cut down elevator time, is located near the ground floor. If they have the item in the vault, they just pull it and give it to a messenger together with a delivery bill. When Sali gets the security, they stamp a copy of the delivery bill saying that they got it; later, they wire us the funds. There are far fewer steps to track when we self-clear than when the clearing bank gets into the act." To which he added, "Everyone on the Street who is of decent size will end up self-clearing [physicals]."

Dealer accounts at the Fed

It has been suggested that the Fed should permit dealers to have accounts, as banks do, with it. That would enable dealers to self-clear trades in book-entry securities. This proposal raises an important question: would the Fed extend intraday credit to dealers? Currently, the Fed is expressing much concern over the intraday overdrafts that top-tier, highly capitalized banks run with it. There is no reason to believe that the Fed would welcome the running with it of big daylight overdrafts by dealers in governments. Dealers, for their part, would find themselves operating in a straight jacket if they entered into a self-clearing arrangement that precluded them from running, from time to time, sizable daylight overdrafts.

RUNNING A SMALL TRADING OPERATION

Much of our discussion of clearing so far has focused on the clearing of dealer trades. Dealers are typically very active traders of governments and of any other securities in which they make markets; such firms are, however, not the only active traders on the Street. The government market is the habitat of a host of smallish trading operations—*spec accounts* for want of a better term—that behave much like dealer shops except that they have few or no customers; also, their investment horizons are usually exceedingly short: a lot of spec accounts are day traders. Firms of this ilk are important: their trading adds to market liquidity; and the arbs they do, like those that dealers do, work to bring market rates into line with one another.

Relationships

Someone wanting to build a small trading operation must begin with *relationship building:* getting traders at top dealers to trade in size with them and getting top dealers to extend credit to them via reverses. Although dealers are always wanting to do more customer business, the many bankruptcies of small dealers—Drysdale to ESM—that have occurred in recent years have made dealers highly leery, to say the least, of the credit risk to which servicing a small, active trading account inevitably exposes them. "Small" is perhaps not the right adjective to apply to the sort of trading accounts we have in mind, since such accounts routinely assume positions of a billion or more.

To become accepted by major dealers, a *sine qua non* for a trading operation is that it be run by or have as its chief trader someone who is an experienced, successful trader and who is recognized as such by others on the Street. When a trading operation starts calling a Sali or

a Merrill, the latter will, before they agree to pick up on him, want to feel assured that the guy at the other end of the phone knows what he is doing and can be trusted to honor his word. It is not uncommon for a small trading operation to be run by an ex-trader from a big shop, one who is known to and respected by his former peers in the business.

Financing

Normally, a small trading operation in governments has limited capital and, thus, must be highly leveraged to make any money. Such a shop, no matter how creditworthy it may be, is never going to get its name known and its credit recognized in the national repo market. Thus, to obtain financing, the small shop must get dealers who have access to this market to grant it—naturally, after a rigorous credit check—financing lines; once it has such lines in place, the shop can then finance a portion of its positions by reversing them out to those dealers. A shop doing this will try to appear as professional, creditworthy, and profitable as possible to the dealers on whom it relies both to be its counterparties in trades and to finance its positions. For example, such a shop might, when it day trades, make it a point to unwind profitable trades with the selling dealer. Whenever it is able to do so, the shop can settle both a buy and a sell with a pairoff and a difference check; the difference check will, moreover, go from the dealer to the spec account, and the former will see that the latter is making money.

Clearing trades

To avoid a costly pile of fails, an account that trades actively will need a clearing arrangement that provides for a two-minute-or-better turnaround time. Thus, such an account cannot content itself with the sort of custody account at a bank that many institutional investors maintain. Instead, it must set up, at a clearing bank, a dealer-type clearing account, under which it pays for and gets the same level of service that a dealer gets. Also, a small trading shop will need a credit line from its clearing bank because it must look to the latter to be its lender of last resort—the entity that will, for example, finance deliveries that come in after the RP market has closed.

A small trading shop will clear its trades pretty much the same way a dealer does except that it won't get dealer turnaround time (Table 9-1). A trading shop must, like any other customer, get its deliveries out by 2:30 P.M. unless there's an extension of the Fed wire.

For an active trading account, the *slow* speed of the Fed wire can create costly problems. An active account that buys and sells all day,

often for cash settlement, is bound to get some late deliveries. It is, moreover, required, like any customer, to take in any securities that arrive before—even 30 seconds before—2:30 P.M. That requirement creates no problem for an institutional investor, say, a corporate liquidity portfolio that is buying and paying for securities with cash it wants to invest. A spec account, however, is not in the business of investing just its own cash; it expects to repo a lot of the securities it buys. If it is doing its job, it will arrange to repo any securities that add to its financing needs as soon as it buys those securities. So far so good. But what happens if the securities come into the spec account's clearing bank 30 seconds before the 2:30 P.M. cutoff? This may or may not cause a problem.

To illustrate, consider a shop that clears through BONY, which, like the other clearing banks, has a very efficient computer. If that shop has done an RP with some other party who also clears through BONY, then the shop's instruction to shoot out, say, $30 million of bills to that other party as soon as they come in will be in the buffer of BONY's computer; and as soon as the bills come into BONY, they will go out bang—as fast as a computer is—to the party who is supposed to get them as repo collateral. Naturally, BONY will transfer those bills DVP, so the shop, to whom the $30 million of bills were delivered at BONY, gets its money and its bills are financed overnight.

Now suppose that this same shop gets the $30 million in bills 30 seconds before the 2:30 P.M. cutoff and is supposed to deliver them on a reverse to Sali, which clears at Manny. This time the message in BONY's computer that awaits the arrival of the bills is to zap them out over the Fed wire to Manny, account of Sali. Unfortunately for our trading shop, which wants financing, a Fed wire can take several minutes. This means that securities sent before the 2:30 P.M. cutoff time for customer-to-dealer deliveries can arrive over a minute late—so late that the rules of the game say that the receiving dealer may DK the delivery. When that happens, the financing costs of the trading shop mushroom because it has no choice but to finance its securities at whatever rate its clearing bank is charging, a rate that's surely a wide spread over the repo rate.

The above possibility is anything but theoretical. Noted one spec trader, "It's common for me to receive securities that I am obligated to take in 30 seconds before the cutoff for dealer time. It's also common for me to get a delivery message into the Fed wire 30 seconds before the cutoff time and to have that message get to Manny 1 1/2 minutes after cutoff time. If a dealer gets a delivery that late, they 'bounce' it. Once, when this happened, a big dealer's trader called me a scumbag for trying to deliver late. For guys like me, the Fed wire—far from state of the art—is a royal pain in the neck."

The beginning as end

Every trading account has an incentive to make its clearing, back-office, and recordkeeping operations as efficient as possible. In a big shop this requires a big system. In a little shop, it can all be done on a PC with the aid of a programmer who understands how securities are traded and cleared. Said one spec trader, "I am going to get trade tickets and my trade sheet out of the business. Right now, I write down a lot of things on my trade sheet, which is a good document to work off. But as I am writing the sheet, I could key the same information into a PC. If a few more pieces of information, such as the CUSIP numbers [of the securities I trade], went into the record, I'd have the beginnings of a record that could generate every single other thing we need: confirms, clearing instructions, risk measures, P&L results—the whole thing. *The beginning would be the end.*

"Right now I have a girl who calls, each time I do a trade, to make sure the counterparty knows the trade as I do. With my new system, the computer will number each day's trades automatically, and my girl will add, each time she confirms a trade, a check mark not on my trade sheet, but in the computer. At the moment, I am supporting three girls who do a lot of phone and paper work after I do a trade. With my new system, they will have lots of free time, but I still want them there to troubleshoot for me if there are glitches with my computer. So I'm going to turn them into their own profit center. I will teach them to run a matched book operation with lots of emphasis on playing things for fails and on getting into the lending and borrowing of securities—borrowing in a bunch of an issue that you think is going to be tight into a refunding."

Aside: When this prophecy comes true, which it surely will, three more ladies will join a host of successful people in the money market who got into doing what they do by accident, luck, whatever you want to call it. Among that host is, to name one, an ex-secretary, who started calling in commercial paper orders for her boss, the treasurer of a small corporation. As she learned and her company grew, she became a most professional portfolio manager.

BORROWING VERSUS REVERSING IN SECURITIES

In Chapter 12, we said that a dealer, who for one reason or another is short securities that he needs in order to make deliveries, can, in governments at least, usually avoid a fail to deliver either by reversing in or borrowing securities. In this section, we describe briefly the mechanics of each procedure, its pros, and its cons.

Throughout this discussion, it will help the reader to bear in mind that the difference between a reverse and a borrowing of securities is simply this: *In securities lending, the investor swaps collateral for collateral; in a reverse, he swaps collateral for money.*

Reversing in securities

One man's repo is always another man's reverse: the two transactions really amount to the same thing. When a dealer does a repo he is looking to borrow money; when he does a reverse, he is looking to borrow securities. The quid pro quo that a dealer seeking to borrow securities, via a reverse, offers to the lender of the securities is a loan of money. If this seems confusing, recall that the economic substance of either a repo or a reverse is always that the transaction, whatever it is called, is a *collateralized loan.* Also, whether a transaction is called a repo or a reverse, it is always the lender of money who gets margin.

Generally, a dealer will reverse in securities on an *open* basis, which means that the transaction can be terminated at the request of either party; and if the party wanting to terminate the transaction calls before 10 A.M., the securities become returnable the same day. Most securities lending programs operate this way, but some have requirements for next-day termination.

Sometimes, a dealer will do a *term* reverse: take an issue that he thinks—hopes—will become hot and tie it up on term for at least a week. Often, the trader who does this is speculating that the issue will become hot, be shorted by traders, and therefore become *tight* in supply; if this occurs, the issue becomes what is known as a *special*: an issue that is in such demand that it can be reversed out (used to borrow money) at a rate below—perhaps full points below—the repo rate. The trader who wins on such a speculation ends up lending money, when he reverses in securities, at a rate well above the rate at which he borrows money when he subsequently reverses out those same securities. In other words, he ends up earning a positive spread on a two-legged arbitrage.

Borrowing securities

When a dealer borrows securities, it is often from a very conservative portfolio that wants full protection from risk. The standard arrangement is that the dealer borrowing say $10 million of Treasuries gives the lender of securities $10.2 million of other securities as collateral for his borrowing. He also pays the lender of securities a 50-basis-point fee.

A special aspect of a borrowing of securities is that the margin resembles that on a repo, but it goes not to the lender of money, but to the lender of the securities. The reason that the borrower of securities

ends up becoming the giver of margin is that the transaction is driven by his need to borrow securities. A dealer, if he wants to have a viable program for borrowing to cover shorts, must be able to go to an institution holding securities and say, "Look, if you will lend me your bonds, I will make that an extremely safe and attractive transaction for you. I will pay you a fee of 50 basis points so that you don't have to worry about arbitrage, market conditions, reinvestment, timing, moving monies, and so forth. Also, I will give you protection in the form of collateral equal to 102% of the value of the bonds you lend me; and I will maintain that 102% level of collateralization over the life of the transaction."

Historically, banks have been the biggest and best organized lenders of securities. They provide institutional custody, and to make their fees palatable to their customers, they offer a securities-lending service. This is a natural for such banks. They have easy access to the securities and records of what securities are in whose portfolios. Custody banks are not so good at investing the proceeds of an RP, so they would just as soon, if they are lending securities to a dealer, lend for collateral and a borrowing fee of 50 basis points. That fee is split between the bank and the bank's customer.

While banks have taken the lead in securities lending, they have preferred to do business as *agent for an undisclosed third party* rather than disclose to the dealer what portfolio is on the other side of the transaction. One motive a bank has for doing this is that it does not want a dealer, who has borrowed securities from one of its custody customers, to go directly to that customer should the dealer need those same securities a second time. A bank could achieve the same objective by acting as principal in the transaction, but a number of banks have been unwilling to accept the full responsibility for the risks to them that would be inherent in their securities-lending business if they acted as a principal. This situation has made some dealers—post the Drysdale failure, which involved big borrowings of securities and big losses—cautious about which banks they will deal with when they either lend or borrow securities.

Coupon interest and full accrual pricing

Whenever securities pass temporarily, either via a reverse or a borrowing, from one party to another, the current market practice is to price those securities at market plus accrued interest: to use what is called *full accrual pricing* in setting the terms on which particular securities are exchanged either for money or for other securities. If it happens that during the holding period, a coupon date occurs, the coupon interest is paid to the temporary holder of the securities who is obligated to pass on that interest to the true owner of the securities. Normally, after a

coupon payment, the transaction is repriced so that the originally agreed-upon haircut is maintained. These arrangements are designed to minimize credit risk.

Which to do and why

Some years ago, the market swung in favor of reverse RPs over borrowing securities. The primary advantage of a reverse over a borrowing of securities is that a reverse is operationally simpler: A reverse requires only *one* delivery of securities, whereas a borrowing requires *two* deliveries. Still, both types of transactions commonly occur depending on the particular circumstances under which a deal is struck.

Normally, an investor dealing directly with a dealer won't want to go to the bother and cost of doing a reverse unless he can pick up at least 50 basis points on the deal. Often, an investor holding securities has an arbitrage lined up where he expects to get at least a 50-basis-point spread between the rate at which he borrows money from the dealer and the rate at which he can invest that money. Such an investor will want to reverse out, rather than lend, securities to a dealer. In the other cases, the investor says, "Give me collateral, not money, and I'll take my 50 basis points as a fee." Some investors won't do reverses because they lack reinvestment capabilities and don't, therefore, want cash.

Some investors are set up both to reverse out and to lend securities. They will go the reverse route if the spread on the arb is more than 50 basis points. If it is not, they will go the securities-lending route.

A dealer wanting to cover his shorts must be prepared to go both ways, to reverse in securities or to borrow them. How a given deal is struck involves both an investor, who holds securities, and a dealer, who wants securities, responding to relative rates and to availability in deciding what they want to do.

Since a lot of borrowing of securities by dealers is done to prevent "fails to receive" from creating "fails to deliver," a lot of dealers borrow securities from other dealers 10 minutes before the close of the wire or during the reversal period.

THE NEXT CHAPTER

In the next chapter, we describe in detail some key topics that we have, up to now, mentioned only cursorily: dealer safekeeping, third-party custody, and tri-party RPs.

Dealer safekeeping, tri-party RP, and third-party custody

IN THIS CHAPTER, WE DESCRIBE VARIOUS ARRANGEMENTS under which a customer of a dealer may choose to hold securities: in dealer safekeeping, in a tri-party RP if the securities are repo collateral, and in a bank custody account. We describe, first, traditional market practices and then, at the end of the chapter, certain modifications in these practices required as a result of regulations implemented in 1987 by the Treasury pursuant to the 1986 Government Securities Act.

DEALER SAFEKEEPING: PRE-1987

Sometimes customers, instead of taking delivery of securities they buy or of repo collateral, leave their securities with their dealer for safekeeping. Many, if not the majority, of major losses that have occurred in connection with dealer bankruptcies have occurred in connection with dealer safekeeping, a controversial but common practice.

Reasons for dealer safekeeping

Some, but not all, dealers offer to safekeep securities for customers at no charge. One reason a dealer may do this is to nurture customer

relationships by providing his customers, at no cost to them, a service that they would otherwise have to buy. A second reason some dealers prefer, on overnight RPs, to safekeep customer securities, especially physical GNMAs, is that delivery would, relative to the interest paid on the RP, be costly to both parties. A third reason some dealers prefer to safekeep customer securities is risk of a subsequent fail. Dealers reason, "If I deliver out, as collateral for an overnight RP, $10 million of bills to XYZ Corp., I must worry about whether XYZ will return my collateral tomorrow in time for me to redeliver it to another RP customer or to an outright buyer. If, alternatively, I safekeep, overnight, for XYZ his collateral, I know that, tomorrow when my RP with XYZ comes off, I'll have my bills in time to make good delivery of them to another customer." Still a fourth reason why dealers like dealer safekeeping is that, under this arrangement, it is the dealer, not the customer, who will profit if the dealer is *failed to* on a delivery of securities that he [the dealer] has promised to safekeep for the customer. In this case, the dealer will honor his promise to safekeep his customer's securities only when those securities finally come in, which may be a day, or many days, after his trade with the customer settles.

Exempt versus regulated securities

In discussing dealer safekeeping, it is important to distinguish between regulated and exempt securities. The SEC legislation passed in the 1930s brought under federal regulation trading in corporate stocks and bonds, but not trading in most money market instruments. Today's roster of *exempt securities* comprises government and federal agency securities, BAs, CDs, commercial paper with an original maturity of 270 days or less, and municipal securities. Regulation of municipal securities, introduced in 1975, is carried out by the Municipal Securities Rulemaking Board (MSRB), not the SEC.

Regulated securities. Any broker/dealer who deals in *regulated* securities is required by Rules 15c2-1 and 15c3-3 of the Securities Exchange Act of 1934 and by Article III Section 19(d) of the Rules of Fair Practice of NASD to hold all fully paid-for securities that he safekeeps for customers in a denominated, segregated account in which the customer is afforded significant protection. In particular, a broker/dealer holding securities in such an account may neither hypothecate nor negotiate such securities unless he is specifically instructed by the customer to do so. Also, a customer who holds fully paid-for securities with a regulated broker/dealer for safekeeping may, at any time, demand immediate delivery of those securities. Normally, a dealer will maintain a safekeeping account for customer securities at his clearing bank, either

in the clearance area or in the custody area. A dealer who does so must, to ensure that he can meet a customer's demands for securities, create, for each security not in his actual custody, records that indicate both where the security is located and how it may be identified as belonging to a specific customer. Also, a dealer must ensure that his records match customers with their securities and that his clearing bank employs a system that permits retrieval of each security upon a customer's request.

Margined securities held by a regulated broker/dealer for a customer are afforded less protection. A broker/dealer may hold such securities in his clearance account and he may hypothecate them; this makes sense, since the principal way broker/dealers get the cash necessary to finance their customers' margin accounts is by borrowing against the securities that their customers buy on margin.

Exempt securities.   Prior to the passage of the Government Securities Act (GSA) of 1986, firms that dealt solely in exempt securities, including the GSI subsidiaries (Government Securities, Inc., subs) that some broker/dealers created to deal in exempt securities, did not have to register with the SEC, or with anyone, for that matter. Moreover, most SEC rules arising out of the 1934 Act, with the exception of the antifraud provisions of this Act, did not apply to such firms. SEC rules with respect to the safekeeping of customer securities did not apply to firms dealing in exempt securities. Passage of GSA changed this.

Operation of dealer safekeeping

Dealers who dealt solely in exempt securities and who offered dealer safekeeping could and did use various arrangements for holding customer securities. Some such firms, mainly smaller ones, simply held customer securities in their clearing account. This tack saved a dealer money, because a clearing bank charges a fee each time a dealer moves securities either from his clearing account to his safekeeping account or vice versa. (The fee for such a transfer is approximately two-thirds of the normal clearing fee for wireables, much less than two-thirds of the normal clearing fee for physicals.)

Despite the fees that a dealer incurs when he opens a safekeeping account for customer securities, most unregulated dealers who were, prior to 1986, safekeeping securities for customers did have a safekeeping account at their clearing bank. Under the most typical arrangement, the dealer was and still is free to move securities into and out of this account at will. The clearing bank had and still has *no* information about which customers' securities are in the dealer's safekeeping account; the clearing bank knows the account solely as one of several accounts the dealer maintains and over which he exercises *sole* control.

Dealer safekeeping of this ilk is referred to as *trust-me* safekeeping; to give customers a greater level of comfort, some dealers in exempt securities have set up customer safekeeping accounts that contain various safeguards akin to those associated with safekeeping accounts maintained by broker/dealers who deal in regulated securities. If there is one generalization that holds about the safekeeping practices followed by dealers in exempt securities, it is that these practices *did lack and still do lack uniformity.*

Clearing bank responsibilities

We said above that, when a dealer in exempt securities sets up at his clearing bank a safekeeping account, that account is under the dealer's sole control—the fact that the account bears the title "for the sole benefit of customers" notwithstanding. Moreover, the dealer's clearing bank has *no responsibility under securities law* to police movements of securities into and out of that account. Since the latter point has been the subject of several suits and a source of misunderstanding to many investors, the point is worth restating with emphasis.

With respect to a clearing bank's responsibilities, a Washington securities lawyer, formerly with the SEC, noted, "We've done work in connection with a major dealer bankruptcy and have gotten into this. Independent of any regulation, the government securities dealer, through contractual relationships with the clearing entity, works out some kind of arrangement to safekeep securities. From that standpoint, some obligations [on the part of the clearing bank] may be created by contract law, but *I have come across nothing, in what I've read or seen, where those obligations were required by securities laws."*

A respected clearing banker seconded this opinion by describing, with the following example, what he thinks are his responsibilities: "Suppose that the first transaction a dealer ever does with us occurs when $1 million of bonds come into his account and $1 million of cash goes out. We've got a $1 million cash overdraft, but we've got $1 million of collateral in the dealer's account. The dealer then tells us that he sold those very same securities to a customer and would we be good enough to move them from his dealer account to that customer's account. We would do it only when and if he funded that $1 million shortfall in cash. Now, assume that he did, that he took the $1 million the customer paid him and paid us. We would cover his overdraft with the cash, and, thereafter, we'd view his security as excess collateral; we'd put it anywhere he told us to put it. If he told us to put it into a safekeeping account held exclusively for the benefit of his customers, but not specifically for the account of customer XYZ, we'd be happy to do that. If, on the next day, he [the dealer] gave us instructions to take $500,000 of those securities

from the customer [safekeeping] account and put it back into his dealer account, we would absolutely do it without question.

"In the clearing environment, we operate on a value-for-value basis. We would hesitate moving a security from a dealer's account to a safekeeping account if, in fact, we had a lien on those securities. That's the only way we would object."

Meaning to a customer of dealer safekeeping: Exempt securities

In discussing the meaning of dealer safekeeping to a customer, it's important to distinguish between what a customer thinks he is getting and what he is actually getting—the two often differ totally. Many customers who utilize the safekeeping facilities offered by dealers in exempt securities are small and unsophisticated.

The customer's view.   The small money market investor who leaves securities with his dealer for safekeeping typically underestimates the resulting credit risk. He often thinks that dealer safekeeping means that his securities are tucked off somewhere safe for him and that they will, under *all* circumstances, always be there whenever he wants them.

Many small investors also have—their depositions in dealer bankruptcy cases so indicate—the notion that dealer safekeeping must generate some paper trail outside the dealership. In particular, such investors, if they deal in book-entry securities, often think that the Fed must have a record of what securities have been delivered on their behalf over the Fed wire. Such investors also often think that the dealer's clearing bank must have a record of what securities the dealer is holding at that bank in safekeeping for them.

The truth: trust me.   In truth, dealer safekeeping is a *trust-me* arrangement. It generates no customer-specific records outside the dealership. Consequently, regardless of what a dealer does with a customer's securities—place them in a safekeeping account, place them in his clearing account, hypothecate them, or sell them—his act is, from the customer's point of view, an *unverifiable* event.

Should the customer who believes otherwise go to the Fed, he will find that the Fed has *no* record of its having moved securities from Bank X to Bank Y to be placed in a dealer safekeeping account for the customer's benefit. As noted, the only information in a securities wire with which the Fed concerns itself is (1) what securities are to move, (2) from what bank to what bank they are to move, and (3) what money, if any, is to move.

If the customer asks the dealer's clearing bank for information concerning securities being held by his dealer in safekeeping for him, he

will probably receive, as have a number of investors, a letter telling him to direct his request for information to his dealer. Generally, this is all a clearing bank can do, since it has *no* information as to which of a dealer's customers hold which of the securities that the dealer may have in its safekeeping account at the bank.

Since neither the Fed nor the clearing bank maintain any paper trail that would indicate where the customer's securities are, the only way the customer can find this out is to ask the dealer. If the dealer says the customer's securities are at the dealer's clearing bank, the customer is back where he started—with a trust-me arrangement with his dealer.

Since dealer safekeeping is an unverifiable arrangement, any investor who leaves securities with a dealer has made the risk equivalent of an unsecured loan to that dealer.

Fraud associated with dealer safekeeping

In recent years, a string of dealer bankruptcies has shaken the government market. The list of firms no longer with us includes the following somewhat familiar names: Drysdale Government Securities, Lombard-Wall, Lion Capital Group, Comark, RTD Securities, E.S.M. Government Securities, and the Bevill Bresler and Schulman Group. While not all of these firms used precisely the same techniques for getting their fingers into other people's pockets, a number of them discovered that unverifiable dealer safekeeping combined with the trusting nature of many of their smaller customers provided them with an easy means of generating, via various frauds, hundreds of millions of dollars to enhance their capital and eventually to cover their cumulative trading losses—losses that each firm had and that each firm earnestly prayed would vanish, if not today, then tomorrow.

It has been suggested that a few sharp souls migrated to the government market to become dealers primarily because the opportunity to combine doing repos against governments with unverifiable safekeeping of customer securities provided them an irresistible opportunity to steal. However, it is more likely that no dealer in government securities ever set up shop specifically to make a living from defrauding his customers. Probably in every or almost every case, a dealer who eventually engaged in fraud started out intending to make money running an honest business; then, due to his incompetence and/or to a few unfortunate bets he made on the market, he lost money and ended up broke or worse. At that point, he succumbed to the temptation to reason, "I'm bankrupt at the moment, *but,* if I just borrow from customers for a little while, I can recoup my losses." And, thus, started the fraud, the creative accounting, and the deceit. Noted one dealer, "Covering up widespread

fraud is such a time-consuming and troublesome chore that it's hard to believe that any dealer would, in a market where it's possible to make money honestly, choose, except under duress, to be dishonest."

BEYOND TRUST-ME REPO

Large, profitable, well-capitalized dealers have sought some means whereby they could minify the deliveries associated with RPs—especially in situations where the pieces serving as collateral were small—and yet give their customers a far greater degree of assurance and safety than that provided by straight dealer safekeeping.

Letter RP

Letter RP, a form of nondelivery RP, is one way some big houses on the Street have sought to achieve operational efficiencies and yet provide safety to customers.[1] An operations person at one major dealer—a Cadillac credit—described how his firm got into letter RP. "Ten years ago, when we did RP it was always DVP, and delivery on a repo was just like delivery on an outright sale. Typically, at the end of the day, we had very large money amounts of securities in small pieces. We used to dump that stuff into a bank loan at the end of the day, which was expensive. Then one of our guys said, 'Why can't we repo this stuff without having to do all of this paper work?' So we devised a way to generate, via a computer, a confirm to a customer, but without writing a trade report—it was a different system.

"Today, the way our system works is that we enter into our computer all day the dollar values of the letter RPs customers want to do with us; the computer knows what classes of securities each customer will accept. At 3:30 or 4 P.M., we press a button and say, 'OK computer, allocate.' The computer spits out confirms to customers and instructions to our clearing bank. The bank then takes the collateral we have assigned to letter repo and moves it out of our clearing account into a customer safekeeping account.

"We know that our bank knows that the collateral is pledged to a customer as part of a letter repo. We next make up a letter of confirmation to each [letter] repo customer, slap onto it a listing of paper the collateralizing his repo, and then send that confirm off in the mail to the customer. When the customer gets his paper confirm, he reads that, on Monday, he lent us $100 million and that this was the collateral. The

---

[1]Every firm calls letter repo something else. Some call it a due bill, others call it hold-in-custody repo, and still others call it a premise repo.

customer can use that document to go back to the bank and ask if that collateral was really in our customer safekeeping account. Occasionally, customers send in an audit guy to do just that.

"The paper work on the sales desk is quite similar for delivery and for nondelivery repo, but there's a big difference in the back-office work associated with the two. The collateral behind a letter repo may be in our own vault rather than at our clearing bank. So we have customers' auditors waltzing, now and then, into our vault as well as into our bank."

Tracking OPM.   In the course of the many different transactions that dealers do with different customers, they sometimes end up temporarily holding for various reasons customers' money. To avoid the temptation to use *other people's money* (*OPM*) to lever their own operations and also to minimize the opportunity for employees to be tempted to engage in hard-to-detect thefts of such money, tightly run shops go to considerable lengths to hold down the amount of OPM that they hold. For example, in a shop that is a big Ginnie Mae trader, unclaimed interest on Ginnies (Chapter 18) can build up to a significant sum unless the dealer goes to extreme lengths to get rid of it. To clean up unclaimed pass-through interest, a dealer may, when the problem gets out of hand, request that his operations people put in overtime and direct them to use that time, first, to figure out whose interest he is holding and, second, to request of those people that they claim all monies due them. Inefficiencies in the back office of one dealer can lead to a build up, at other shops, of OPM owed to the lax dealer.

Speaking of this problem, one operations person said, "We keep a record called OPM, other people's money, so that our cashier knows the total of it that we have from all sources. In years gone by, whenever we ended up with customers' money for any reason, we always collateralized it. We never allowed a dollar of customers' money to get into our pipeline. We never wanted to overleverage ourselves. We wanted to be assured that the only capital we were using was the firm's own money. When securities were all physical, we used to sit up until 8 P.M. doing that [collateralizing OPM]. As we got computerized and more sophisticated, we continued the same policy. So did the other major dealers. We all have the same mentality." Note the sharp contrast between this mentality and that of some of the smaller dealers who failed; those dealers did not seem to think that they had to collateralize individual trades.

Letter RP and OPM.   A problem with letter repo is that it tends, in the morning of each business day, to generate in a dealer's shop large balances of OPM in a fashion that makes the regulators less than fully happy. Regulators, who have been concerned about repo because of all the losses to repo customers that arose out of recent dealer bankruptcies

have no problem with letter repo as described above. Their problem is with what occurs the morning the repo comes off. At the time, the dealer takes all of the securities he has used to collateralize letter repo back into his free box—he needs it to conduct his business. If simultaneously his customers were to get all of their money back, the regulators would be happy. Sometimes this occurs, because the customer wants his money back first thing in the morning. More often, however, the customer does not know what he wants to do with his money. He may think that he'll probably want to do another repo, but must wait to decide the dollar value of that repo until later in the day. It may be 1 P.M. before the dealer has instructions from the customer either to pay the guy his money or to do a new repo. If the instruction is to do a new repo, that information goes back to the dealer's computer and waits for collateral to be allocated.

The fact that a dealer doing big letter repos ends up holding, intraday, uncollateralized customer monies gives the SEC fits. They view RP collateral as fully paid-for customer securities and have argued, on the basis of rules designed to protect customers investing in equities, that the dealers should not be doing what they are doing, which, if they were handling equities, they would be specifically prohibited from doing. A dealer's response to this is, "Hey, wait a minute. I have not got customer securities. This is a financing transaction."

Note that repo has never been defined in law. The law talks about securities transactions and about loans; it is silent on RPs. Since RPs have certain of the characteristics of a collateralized loan and certain of the characteristics of a securities transaction, they are in truth a sort of legal jackass: part horse (securities transaction) and part donkey (collateralized loan). In one securities case after another, lawyers for the opposing parties have argued *position one:*

Repo is a securities transaction because the key *indicia* [legalese for characteristics] of repos are those of a securities transaction.

versus *position two:*

Repo is a collateralized loan because the key *indicia* of a repo are those of a collateralized loan.

Credit Risk in Letter Repo.   It is true that a customer doing letter repo has less certainty than one taking delivery of his collateral that his collateral is really all there all the time. Perhaps being able to verify that one's collateral was in fact there after the fact, the next morning, smacks of being a touch too late to assure 100% safety, but, at some point, one must recognize that managers of major portfolios make unsecured loans all the time to top-rated—by Moody's, Standard & Poor's, and Fitch— companies, financial and nonfinancial, by investing in commercial paper,

which is nothing other than short-term, unsecured corporate IOUs. Who is to say that these same sophisticated investors should not also make unsecured, short-term (typically overnight) loans to world-class, highly capitalized dealers so long as they have their eyes open, know what they are doing, and have the inclination and resources to examine the credit? Here's how trouble has erupted, again and again in the past: A small investor—who would not dream of making an unsecured loan to some small outfit, say, Widget Inc. down the street—merrily lends, in effect, on an unsecured basis to some small dealer, who probably hasn't been around very long and whom the small investor doesn't know very well, $10 or $20 million on the basis of some outdated and well-window-dressed financials.

Tri-party RPs

A second way big dealers seek to do nondelivery RPs—while at the same time providing the customer full assurance that his collateral is there, backing his repo, when it is supposed to be—is by doing *tri-party repos*.

It is becoming increasingly common for large investors to negotiate with their dealer and with their dealer's clearing bank tri-party repo agreements in which the clearing bank not only knows both sides of a repo transaction, but holds the repo collateral put up by the dealer in custody for the investor for the life of the repo. Such an agreement has several advantages. It obviates the need for delivery of collateral, while protecting the interests of the investor whose credit risk becomes that of a major bank rather than that of the dealer. A tri-party RP also reduces the clearing costs associated with a large repo and makes substitution of collateral on such a repo cheaper and simpler for both the dealer and the investor.

On a tri-party RP, the dealer pays the clearing bank a fee, but the investor does not. Typically, tri-party RPs are done for large sums; such RPs may amount to a billion or more when the investor is a money fund.

Big investors, who do tri-party RPs, may and sometimes do send their auditors around to check whether the clearing bank has in fact segregated their collateral. On such an RP, the dealer's collateral does not come back to him until he repays his loan from the investor.

Operations people at dealers that make use of tri-party repos tend to be very happy with the arrangement. Said one, "Merrill makes a lot of use of the tri-party RP agreement that Manny offers. We think Manny's approach is terrific. It cuts the amount of securities that have to be shipped. In such a repo, Manny always knows who the customer is, since all three parties must sign the same agreement and thus must know who their counterparties are. When such a deal is done, first there are negotia-

tions, perhaps for several months among the lawyers. Once the paper is signed, trades can occur.

"For Merrill to do a tri-party repo with Portfolio XYZ, both Merrill and XYZ would have to open an account with Manny. Manny is fully responsible for the operation of the agreement, and they are responsible that repos done under the agreement are fully collateralized—they are pretty strict about that too.

"If we do an overnight repo, Manny will, at the end of the day, move say $200 million of collateral over to XYZ's account with them and whatever collateral is needed to cover the haircut. At the same time, they will move $200 million of cash from XYZ's account to Merrill's account. The first thing they do the next day at 9 A.M., is to move back the collateral and the money to the accounts from which they were taken. Tri-party repo is very clean and very simple. There are no big deliveries involved.

"From the client's point of view, the good points are that they get a slightly higher rate and they are not subject to collateral changes that might otherwise occur during the day. On a straight repo for $200 million, Merrill might give the client 10 different issues; and, if sometime during the day, one of these issues were sold by one of Merrill's traders, Merrill would have to substitute. When a dealer who assigns collateral in the morning must make deliveries, substitutions become a real possibility. That is a nuisance. With a tri-party agreement, neither party has to worry about this so long as they trust Manny. The savings we realized on wires are reflected in the rate that the client gets. Also, the arrangement is much cleaner for the client. He does not have to be on the phone all morning getting lists of collateral because he knows that Manny will send him a nice clean list the following morning telling him what securities collateralized his RP. The whole arrangement is clean, simple, and safe."

The importance of tri-party RPs to major dealers is indicated by the comment of one such dealer, "Yesterday we cleared, exclusive of pairoffs, $14 billion of securities over the wire versus payment, and we did another $4–5 billion of tri-party financing."

THIRD-PARTY CUSTODY

The alternative to dealer safekeeping that large portfolio managers typically use, except perhaps when they do letter RP or tri-party RP, is to hire a *custodial agent* (always a bank with access to the Fed wire) to hold their securities and to clear their trades. Recall our example (Chapter 10) in which Ford used Morgan to hold its securities in custody and to clear its trades. This approach, which totally eliminates the portfolio manager's credit risk vis-à-vis the dealer, costs money; it also involves, relative to dealer safekeeping, extra steps for both the portfolio manager and the dealer.

The agreement and the mechanics

Institutional investors that aren't depository institutions cannot hold book-entry securities themselves, and most of them don't, for various reasons, want to hold physical securities themselves. Thus large, sophisticated investors, financial (e.g., life insurance companies and money funds) and nonfinancial, use an agent bank or banks to clear their securities trades, to hold securities for them, and to collect and credit to their accounts monies due them when the securities they own pay interest or dividends or, in the case of fixed-income securities, when they mature.

An investor wanting to use an agent bank begins by negotiating and signing a lengthy and complex agreement with a major bank (or several such banks); in this agreement, the investor and the bank stipulate that the bank shall act as the investor's clearing and custodial agent for various securities and that, in doing so, the bank shall assume various responsibilities. As part of the agreement, the bank also stipulates that it will indemnify the investor should it lose the customer's securities, should a bank employee steal the customer's securities, or whatever. Banks that do custody business carry *bankers' blanket bond insurance* to cover any losses they might incur due to this commitment. The amount of such insurance carried by a big money center bank is probably several hundred million dollars. Currently, bankers' blanket bond insurance is difficult to get, and some banks have to take high deductibles to obtain it.

To get around the we-need-a-corporate-board-resolution-to-sell-registered-securities problem, a corporate investor who uses a custodial agent often issues to that agent a standing instruction directing it to transfer any registered securities the corporation buys into the name of the nominee created and used by that agent. The nominee arrangement for registration applies only to a limited range of securities; it is not used for governments and most money market instruments.

From the point of view of the investor, registering a security owned by the investor in the name of a nominee is much like decking such a security with a *transparent veil;* the investor would never notice the name or even the existence of the nominee if he did not otherwise know that it existed. When he trades securities in street name, the investor operates in precisely the same way, and with precisely the same ease and speed of execution, that he would if he were trading bearer or book-entry securities.

Actually, holding a security, registered in street name, at a custodian gives an investor one important advantage: He gets the cash payments thrown off by that security faster than he would if the security were registered in his name. On securities registered in street name, the issuer transfers to the nominee, on a coupon or other payment date, *good*

(*immediately available*) funds equal in amount to the sum due on whatever of his securities the nominee holds. These funds are immediately credited to the custodial agent which in turn credits them to the accounts of the beneficial owners of these securities. Consequently, an investor who holds bonds in street name will, for example, get good funds on a coupon date. If the investor held, alternatively, the same securities in his own name, he would, before he got good funds, have to wait for the issuer's check to arrive in the mail, then deposit that check in his bank account, and finally wait for that check to clear. For an investor who has hundreds of millions of dollars invested in physical, registered securities, getting good funds on the date a payment is due is worth real money.

An aside: The book-entry system is set up so that, on each coupon date, holders of Treasury notes and bonds in book-entry form should, assuming no computer glitches, have credited to their bank accounts good funds equal in amount to any coupon interest owed them. If the coupon date is the 15th, the Treasury takes the holder of record of the securities to be the entity that held that security as of the close of the Fed wire on the 14th. Actual coupon payments are made, by the Fed on behalf of Treasury, in Fed funds the morning of the 15th.

Speed of execution

With respect to bank custody, it is important to note that an agent bank is not a clearing bank with a guaranteed two-minute turnaround time. A custody officer at a New York bank commented, "Sometimes Canadian dealers will try to use custody accounts with us like clearance accounts. We miss several times and they get very irate. We tell them that, if securities get into their accounts before noon, we will deliver out those securities before 2:30 P.M., but only on a best efforts basis. Our bank opens *custody accounts* for customers. If a bank opens a *clearing account* for a customer, that bank is on the hook; it must meet its performance guarantee [with respect to speed of execution] or eat the fail."

Cost of custody

Custodial fees vary from bank to bank. At one New York money center bank, fees are approximately as follows: $1,500 a year to open an account, go through the legal documentation, and obtain an account number; $30 a year per issue to hold wireable securities at the Fed or at DTC (the next chapter explains DTC); $75 a year to hold a physical item; $20 to wire in or deliver out a wireable security; and $45 to receive or deliver a physical security. The $1,500 fee covers a report that the bank prepares for the customer's portfolio showing interest income, dividend income, capital gains and losses on securities transactions—everything

an accountant would need for financial reporting purposes. For a further fee, the bank would do other analyses of the customer's portfolio that the customer desired.

It is hard to say what total amount of customer fees a portfolio will incur because that depends on what bank it uses (some banks have lower fee schedules than the one cited above), on how big the portfolio is and on how many issues it holds, on how actively the portfolio is traded, and so on.

An important point to make is that the fees we have just cited are fees that a major portfolio that used as its custodial agent a money center bank would pay. A smaller regional account would be better off using as its custodial agent a regional bank. On this point, a New York bank custody officer noted, "Say I am the Alamo S&L in New Galos, Texas. I could have a custody account with a Houston bank. The Houston bank would have its own account with the Fed to hold wireable securities; it would also have an account with DTC to hold corporate securities. However, to hold [nondepository-eligible] physical securities, the Houston bank would have to have a custody account with a New York bank.

"Probably, it would be a little cheaper for the Alamo S&L to use the Houston bank as its custody agent than to use a New York bank; Alamo S&L would not be coming into New York with big positions, and there are economies of scale for a New York bank in providing custody services, economies of scale that are reflected in the bank's pricing. The big thing that Alamo would get, however, by using a Houston bank rather than a New York bank as its custody agent would be more personalized service. If Alamo used a Houston bank, they would have an account officer right there in Houston, which is maybe only 100 miles from New Galos. Alamo would get attention from the Houston bank in part because they would probably have other business with that bank. They would have more clout with the Houston bank and therefore get better service. Alamo needs only one thing in New York, custody of physicals. If they choose a New York custody agent, who will visit them? Why would a New York bank pay attention to them given their small volume? Who at the New York bank would they call? They would have at a New York bank no account officer who would really make an effort to give them good service.

"Alamo, however, needs and gets other services locally: checking accounts, money transfer accounts, and so on. In the Texas area, Alamo is probably a pretty big account. Chances are the Houston bank is providing Alamo with a whole raft of correspondent banking services. When Alamo calls the Houston bank, it knows who they are. Alamo is a big deal to that bank. If Alamo has a problem with a physical security ("Why didn't a GNMA get delivered?"), the Houston bank will call its New York agent for whom it is a big customer and get attention to that question. *For a smaller account, the big difference that results from the choice*

of a local rather than a New York custody agent is the difference in service, not the difference in cost."

Safety of bank custody

An overriding concern of all large, sophisticated portfolio managers who open bank custodial accounts is safety for their valued securities, and such safety is precisely what they think bank custody affords them. With third-party custody, as opposed to dealer safekeeping, the investor gets a separate custodial account and clear identification of the securities in that account as his. A dealer safekeeping account, in contrast, is typically of an omnibus-type nature. Moreover, the clearing bank's contractual relationships run solely to the dealer, so the clearing bank is, in effect, circumscribed in what duties it presumably owes to the ultimate owners of the securities in that account.

The manager of a major U.S. corporate portfolio, who's a most conservative fellow, explains what he believes are the safeguards of bank custody: "When I enter into a custodial-agency agreement with say Chase or Citi, that bank acts, under that agreement, as a fiduciary for me. They examine the authenticity of the securities upon advice from me, confirmed in writing; they also will act only on my specific instructions. If I tell them that I expect $100 million in government repo coming in from dealer X, they will not pay out until that occurs. The principal reason I like to have an agency bank is that it will be fully responsible for the validity of the securities and, also, will disburse funds, in accordance with our agreement, only after the securities have been examined, found to be in good form, and identified as being in fact what we described. They [the bank] look at the securities and then pay out funds on the basis of delivery.

"I have never left securities with a dealer for three reasons: (1) I don't know whether the dealer actually has the securities or not; (2) if the dealer is trading these securities actively, my account may never be credited with these securities: and (3) I have found that, due to the frequency of fails in repo, dealers often don't have securities to deliver to customers because they've been failed to themselves. When a dealer fails on an RP with us, we have the use of the funds *and* the dealer is required to pay us interest; we end up being double invested because the dealer pays me and we still have the funds."

The same portfolio manager continued, "At the least, I require dealers to make delivery. It's not because of the opportunity to double dip, but because I want to be sure funds are not paid out against nothing. I feel this way because, *regardless of who the dealer is, regardless of what the SEC says about them,* I want to have my own agent physically involved in the collection of the securities, the holding of the securities for my

account, and then the disbursing of funds in accordance with the delivery of the securities.

With respect to credit risk vis-à-vis the custody bank, our conservative portfolio manager observed, "Should my bank, as fiduciary agent, go belly-up, where do I stand? Well, I have a trust arrangement with the bank whereby the securities are segregated assets of the bank. While this point may not have been tested in court, I feel that under the agreement contemplated in our agency agreement, namely, physical delivery of the securities and housing in a separate area in the bank—in the bank vaults, segregated for customer accounts—that these securities clearly are not part of the bank's portfolio. The bank statements I get are produced by a trust department. The trust department laws and the laws of fiduciary would confirm that these securities would never be commingled with the bank's, and, if they were, inadvertently, commingled, we could clearly identify the portion of the securities that belonged to us. If they [my securities] were commingled [with the bank's] in the event of fraud, we would still have to fall back on our fiduciary contract with the bank. Under the 'Chinese Wall' that the banks must observe, segregating trust assets from bank assets, we would have a case against our bank for the delivery of the securities. In a fiduciary type of agreement, lawyers take care to assure that the bank is on the hook in the event of any sort of fraud.

"A bank can get away with minor things that are not the bank's fault. In all my experiences, without question, I have never had to ask a bank to make funds available; the bank has always done so on its own initiative. Our securities, unbeknownst to me, may have been misplaced, stolen, etc., but we have never noticed it because the bank, in fulfilling its contractual obligations, has always credited our account. Our agreement provides that we secure immediate payment when payment is due. Back in the 70s, it was quite scandalous with all the securities fails and losses. During that time, there never was a day when our account was not credited when we expected it to be. With our agreement, we are fairly well isolated from day-to-day mismanagement."

A super worry bug might go on to ask, What if, due to some terrible mismanagement, fraud, or whatever, a custody bank failed and somehow took its trust area down with it? The answer is that most major portfolio managers use a big (top 25) bank as a custody bank, and the general view is that the Fed is the de facto guarantor of any such bank. If such a bank were allowed to fail with major losses to depositors, not to speak of custody customers, everyone would have a lot to worry about.

Who can afford custody?

Some smaller investors (banks, S&Ls, and municipal bodies) have the notion—so indicate their depositions in dealer bankruptcy

proceedings—that they cannot afford bank custody for their securities and that they therefore have no choice but to use dealer safekeeping. For an institution with even so little as $5 or $10 million of securities, not to speak of $40 million of securities (the amount of securities that the Worthen Bank was safekeeping with Bevill, Bresler and Schulman at the time of the latter's bankruptcy), to say that it cannot afford a few thousand dollars in custody fees makes *no* sense in the same way that it would make *no* sense for a New Yorker with a car and some other assets, which could be taken away from him in a liability suit, to say that car insurance in New York City, which is expensive, is not for him, but only for the Rockefellers and other big-buck boys.

THE GOVERNMENT SECURITIES ACT OF 1986

In 1975, Eldin Miller's Financial Corporation, a fledgling government securities dealer, went belly-up with estimated losses of $15 to $25 million to investors. At the time, the flap over this bankruptcy was so great that one could hope that some lessons had been learned: know thy counterparty in an RP; ensure that RPs and reverses are properly collateralized; and so on. Alas, memories are unfortunately short. A few years later, there were lots of new faces in the money market—*and* they were people who had never heard of Eldin Miller.

From the late-1970s on, when interest rates were often far higher and far more volatile than they had ever been, a number of smaller dealers—some new, some who had been around for awhile—went bankrupt with large losses to investors. It is estimated that the failure of Drysdale Government Securities in 1982 cost banks and investors $270 to $290 million, that the failure of Lombard-Wall, Inc. in 1982 cost investors $20 million, that the failure of Lion Capital Group in 1984 cost investors $40 million, that the failure of RTD securities in 1984 cost investors $1.7 million, that the failure of E.S.M. Government Securities in 1985 cost investors $300 million, and that the failure of Bevill, Bresler and Schulman in 1985 cost investors yet another $150 million.

These bankruptcies and others followed a variety of patterns. However, a reasonable generalization is that losses to customers typically resulted from one or both of several factors: (1) the failing firm treated securities, including RP collateral, that it was holding in safekeeping for customers loosely to say the least—sometimes such securities were hypothecated more than once, sometimes they were sold; and (2) the failing firm gave inadequate collateral to customers when it repoed securities out to customers and/or it demanded excessive collateral when it reversed in securities from customers.

It's important to note, with respect to the above failures, that no investor ever lost so much as a penny due to credit and other problems

at a major dealer. While the big boys may at times have lost a lot of money due to market turbulence, they stayed, to a man, squeaky clean in their dealings with customers. Another point to note is that, with the exception of the losses by Chase and several other N.Y. banks during the Drysdale bankruptcy (losses due, at least in the case of Chase, to an admitted failure of the bank's internal controls), no major investor or dealer lost a penny because of the bankruptcies we have listed. It was small investors—school districts, S&Ls, and so on—who saw their money vanish as small dealers in governments went down the tubes. The big, sophisticated players had all protected themselves by following old and respected rules of prudence. To the extent that they dealt at all with the second- or third-tier dealers that failed, the big players to a man had said, "We will buy securities from you, sell securities to you, and do RP with you, but only on a strictly DVP basis and on a basis of reasonable margin." It's hard for a market player to lose big bucks because of a dealer bankruptcy if his rules are: never give a dealer money except against securities due; never give him securities except against money due; and never do RPs and reverses with him except when margin is set and maintained at a reasonable level consistent with accepted market practices.

The Fed acts

Naturally, the problems we described briefly above raised a brouhaha in Washington and elsewhere. Despite the fact that recent bankruptcies of government securities dealers raised only a rather narrow issue—how to protect *smallish* investors from hanky panky by *smallish* dealers in exempt securities—cries went up for imposing new rules and regs on *all* dealers in governments.

The Fed took a crack at solving the perceived problem by coming up with complex "voluntary" guidelines on capital adequacy, which were supposed to apply to all dealers in governments except the primary dealers whose activities the Fed was already overseeing. The Fed's guidelines, which are extremely complex, require that a dealer maintain sufficient capital to cover (1) the credit risk of its receivables and (2) the market risk of its securities inventory where the latter is calculated, for different types of securities, on the basis of the historic volatility of the prices of those types of securities. This sounds reasonable: make a dealer back his holdings of a safe asset with 2% in capital, his holdings of a more risky asset with 5% of capital, and so on. There is, however, as a wise banker once noted, a fallacy in this approach: risk can be accurately gauged only *ex post*. A glance at how various money market participants have lost big (to them and to their regulators if they had them) sums of money suggests the truth in this dictum. In the early 1970s, thrifts lost money by selling GNMA puts because neither they nor their

regulators appreciated that this means of garnering *fee income* involved placing a risky bet on the direction of interest rates. Wiser firms have lost bundles learning the risks inherent in *new* products and, when markets were volatile and changing, in *old* products as well. If capital requirements alone sufficed to keep financial institutions afloat, a lot of now defunct banks and thrifts would still be around.

Congress acts

While the Fed was experimenting with new capital rules, Congress, in a typical political response, was debating what *it* should do about dealer bankruptcies. Despite the fact that only a narrow group of dealers had caused losses to investors—by lying about their financial strength, by double pledging securities in the repo market, by demanding excessive collateral on reverses, and by playing other games—Congress felt called upon to focus on the "great problems with respect to *unregulated* government securities dealers"—*all* of them.

After much debate and delay, Congress finally passed, in October 1986, the Government Securities Act of 1986. This act ostensibly fixes a lot of things, many of which were not broken in the first place.

The act requires a number of things. First, all government securities brokers and dealers except registered broker/dealers and financial institutions (domestic and foreign banks, and federally insured thrifts) are required to register with the SEC. Primary dealers as a class are not excepted from this registration requirement. Registered broker/dealers and financial institutions that deal in governments are required to file a notice with their appropriate regulatory agencies (ARAs).

Second, the act requires that the Secretary of the Treasury, in consultation with the SEC and the Fed, promulgate rules regarding the activities of brokers and dealers in governments. These rules relate principally to capital adequacy, custody and use of customer securities, the mechanics of repos and reverses, the carrying and use of customer deposits or credit balances, financial reporting, and recordkeeping.

Capital requirements

Under the new regulatory regime, broker/dealers who deal directly (not through a GSI) in governments will continue to be subject, as they were before, to the capital requirement imposed by the SEC under 15c3-1 of the Securities Exchange Act of 1934; banks that deal in governments will be subject to capital requirements imposed by bank regulators; and other dealers will be subject to new capital requirements fashioned by the Treasury, which used as its model the complex, voluntary capital guidelines created by the Fed for government securities dealers. SEC

capital requirements follow a different format than Treasury capital requirements, but one is not clearly more onerous than the other.

Financial reporting

Besides respecting a new net capital rule, dealers who were previously unregulated will now be required to have annual audits of their financial statements, a procedure that will be overseen by the National Association of Securities Dealers (NASD).

Repos, reverses, and safekeeping

Several things were done by the Treasury and the SEC in their regulations to pare the risks associated with repos and reverses. In particular, both the Treasury and the SEC imposed complex capital charges on repos and reverses. One purpose of these requirements was to create incentives to encourage dealers doing repos and reverses to operate as follows: collateral is to be reasonably priced; the amount of money that changes hands is to be a reasonable percentage of the collateral's market value; and, finally, margin calls are to be made if significant changes occur in that market value.

Also, under the new regs, a dealer, before doing repo with a customer, must send to the customer a written agreement that includes a specifically worded disclosure regarding the dealer's right to substitute collateral. A dealer must also send to a customer confirms on all transactions, including repos and reverses. Also, a dealer must segregate in a safekeeping account at his clearing bank and on his books any customer securities, including repo collateral, that he holds for customers. On hold-in-custody repos, a dealer, on his confirms to customers, is supposed to list collateral separately—he can no longer write "various." Also, he is supposed to state the market value of the securities that he is giving to the customer as collateral.

The difficulties that regulatory authorities experienced in setting up new regulations under the Government Securities Act of 1986 suggests that such regulations will be subject to evolution over time.

THE NEXT CHAPTER

In the next chapter, we turn to the issuance of commercial paper, a sort of intricate issuer-bank-dealer minuet that goes on each business day in New York City. We also discuss briefly the issuance of CDs and of municipal notes.

Chapter 15

Issuance of commercial paper notes and other money market paper

COMMERCIAL PAPER IS, RECALL CHAPTER 2, *unsecured,* short-term, corporate notes—in effect, IOUs of various corporations. The major issuers of commercial paper are industrial firms (who were the first issuers of such paper), finance companies, and bank holding companies. Many foreign entities also borrow in the U.S. commercial paper market, and so do some municipal bodies. Almost all commercial paper is rated with respect to credit, and most paper sold has a top rating, A1 or P1, from one of the rating agencies; investors in commercial paper are averse to credit risk. As a matter of practice, maturities at issue of commercial paper are very short, typically 30 days and under. Only occasionally is paper with longer original maturities sold; the frequent quoting of rates on 3- and 6-month paper notwithstanding, such long rates lack meaning because little or no business is done at them.

Today, the total amount of commercial paper outstanding in the U.S. market is approximately $320 billion (Table 15-1). That's about twice the dollar amount of such paper that was outstanding only four years ago. Growth in the commercial paper market has been and remains explosive.

TABLE 15-1
Commercial paper outstanding in January 1987 ($ billions)

All issuers	$336.9
Financial companies*	
Dealer-placed paper†	
Total	101.7
Bank-related	2.3
Directly placed paper‡	
Total	157.3
Bank-related	45.0
Nonfinancial companies§	78.0

*Institutions engaged primarily in activities such as, but not limited to, commercial, savings, and mortgage banking; sales, personal, and mortgage financing; factoring, finance leasing, and other business lending; insurance underwriting; and other investment activities.
†Includes all financial company paper sold by dealers in the open market.
‡As reported by financial companies that place their paper directly with investors.
§Includes public utilities and firms engaged primarily in activities such as communications, construction, manufacturing, mining, wholesale and retail trade, transportation, and services.
Source: *Federal Reserve Bulletin.*

Commercial paper is almost exclusively *bearer paper,* and transactions in such paper are normally settled same-day in Fed funds.[1]

DEALER PAPER

Today, about 55% of all commercial paper sold is placed through various dealers, the largest of which are Goldman, Merrill, Sali, First Boston, and Lehman.

The dealer

When a corporation decides to borrow in the commercial paper market, it must first choose a dealer. Typically, a corporation will issue all of its paper through a single, exclusive dealer. That dealer does several things for the issuer. First, the dealer, who is in close contact with market conditions, will each day advise the issuer, if the latter wants such advice, on what rates the issuer should post that day on the various maturities of his paper that he wants to sell. Second, the dealer will post the issuer's offerings—maturities, rates, and amounts—to his salespeople, who typically are located not just in a N.Y.C. office, but in regional offices around the country. The dealer's salespeople, who have contacts with

---

[1]The exceptions: Citibank's holding company issues some registered commercial paper. At issue, commercial paper is traded for same-day settlement, but a trade of such paper in the secondary market might be done for later settlement.

a wide range of investors, will then seek, via calls to investors, to sell the issuer's paper. Once sales of the issuer's paper are made, the dealer's third responsibility is to see to it that all such sales (trades) are cleared.

Each day, a dealer's final responsibility to an issuer may be to position any paper that the issuer tried but failed to sell that day. Generally, dealers are not keen to position paper. The attitude of a commercial paper dealer is typified by the following comment by a dealer, "We are like a candy store: we buy it [commercial paper], we sell it, we have *no* interest in owning it." However, if an issuer takes a dealer's advice in pricing his paper—sets what the dealer thinks are reasonable rates for reasonable amounts of paper, the dealer will agree, as part of his relationship with the issuer, to position any of the issuer's paper that remains unsold. The amounts involved are usually small, and the positions assumed are usually only overnight.

The issuing bank

A second important decision that an issuer of commercial paper must make is what bank it will use as its *issuing and paying agent*. Morgan, Citibank, Irving, Manny, Chase, Bankers Trust, and Chemical are biggest and best in the agent-banking business, but all of the 11 New York Clearing House banks do at least some of this business. So, too, do certain out-of-town banks, such as the Bank of America; such non-N.Y.C. banks all perform whatever agent-banking business they do out of offices located in downtown New York City.

Most issuers choose an agent bank on the basis of previous relationships with that bank. Noted one dealer, "We sometimes recommend several possible agent banks to a new client. The latter, however, will often pick some other bank with which it has had previous relationships."

The agent bank is responsible for printing up the issuer's notes as they are sold, for affixing a proper signature on each of these notes, and for then delivering the notes to the dealer or bank who is to clear sales of the issuer's paper. The agent bank is also responsible for collecting monies due for the paper it delivers out and for redeeming at maturity all paper issued through it.

A commercial paper note looks more like a check than a classy stock certificate. (See Figure 15-1, issuer, XYZ Corporation, issuing agent, Morgan Bank.)

The custody banks

With rare, if any, exceptions, commercial paper is delivered to the custody bank of the investor who buys it. Banks that are active in the custody-of-physical-securities business, N.Y.C. banks as well as of out-

FIGURE 15-1
Sample commercial paper note—issuer XYZ Corporation; issuing agent Morgan Bank

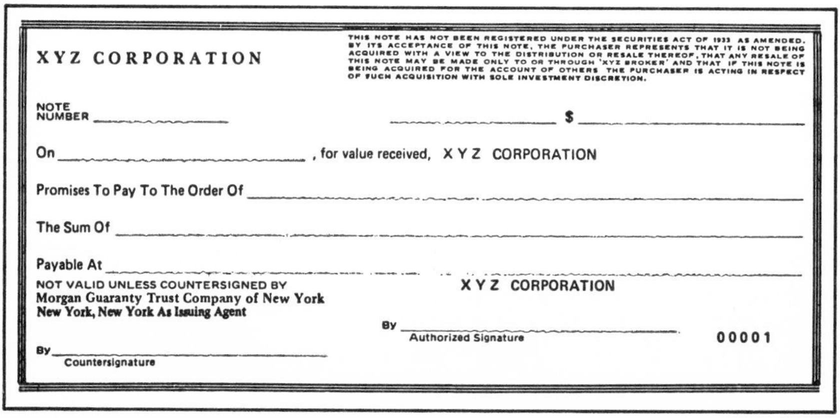

XYZ CORPORATION

THIS NOTE HAS NOT BEEN REGISTERED UNDER THE SECURITIES ACT OF 1933 AS AMENDED. BY ITS ACCEPTANCE OF THIS NOTE, THE PURCHASER REPRESENTS THAT IT IS NOT BEING ACQUIRED WITH A VIEW TO THE DISTRIBUTION OR RESALE THEREOF, THAT ANY RESALE OF THIS NOTE MAY BE MADE ONLY TO OR THROUGH 'XYZ BROKER' AND THAT IF THIS NOTE IS BEING ACQUIRED FOR THE ACCOUNT OF OTHERS THE PURCHASER IS ACTING IN RESPECT OF SUCH ACQUISITION WITH SOLE INVESTMENT DISCRETION.

NOTE NUMBER ______ ______ $ ______

On ______, for value received, X Y Z CORPORATION

Promises To Pay To The Order Of ______

The Sum Of ______

Payable At ______

NOT VALID UNLESS COUNTERSIGNED BY
Morgan Guaranty Trust Company of New York
New York, New York As Issuing Agent

By ______
Countersignature

X Y Z CORPORATION

By ______
Authorized Signature

00001

of-town banks—including the biggest custodian, Boston's State Street Bank—all do their custody business out of an operation located within the narrow confines of the downtown, N.Y.C. financial district: on Wall Street or a few blocks off it.

This results in a tidy arrangement: The big players in commercial paper—any dealers who self-clear, the agent banks, and the custody banks—are all located at the center of the market in downtown N.Y.C. Commercial paper is cleared in accordance with a tight set of cutoff times set by the New York Clearing House. To respect these cutoff times, the big players in commercial paper must be located within short, walking distances of each other. Said a Merrill operations person, "We will *not* deliver commercial paper outside of what is regarded as the Wall Street, downtown area, which may be all of one square mile."

The mechanics of issuance

The issuance of dealer paper, when it goes smoothly, is something like a well-choreographed dance with the full company on the stage. This has to be because so many players are involved: the issuer, his dealer, his agent banker, the investor, his custody bank, and usually a clearing bank.

The dealer's trader. An issuer who uses a dealer begins his day by consulting with that dealer about what amounts and maturities of paper he should issue and what rates he should post. The person with whom

he speaks is a *trader* who is responsible for one or more of the dealer's commercial paper accounts. This trader—the middleman between the issuer and the dealer—advises the issuer about what he thinks—given his close knowledge of the market and his perception of market's appetite for the issuer's paper—is reasonable for the issuer to do. Such advice is likely to depend on many variables, including how much paper the issuer has been putting into the market of late. When the paper that the issuer has decided to issue comes into the dealer's shop, it goes into the trader's position just as if he were a bill trader who had bought bills. From that point on, that paper is the trader's responsibility: The trader runs his own book, keeps his own P&L statement, and is judged on how profitable his activities are to the firm.

From early morning until around 12:30 P.M., the dealer's salespeople contact their many institutional accounts seeking to sell the issuer's paper. Each time a salesperson makes a sale, he will record the name of issuer, the amount, the maturity, the rate, the investor, and the custody bank to which the investor wants the paper delivered. This information is conveyed back to the trader, who must track his position, and to the issuer's agent bank, which is printing up the notes and delivering them to the party responsible for clearing the trade.

The issuer's agent bank. To illustrate the agent bank's role, let's use an example. Suppose that Chevron is the issuer, Merrill the dealer, Chase Manhattan the agent (issuing) bank. Early in the day, Chevron will have given Merrill its marching orders for the day: I want to sell, in each of these maturity ranges, these amounts of paper at these rates. That information also will have gone to Chevron's agent bank, Chase, so that Chase—actually its computer—can double check that no slip-up somewhere along the way causes paper to be issued that differs from what Chevron wants to issue.

As Merrill's salesforce places Chevron's paper, Merrill will call Chase, the issuing agent, and say, "We want to take down $100 million of paper today: these are the deal obligations, these are the maturities in which we want to see them, and so on." Merrill will give Chase all the specifics as to how the paper should be issued.

A dealer, like Merrill, can go to the issuer's agent bank in several ways. Until recently, the dealer would call the issuer or its agent and say, "I have sold $20 million maturing on date X; I want that paper in 20-by-1 or 4-by-5 pieces; and so on." Today, however, the large issuing agents such as Irving, Manny, and Chase have installed computer facilities that permit a dealer to dial up their computers and to transmit directly to those computers their issuing instructions. The bigger issuing banks sell this service aggressively.

The innovative dial-up system significantly simplifies the transmission of information by the dealer to the issuing bank; and as the dealer goes into the bank's computer, the paper requested by the dealer is cut almost immediately. When the bank's computer gets instructions from the dealer, it automatically checks these against the parameters for the day given to it by the issuer. Also, as instructions come in from the dealer, the agent bank's computer keeps running totals of the paper that has been issued in each maturity range, and it checks that the dealer does not sell paper at rates above or below those set by the issuer or in maturity ranges other than those in which the issuer desires to sell. The agent bank's computer also automatically records the numbers on the notes that are issued. Every note issued carries a certificate number as well as a note number for the bank's internal recordkeeping.

If an agent bank has a dial-up system attached to its computer, the issuer can, at any time, dial into that computer to check what amounts and what maturities of its paper have been sold so far during the day. Such a dial-up system, combined with appropriate software, can provide the issuer access to current-to-the-minute management information: the average maturity of his paper outstanding, data on his cost of funds, and so on.

For an issuer whose agent bank lacks a dial-up system, other alternatives exist. The dealer may be instructed to transmit information on sales by placing a phone call to the agent bank or directly to the issuer himself who in turn would phone in instructions to his issuing agent or send his issuing agent a *delivery manifold* instructing the latter what paper to issue.

Clearing commercial paper through a clearing bank. Banks that get involved at one stage or another of a sale (at issuance) of commercial paper may be wearing any one of three hats: agent bank, clearing bank, or custody bank. We have talked about the functions of an agent bank. Once that bank has cut the notes sold by the dealer, it is time for a bank wearing its clearing bank hat to enter the stage.

Most, but not all, dealers use a clearing bank to clear their sales of commercial paper. A dealer who uses a clearing bank to clear his commercial paper trades instructs the issuer's agent bank to deliver the notes that it cuts to that clearing bank. At the same time, the dealer sends instructions to the clearing bank: (1) instructions to receive in the paper ("Take in for our account these size pieces, these maturities. . . ."), and (2) instructions as to where to deliver that paper, for example, the pieces by size, the monies due, the customers, and the latter's delivery instructions.

The reader who recalls our description in Chapter 11 of how trades in physical securities are cleared should be starting to get a feeling of

déja vue. And well he should, since once the agent bank has cut the paper to be issued, things proceed much as they would if any other physical security, say a CD or a BA, were being cleared.

Agent bank to clearing bank.   The agent bank sends by messenger the notes it has cut, which are now valuable bearer paper, to the dealer's clearing bank along with a delivery bill. The messenger delivers the notes in over the window at the clearing bank; a clerk there time stamps the delivery bill presented by the agent bank's messenger. Next, the clearing bank examines and counts the notes it has received to see if the delivery is in good order. If it is, the clearing bank sometime later will wire to the agent bank, account of the issuer, the money due to pay for this paper.

Daylight overdraft: issuer and agent bank.   The "sometime later" in the previous sentence is a big source of daylight overdraft for agent banks vis-à-vis the Fed. An issuer selling paper on a particular day will need to begin, early in the day, to spend the money he is raising that day. The issuer's first big need for funds will be, starting early in the day, to meet redemptions of his maturing paper. From the agent bank's point of view, this means that the issuer will, during much of the day, run a large daylight overdraft (OD) in its money account at the agent bank; that OD will, moreover, contribute to the agent bank's daylight OD at the Fed. When the clearing bank finally pays the agent bank for the issuer's paper that the agent bank delivered to it earlier in the day, the issuer's daylight overdraft with its agent bank will wind down, which in turn will diminish the agent bank's daylight OD with the Fed.

Daylight overdrafts, as we've described them, must occur because of the way the system is set up: The agent bank will not get the new notes that the issuer sells during the morning to the clearing bank until maybe 2:15 P.M., and the clearing bank will probably not wire, to the agent bank, the funds due it for those notes until 4 or 5 P.M.; the "sometime later" we spoke about above may be as much as three hours later.

The clearing bank's role.   To illustrate the clearing bank's role, assume the following: The issuer is a client of First Boston, the clearing bank is Irving, and the agent bank is Morgan. First Boston will have alerted Irving to anticipate delivery from Morgan of such and such notes for a particular issuer. Once that paper comes in over Irving's window, it will be given to a receiving clerk on Irving's First Boston desk, who will check it, record that Irving has received it, and then literally dump it into a delivery bin on the desk of a delivery clerk, also on Irving's First Boston desk. That clerk, in turn, will check the paper in his bin against what First Boston says investors have bought, and when he gets a match, he will shoot out a note to the buyer's custody bank. Said one clearing banker, the biggest in commercial paper, "We have a messenger section with 90 people and dispatchers like a taxi company."

Arrival custody bank. Naturally (recall Chapter 11), the clearing bank's messengers, who deliver commercial paper from the clearing bank to various custody banks for the accounts of the investors who have purchased this paper, carry along a delivery bill for each note delivered. The custody banks have been alerted by their investor clients to expect delivery of, to take in, and to pay for whatever paper these clients have bought. Thus, once the paper arrives over a custody bank's window, that bank receipts with a time stamp the delivery bill that accompanies the paper being delivered, takes in the paper, examines and counts it, and then, if the delivery is in good order, wires payment to the dealer's clearing bank for the account of the dealer. At the same time, the custody bank debits by a like amount the cash account of the investor for whom it has received in the new commercial paper; credits, in its computer records, the investor's portfolio with his newly purchased paper; and physically places the paper in its vault, in safekeeping for the customer.

Daylight overdraft at the clearing bank. Here's daylight overdraft again, this time at the clearing bank. A banker, big in commercial paper clearance noted, "After we pay, between 4 and 5 P.M. for paper coming in from agent banks, we are out that money until we get paid by custody banks for paper we have delivered out to investors. That gives us daylight overdraft, and also a risk. The latter, however, is minimal because, if we deliver paper to a clearing house bank, the rule of the clearing house is that, if we don't get paid, the securities must be returned to us. Usually, we don't get paid for everything because of clerical mistakes; in such cases, the mistake is later corrected, and we get paid with interest.

Multihatted banks. Most banks that are big at wearing one of the three hats we described above are also big at wearing a second hat. Irving, for example, is a big agent bank, *and* it also clears more commercial paper than does any other bank. Irving now clears commercial paper for Sali and First Boston, and for years it did so for Merrill. If Sali happens to sell commercial paper for a client who uses Irving as agent bank, then the new notes that Irving is asked to cut will be moved internally by Irving from its issuing operation to its commercial paper-clearing operation. Moreover, if a buyer of such paper happens to use Irving as its custody bank, delivery of the paper to the buyer's account is again internalized within Irving—the paper is simply moved from Irving's clearing operation to Irving's custody area. Of course, Irving is not lucky enough to have all of its deliveries of commercial paper internalized, so it must employ a flock of messengers to deliver new notes, as appropriate, to other clearing banks, to other custody banks, and to dealers who self-clear their own sales of commercial paper.

Clearing commercial paper is labor-intensive. Said a clearer of such paper, "If I clear 1,000 book-entry government transactions a day, I may

need only two people to process that. To do the same number of commercial paper transactions a day, I would need a small army plus messengers."

Self-clearing commercial paper. Some dealers, Goldman and Merrill to name two, self-clear commercial paper that they sell. To do so, a dealer must get a sizable line for unsecured loans from its bank. One reason why more dealers do not clear their own paper is that clearing banks feel far more comfortable extending to a dealer a loan that is secured by commercial paper delivered to that dealer's clearing account than they do extending to a dealer an unsecured loan.

Merrill now self-clears commercial paper that it sells. To illustrate self-clearing, suppose, to continue our earlier example, that Merrill sells Chevron paper to Ford, which has a custody account at Morgan. The deadline for delivery of physical securities to a buyer's custody bank is 3 P.M. Assume that Merrill delivers by 3 P.M., the paper to Morgan, account of Ford. Morgan takes in the paper as it would any other delivery of a physical security to it for a customer, verifies that the paper is what the customer said was to come in, and then wires the funds due for the paper to the account of Merrill at Irving. That payment must be in before the Fed wire closes.

A dealer that self-clears commercial paper tries to manage its position so that the bank overdrafts it incurs in connection with the clearing of its commercial paper sales are largely intraday, and it therefore does not have to take out any large end-of-day loans with its bank. A dealer who self-clears its commercial paper sales cannot help, however, but build up large intraday overdrafts. A bank with which a dealer builds up a big daylight overdraft in connection with its clearing of commercial paper typically does not charge the dealer an explicit rate of interest on that overdraft; instead it will tell the dealer that it builds into its per-transaction charges an undisclosed factor to compensate it for the daylight exposure it has vis-à-vis the dealer.

Dealers who choose to self-clear their sales of commercial paper do so for pretty much the same reasons that they self-clear other physicals: They think that they can do the job cheaper and more efficiently on their own. Said one such dealer, "Suppose things are running late at an issuer's agent bank. The issuer's paper comes into the clearing bank's window. That bank must call us and say, 'The paper is here late. Do you want to take it in?' Then we have to call the trader who is responsible for the issuer and ask him if he wants to take in the paper late. Because it is late, we have no obligation to accept that paper, but the trader, perhaps for some relationship reason, may want to do so, hoping that the paper can be delivered by cutoff time to buyers [if it isn't, the dealer is stuck with fails and financing costs]. By self-clearing," continued the dealer,

"we can cut the time lags involved in making and implementing the decision to accept or not to accept. There are fewer phone calls to make, and we can come to a quick decision."

Cutoff times. As our remarks so far suggest, the various steps—tasks—involved in issuing commercial paper must be accomplished according to fixed deadlines, which must exist or such transactions would never get done. Most issuing agents have a cutoff time of 1 P.M. for taking instructions. Dealers try to cut off taking orders from investors by 12:30 P.M. The issuing agent, once it has cut new paper, must deliver that paper either to the dealer or to his clearing bank by 2:15 P.M., a deadline set by the New York Clearing House. Once the dealer or his clearing bank receives paper from an agent bank and has examined and counted that paper, that entity immediately redelivers the paper to various custody banks so that the latter have time to take in the paper, to examine it, and, assuming the delivery is in good order, to wire payment for the paper before the Fed wire closes for the day. The deadline for delivery of commercial paper to a custody bank is 3 P.M. Often, because of the many steps that must be carried out from the time that an investor orders, in the early morning, commercial paper for his account until the time that that paper actually ends up in his custody account, payment is not made by the investor's custody bank for the paper until 4 P.M. or later.

Secondary market trades. Except perhaps for big blocks of paper issued by the biggest of the direct issuers, there is little secondary market trading in commercial paper, and such paper is therefore illiquid. An investor who has bought paper from a dealer and wants later to sell that paper before maturity will find that his best bet is to ask the dealer who sold him the paper to give him a bid on it; normally, a selling dealer will do that. If a customer buys commercial paper from, for example, Merrill and then wants to sell it, it is the Merrill trader who handles that issuer who will decide what bid to give the customer for his paper.

Redemption of commercial paper

In a short time, the Chevron paper that we supposed Merrill sold Ford will mature. On the maturity date, Morgan, Ford's custody bank, will send by messenger the matured paper to Chase, the paying agent for redemptions of Chevron paper. Chase, when it receives this paper, will wire the funds to Morgan, account of Ford, and debit the issuer's (Chevron's) account at Chase.

Dealer financing of paper taken into position

If a dealer ends up having to position paper at the end of the day, either because it sold less of an issuer's paper than the trader for that issuer thought it could at the rates posted or because fails to deliver occurred—there was a slip-up and a deadline was missed—the dealer may use one of several financing mechanisms. He might, for example, borrow from the firm's holding company money that the holding company itself might have raised via the sale of commercial paper, or he might do either a delivery repo or a letter repo.

A letter RP (called a due bill by at least one big dealer, Merrill) is simply an IOU from the dealer to the lender of money. If the due bill were issued by Merrill, it would say, "We [Merrill] owe you [the lender of money] the following securities for the following money you are sending us." The due bill, which physically is an ordinary letter, is sent by mail to the investor by the dealer. By doing a due bill, the dealer eliminates the need to and cost of delivering out today and receiving back tomorrow a bunch of physical securities; for that reason, the dealer is able, when he does such a transaction, to give the customer a better rate than he would if he delivered to the customer the commercial paper notes that serve as collateral for the due bill. For a customer who isn't fussy about the kind of collateral he gets, one who does not say "governments only" but is willing to take money market paper, a due-bill transaction is a natural. On such a nondelivery repo, the customer gets a higher rate, *and* he also escapes both receive and delivery charges. Normally, due-bill transactions are done on a *strictly overnight basis.*

Stops and stolen or lost paper

A commercial paper note that is lost, stolen, or mutilated is relatively easy to replace. Each commercial paper note bears the name of the issuer, a specific certificate number, a specific maturity date, and a specific face amount. It is, moreover, a crucial part of control procedures at every institution that handles commercial paper to write down certificate numbers both for notes being received in and for notes being delivered out (recall our emphasis in Chapter 11 on the importance of doing so).

If a commercial paper note is lost, mutilated, or stolen, the institution that has experienced the loss must report, to the issuing agent, all the information needed to uniquely identify the missing paper: issuer, certificate number, maturity, and face amount. At that point, the agent bank will put a stop on the paper and notify the issuer of the loss. Before is-

suing a replacement note, the agent may want a letter of indemnification or a bond.

For entities that handle commercial paper, being able to get a replacement note is handy. Thefts of such paper are rare to nonexistent; commercial paper spends most of its life in a bank vault, and it could not be sold to an alert broker/dealer even if it were stolen. However, other strange things do happen to commercial paper. The biggest agent bank sent off on a very windy day, of which there are many on Wall Street, a messenger with some commercial paper notes; the notes to be delivered just plain blew away, millions of dollars of them—all bearer instruments.

Smoothness of operation of the system

The current system for clearing commercial paper sounds and is archaic, but, according to operations people who must live with it and make it work, the system works well. The system is based more on trust and good relationships than on anything else. Any dealer who wants to play in the market must maintain those good relationships—more precisely, the dealer's operations people who are responsible for the physical settlement of these securities must do so. Said one dealer in commercial paper, "Most of the people who work for me have contacts on the Street at issuing and custody banks, and they are constantly talking to each other because it is necessary. Computers sometimes break down, and you are going to miss deadlines. If you know that that is going to happen, then you had better call your counterparts on the Street and talk to them or you might, one day, be hung up—not be able to move a whole lot of paper or money. Sometimes, operations people must, on a best efforts basis, step outside of regular guidelines; I am not, however, going to take in paper late if I cannot turn it around. In our business, a lot of favors are asked of people in the spirit: You wash my hand, and one day I'll wash yours. Trust and relationships make the system work."

DIRECT PAPER

So far, we have been speaking of commercial paper issued through dealers. A number of firms that regularly sell large amounts of commercial paper (e.g., GMAC, big finance companies, and certain bank holding companies) by-pass the dealers and sell their paper directly to investors. GMAC and a few other direct issuers are so large that they don't even need an agent bank. GMAC has its own system for selling its commercial paper; It instructs the customer where to wire funds and delivers, itself, the paper it has sold to the custody banks of its customers. Tier-

two, direct issuers use an agent bank to cut their notes, deliver them out, and redeem them. Morgan, which is the issuing agent for 15 to 20 directs, is the biggest bank in this business, but Citi, Irving, and all the other N.Y.C. clearing banks are also in the business.

A lot of direct paper is sold by banks that offer to sell governments, agencies, and money market securities to investors. Such banks post the rates being offered by big directs in various maturity ranges. Banks do this to further their relationships with the issuers. Also, they are glad to sell a steady investment customer occasional pieces of commercial paper that fit a special need of the customer—perhaps to invest a specific amount for a specific maturity. Selling, getting, and delivering direct paper to investors costs a bank money, and some banks charge a buyer who is not a regular customer a small fee for this service.

Several big New York banks have been fighting for years with the Fed and in the courts against nonbank dealers over the question of whether they may *underwrite* commercial paper. The nonbank dealers claim that to permit banks to underwrite commercial paper would violate the Glass-Steagall Act; the Fed, nonetheless, gave Bankers Trust Co. authority to sell commercial paper on the grounds that commercial paper is not a "note" for purposes of Glass-Steagall, which says that banks may not underwrite notes or securities.

Currently, the Fed seems determined to poke further holes in Glass-Steagall with or without the help of Congress and in the face of stiff court opposition from the Securities Industry Association (SIA), comprised of nonbank dealers. In 1987, the Fed gave Bankers Trust New York approval to sell commercial paper through another subsidiary, BT Commercial Corp.; it also gave Bankers Trust New York, Citicorp, J.P. Morgan & Co., and Chase Manhattan Corp. permission to underwrite various securities through subsidiaries.

COMMERCIAL PAPER OUTSIDE NEW YORK CITY

A final note: We have said that the commercial paper market is really a New York market, but to this we should add that there is some issuance of commercial paper in financial centers elsewhere in the country, for example, in Chicago and San Francisco. Whenever paper is issued at a place other than New York City, that paper is normally safekept in the same place. This is particularly true of paper issued through smaller regional banks for small, local issuers who sell their paper to local investors. Besides cost and convenience, another reason for commercial paper to be safekept at the same geographic location at which it is issued is that such paper is sold for same-day settlement, which could not be effected if the paper were delivered any distance.

GOING DEPOSITORY

While operations people who are involved with the issuance and redemption of commercial paper notes claim that the system of issuance we described above "operates smoothly," it is nonetheless obvious to an outsider that this system is a needlessly people-intensive, costly, horse-and-buggy arrangement. Surely, the people who must use the system put up with it only because they have never experienced anything better—just as cowboys used to put up with having to ride everywhere on horseback until someone invented a pickup truck with air conditioning and 4-wheel drive.

Today, there is talk—so far, little action—about immobilizing commercial paper in a depository. If that were done, commercial paper would go book-entry, and the costs associated with issuing, trading, and redeeming commercial paper would drop dramatically. Not every issuer, however, is enthused with the prospect. Said one clearing banker, "The big directs like to issue commercial paper through a bank because it fosters their relationship with their bank. Such a corporation says, 'Who needs a good relationship with a depository [e.g., DTC, subject of next chapter]?'"

One of several fledgling efforts to get commercial paper has been made by Citi, Sali, and CEDAL, a Luxemburg clearing organization. This system handles in a paperless environment Euro commercial paper issued by Citibank and sold by Sali.

THE ISSUANCE OF CDs

Since we have said so much about the issuance of commercial paper, we can cover the issuance of CDs simply. Big New York City banks print up and deliver out to appropriate New York City custody banks any new CDs of their own that they have sold to investors either through their own sales force or through a dealer. Big non–New York banks are likely to have a New York office through which they can issue their bank's CDs in the New York market.

There are, however, many—they number in the hundreds—second-tier, regional banks that use a New York City bank as an agent to issue their CDs in the New York market. For example, the Bank of Hawaii and a number of Texas banks do so. The drill that a regional bank goes through when it issues CDs via a New York City agent bank is *identical* to that through which a seller of commercial paper goes when it issues paper via a New York City agent bank. Enough said.

With respect to CDs, as opposed to commercial paper, there is still a fourth hat that a New York City agent bank may wear. Such a bank might call a good, but second-tier, U.S. bank or a Japanese bank and say, "Show us your paper—tell us the price at which you will issue—and we

will sell or even underwrite your paper for you. A bank wearing that fourth hat expects to earn for its trouble 5 basis points ("a nickel" or an "oh five").

A physical CD has none of the glamor of a stock certificate (Figure 15–2).

THE ISSUANCE OF BAs

BAs are *two-name* paper, notes signed by the borrower and by the guaranteeing bank (Figure 15–3). Because of this feature, a San Francisco bank can't give a New York bank a stock of its blank BAs and ask the latter to be its issuing agent in New York for such paper. Consequently, BAs tend more than other paper to be sold and safekept in the geographic locality in which they are originated. Thus, there is, for example, a San Francisco market for locally originated BAs.

Nonetheless, at least one New York bank attempted to sell in the New York market BAs originated by Japanese banks on the West Coast. The procedure it used was as follows: The New York bank had the paper delivered to its West Coast agent, the Bank of America; that bank took in the paper, counted and verified it, and then paid the Japanese issuer for it; finally, the paper was flown to New York to be sold in the New York market for delivery to New York custody banks. This procedure was high in cost and cumbersome in nature; also, the New York bank that was "importing" West Coast, Japanese BAs was sometimes forced by plane delays into costly fails to deliver to buyers; consequently, it eventually quit the BA-import business. Probably, however, some BAs are still being flown from their place of origination to some other place of sale, for example, between Edge Act subs and the parent bank; commercial paper, in contrast, rarely, if ever, travels far.

FIGURE 15–2
A CD issued by the Continental Bank

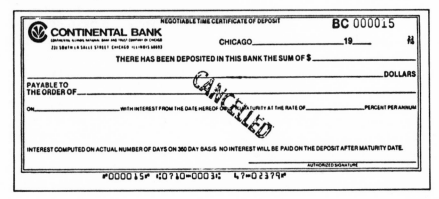

FIGURE 15–3
A BA issued by the Harris Bank

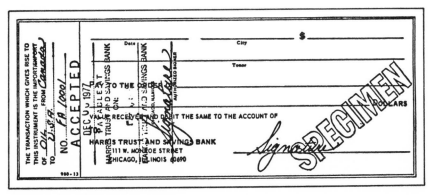

MUNICIPAL NOTES

Municipal issuers issue muni notes to obtain short-term financing; for example, an issuer might sell a BAN (bond anticipation note) with a year's maturity to provide short-term financing for some capital project. Municipal note issues vary considerably in size. Big new issues are sold through a dealer or syndicate of dealers, who most times have obtained the right to distribute the issue through competitive bidding.

Right now, about 60%, maybe 80%, of muni notes clear physical (Figure 15–4 shows a physical muni note). However, some progress was supposed to be made in 1987 in moving muni notes into a book-entry environment by placing them in a depository (Chapter 16). One reason why the movement of muni notes into a depository has been slow is that the MSRB (Municipal Securities Rule Making Board), a self-regulatory body for municipal securities, does not require muni issuers to put a CUSIP number on their note issues. Getting a CUSIP number from S&P is a bit of a hassle and costs money, so muni issuers are inclined to ask, "On a short-term issue, why bother?" As a result, most muni notes have no CUSIP number and, consequently, are not depository-eligible.

When a new muni issue is sold by a syndicate, sales of that issue settle on the day that the issuer is supposed to get his money. In the secondary market, however, most notes trade either for next-day settlement or for *corporate settlement;* the latter term means that the trade settles five business days after it is done. It is up to the buyer and seller to decide how they want to settle. Probably 80% to 90% of the time, their choice is for next-day settlement.

Trades in physical muni notes clear the same way that trades in other physical securities—CDs, BAs—do (Chapter 11).

FIGURE 15-4
A minicipal note issued by New York City

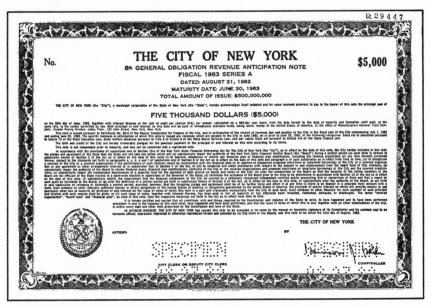

THE NEXT CHAPTER

Is the clearing of either wireable or physical securities as efficient as it might be? The answer is an unqualified *no*. In the next chapter, we examine in some detail the operations of DTC and NSCC, two sister organizations which together clear corporate securities in a highly efficient way. We then look briefly at what the example of these organizations suggests about how the clearing of governments and of other money market securities might be greatly simplified through some radical restructuring of the ways in which such securities are currently cleared.

Chapter 16

The depository approach to clearing: DTC and NSCC

IN THIS CHAPTER we describe the system currently used in the United States to clear trades in corporate stocks and bonds. In all aspects, except for the payments mechanism used, the corporate clearance system is vastly more efficient than the previously described systems currently used in the United States to clear trades in book-entry and in physical money market securities. We also describe how the clearance of municipal bonds has been grafted, albeit so far imperfectly, onto the DTC-NSCC system. We conclude the chapter with a few suggestions as to how the DTC-NSCC approach could be used to simplify the clearing of governments and money markets.

IMMOBILIZATION, MULTILATERAL NETTING, MULTI-ISSUE NETTING, AND CUSTODY

Suppose one were asked to construct a clearing system that would be as efficient as possible, subject to the constraint that some physical securities would still be issued and traded. What attributes would one give such a system?

Several things come immediately to mind. First, paper. It is cumbersome, expensive, and all-around inefficient (Chapter 11) to have paper securities floating around Wall Street, not to speak of around the country. If paper cannot be eliminated altogether, the next best thing to do would be to gather all the paper on the Street together in a *depository* and to link that depository with a clearing system specifically designed so that trades in that paper could be made and cleared with *no* movement of paper—to create, in effect, a back-entry settlement system in which the back entries were "backed" by securities placed in a depository.

Pairoffs

When one thinks of efficiency in clearing, a second key factor that comes to mind is *netting.* Every time a trade is cleared, as things are done today, confirms must move, securities must move, and money must move. All this costs time and money and raises possibilities of errors. Obviously, if one can make *one* transfer of money and securities clear *two* trades, the efficiency of clearing is vastly increased. Dealers understand this, and, as we've noted, they look hard for opportunities to bilaterally net trades, that is, to do what the Street calls *pairoffs.*

Here's a pairoff situation. Sali buys $5 million of the new 2-year note from Merrill for cash settlement at 9 A.M. The market rallies. At 10 A.M., Sali sells $5 million of the same issue to Merrill at a price above the price at which the 9 A.M. trade was done. Sali and Merrill pairoff the two trades: settle them simply by having Merrill send to Sali a difference check, a money wire equal to the difference in the money on the two trades. No one would dispute that such a pairoff is far more efficient and far cheaper for Sali and Merrill than clearing two trades through their respective clearing banks would be. The weakness of pairoffs is that they are but a first step toward realizing the full benefits that can be achieved from netting.

Multilateral netting

To maximize efficiency in clearing, a system is needed that provides for *multilateral netting,* that is, a system that nets all trades in an issue that a dealer does during the day with all other members of the system. To illustrate, suppose that during the day Sali does the following trades in government bonds for regular settlement (settlement next business day): It buys $50 million of issue X from Merrill; it buys $45 million of issue X from Goldman; and it sells $50 million of issue X to Discount Corporation. Under a system of multilateral netting, Sali would be recognized as a *net buyer* of $45 million of issue X. To settle its three trades in that issue, Sali would pay, next day, to the organization respon-

sible for arranging multilateral netting, the *net amount* due on its two buys and one sell; this amount would be:

$$\begin{pmatrix} \text{Amount Sali} \\ \text{owes } \textit{net} \\ \text{on issue X} \end{pmatrix} = \begin{pmatrix} \text{Buy price} \\ \text{due Merrill} \\ \text{for 50MM of X} \end{pmatrix} + \begin{pmatrix} \text{Buy price} \\ \text{due Goldman} \\ \text{for 45MM of X} \end{pmatrix} - \begin{pmatrix} \text{Sell price due} \\ \text{from Discount} \\ \text{for 50MM of X} \end{pmatrix}$$

At the same time it made its net payment due, Sali would receive from the system the $45 million of issue X that, *net*, it had bought for settlement today. That is the simple principle of multilateral settlement of a single issue.

Obviously, if 40 or more dealers trade issue X, two things happen. First, the calculation of each dealer's net positions in cash and securities at settlement gets more complicated, but it remains for a computer a trivial calculation. Second, the potential savings from operation of the system are multiplied by a large factor from what they would be if only two active traders netted bilaterally their trades in issue X.

Multi-issue netting

Going from bilateral to multilateral netting vastly decreases the work involved in clearing trades, but there remains yet one more form of netting that will increase still further efficiency in clearing; it is *multi-issue netting* of monies due on trades. Under multi-issue netting, the netting organization calculates, for example, that Sali is a net buyer of $45 million of issue X, a net seller of $10 million of issue Y, and a net seller of $5 million of issue Z. At settlement, it therefore directs that Sali receive and deliver those amounts of those securities; and that Sali pay or receive, as the case may be, the *net money due* on its one net buy and its two net sells.

We described in Chapters 10 and 11 the many steps that must be followed to clear, on a *one-by-one* basis, trades in book-entry and physical securities. To anyone who recalls these steps, it will be obvious that multilateral, multi-issue clearing would vastly reduce—reduce, in fact, to nearly *nothing*—the number of transfers of securities and of money that would have to be made to clear, daily, among a group of dealers, thousands of trades in hundreds of issues.

Maximum netting plus a depository

As a final step to making clearing efficient, suppose that our multilateral, multi-issue system of netting were combined with a depository in which securities, once there, stayed put physically and moved only electronically, as book-entry securities do from one account

to another. Then, 40 dealers and a single clearing/depository organization could, for example, clear thousands of trades in hundreds of issues, book-entry and physical; and all that would be required for them to settle those many trades would be the passing of 40 wire transfers of money, one between each dealer and the clearing/depository organization. The latter would, of course, also have to track in its backs all changes in ownership of the securities in the depository that occurred as a result of the day's trades among dealers; it would be running a back-entry settlement system for the securities in the depository.

If we throw investors big and small into the system, things need not get much more complicated. For example, dealers might settle with small customers outside the market clearing/depository system and offer to hold any securities such customers bought from them in a regulated book-entry safekeeping account at the clearing/depository organization. Dealers might settle trades with large institutional customers who utilized the services of third-party custodian banks as follows: Each custodian bank would become a member of the clearing/depository system; each such bank would obtain a book-entry account in which it could hold customer securities, and it would become a party to the funds settlement that occurred in the system at the end of each day.

DTC AND NSCC

The system we have just outlined does not yet exist for clearing governments and money markets, but something akin to it does exist for clearing corporates. That system is run by two sister corporations, the *Depository Trust Company* (*DTC*) and the *National Securities Clearing Corporation* (*NSCC*).

DTC

If we ignore some of the more technical points, the operations of DTC and NSCC are easy to explain. We begin with DTC. DTC was established in the late-1960s by the New York Stock Exchange (NYSE), the American Stock Exchange (AMEX), and the National Association of Securities Dealers (NASD). The purpose of DTC was to help brokers of corporate stocks and bonds cope with the painful, fatal-to-some "paper crunch" they were experiencing, at that time in their back offices. During those years, the volume of trading in equities ran 14 to 16 million shares a day, and the exchanges were talking about possibly closing on Wednesday and reducing their trading hours in order to pare the numbers of corporate trades to be cleared.

DTC was set up to serve several functions. A first and crucial function was that it was to serve as a *depository* for most of the corporate bonds and stocks traded by members of the NYSE, AMEX and NASD (to be DTC-eligible, an issue must be assigned a *CUSIP number*). In terms of simplifying the clearing of physical equity and bond certificates, the simple and potent premise on which DTC was built was this: By immobilizing physical securities, DTC would be in a position to allow *book-entry delivery and receipt* of those securities. Basically, DTC created a system for clearing corporate bonds and stocks that resembles the book-entry system created by the Treasury and the Fed for clearing governments and agencies. The principal difference between the two systems is that the Treasury and most federal agencies issue their securities in book-entry form (there are no physical securities on new issues), whereas DTC created and continues to create book-entry credits for securities in its system by taking in physical securities and storing them in its vaults. DTC has not escaped the world of physical securities, but from the point of view of ease of clearing, it has done the next best thing, immobilized physical securities—2.4 trillion of them—in a central place.

DTC takes in both bearer and registered securities. To the extent possible, DTC registers securities it takes in in the name of its namee, Cede & Co.

Two sorts of trades flow into DTC: trades between "professionals" (legalese for broker/dealers) and trades between customers and professionals. We describe the former first.

NSCC

The National Securities Clearing Corporation (NSCC) was formed in 1977 as a result of combining the clearing corporations of three groups: the NYSE, AMEX, and NASD (over-the-counter stocks). NSCC is now owned one-third by each of these entities. It is, however, run and directed by a 16-member board comprised of 2 banks and 14 broker/dealers. NSCC clears and processes about 500,000 to 600,000 trades per day. The equities portion of these trades represents about 90% of the trading done each day in the U.S. equities markets.

In a nutshell, NSCC's mission in life is to clear, with great efficiency, *interbroker* trades by engaging in *multilateral, multi-issue netting* of trades done among broker/dealers and banks participating in the system. Currently, about 300 firms participate as *full settlement members* in NSCC.

To follow how NSCC clears trades, note first that "regular settlement" means, in corporate securities, that a trade will clear *five* business days after its trade date. To describe how an interbroker/dealer trade is set-

tled through NSCC, we will trace a simple example of two broker/dealers settling one trade in one security. To move from there to imagining how NSCC does multilateral, multi-issue settling of trades is simple.

Suppose Sali sells Merrill 500 shares of IBM at $150 a share. The trade is to be cleared through NSCC. Step one is that Sali and Merrill both electronically send, via a computer-to-computer, PC-dial-up-to-computer, or some other hookup, confirms during the night after the trade to NSCC's computer. Merrill's confirm will read, "We bought, today [say, Friday], from Sali for settlement five business days hence [a week from Monday] 500 shares of IBM at $150 a share." Sali will send a similar "We sold" message to NSCC's computer. On Monday morning, NSCC's computer will, looking over the messages it has received since Friday close, say, "Ah ha, Merrill and Sali traded IBM, and their descriptions of that trade match— same money, same dates, etc. That trade is, thus, *compared* [NSCC jargon for both sides of a trade knowing the trade the same way]." At that point, NSCC's computer will shoot out, electronically, as always, confirms to Sali and Merrill telling each that the other agrees to the trade as they know it. At the same time, NSCC's computer will schedule the Sali-Merrill trade for automatic settlement on the following Monday. Should Sali and Merrill not agree on the terms on which they traded, NSCC computer's would tell them that, and the two firms would have adequate time to straighten out the trade and to submit it again to NSCC for comparison before the settlement date.

On the day before settlement, something novel and important occurs: NSCC severs the relationship between the true buyer and seller and places itself in the middle of the trade. Specifically, NSCC says to Sali, "You now have an obligation to deliver, on the next business day, to NSCC 500 shares of IBM for which NSCC will pay you $150 per share." Simultaneously, NSCC informs Merrill that Merrill has a precisely offsetting, from the point of view of NSCC, buy obligation with NSCC.

NSCC assumes the role of principal to both sides of the trade because, by doing so, it becomes the *guarantor* of the Sali-Merrill trade. Merrill, in particular, now knows that it will get its securities even if Sali fails to deliver those securities to NSCC either because it (Sali) just does not have the securities (it lent them and they did not get back in time for delivery) or because it became insolvent before the trade settled. Conversely, Sali knows that it will get its money even if Merrill fails to show up with a check at the appointed hour.

The settlement procedure.   The night before the trade settles, NSCC sends a file to DTC's computer telling it that Sali owes NSCC 500 shares of IBM and that NSCC owes Merrill 500 shares of IBM. In response to NSCC's message, DTC's computer will look at Sali's account with it and ask, "Does Sali have 500 shares of IBM in its account that are not

customer securities and the like, that is, securities that Sali can legally deliver to NSCC?" If the answer is yes, then DTC's computer will transfer 500 shares of IBM from Sali's book-entry account at DTC to NSCC's book-entry account at DTC. No physical shares move. At the same time, DTC's computer will also transfer 500 shares of IBM from NSCC's book-entry account at DTC to Merrill's book-entry account at DTC. That takes care of the securities side of settlement. Sali has been debited 500 shares of IBM, NSCC is flat, and Merrill has been credited with 500 shares of IBM.

Money, too, must change hands as part of settlement. At 3:15 P.M. on the day of settlement (Monday afternoon in our example), a Merrill messenger is supposed to show up at NSCC with a certified check for $75,000 (500 shares × $150/share) made out to NSCC and payable in Federal funds the next business day. Money delivered in a form that converts into good funds the next business day is called *clearing house funds.*

Assume that NSCC has been informed by DTC that the IBM shares were in fact transferred out of Sali's account with DTC into NSCC's account with DTC; NSCC's computer will credit Sali's account for the same sum that Merrill paid it. In terms of money, these transactions leave Merrill, Sali, and NSCC precisely where they would have been if Sali and Merrill had settled their trade directly with each other.

Two things to note. First, NSCC, in its role as clearing house, acts in the same way that a clearing house associated with a futures exchange acts; in each case, the clearing house becomes the guarantor of trades cleared through it. Second, in the course of clearing securities trades, NSCC handles money but not securities; any necessary transfers of securities are done for NSCC by DTC.

Multilateral, multi-issue net settlement.   Naturally, Sali and Merrill do not do one trade a day, but many thousands. Also, NSCC settles, each day, not one trade, but hundreds of thousands of trades. What makes NSCC settlement vastly more efficient than the trade-by-trade sort of settlement that goes on in governments and money market securities is that NSCC clears on a given day all of the trades it is supposed to settle that day on a multilateral, multi-issue basis. Thus, settlement ends up, ideally, with Sali having the following positions: (1) a single net long or short in every issue settled for it that day by NSCC and (2) a single net money sum that is either *due to* NSCC or *due from* NSCC. DTC moves securities into and out of Sali's account with it as required for Sali to settle. So, basically, all Sali must do to settle is send or receive one check. For Sali to clear the same number of money market trades, it would have to make or receive thousands of wire transfers via its clearing bank; and, probably, it would have to deliver or receive a large number of physical

securities. The benefits of settlement through NSCC accrue, of course, not just to Sali, but to *all* brokers/dealers and banks that are full settlement members of NSCC.

A fail to deliver. While NSCC manages to settle, on time, most trades put into its system, some fails inevitably occur. To illustrate how NSCC handles a fail, let's continue our Sali-Merrill example. Suppose that, on its delivery of 500 shares of IBM, Sali fails, for some reason—any reason other than insolvency—to deliver, at settlement, the shares it owes NSCC. NSCC will have no securities to deliver to Merrill, but Merrill's credit risk is minimal because NSCC will *mark the fail to market.*

To illustrate marking a fail to market, suppose that, on settlement day, IBM closes at $151 a share. To mark Sali's fail to market, NSCC computes the difference between what it has agreed to pay Sali for the shares Sali owes it and the current market value of those shares. That difference, $1 per share times 500 shares, equals $500. NSCC charges Sali's account $500 and credits Merrill's account for a like sum. Sali's fail might continue for several days. If so, the fail would be marked to market, each day, using the procedure just illustrated; and each day the fail would be treated, for SEC purposes, as if it were a 1-day fail.

Suppose now, to continue our example, that Sali delivers to NSCC, the day after settlement was supposed to occur, the 500 shares of IBM that it owes NSCC. At that point, NSCC will pay Sali the last price in its system for IBM, which is $151 per share. At the same time, NSCC will collect the initial sale price of $75,000 from Merrill plus the extra $500 it credited Merrill's account; that is, Merrill will pay in effect the current market price of $151 for the 500 shares of IBM that it receives. Simultaneous to these payments, NSCC will instruct DTC to make a book-entry transfer of the IBM shares now in its account at DTC to Merrill's account at DTC. Note that when the $500 that changed hands between Merrill and Sali due to the mark to market is taken into account, the money numbers in our example net back to the dollar amount, $75,000, in the original Merrill-Sali trade contract.

Continuous net settlement. NSCC refers to its method of settling trades as *continuous net settlement.* NSCC settlement is *net* for the reason explained above: NSCC offsets (1) a broker/dealer's buys in each issue against his sells of that issue and (2) all monies due to him against all monies due from him as well. NSCC settlement is *continuous* because, on each settlement day, NSCC offsets, for each issue, any *fails* a broker has from the previous day against any new trades he has in that issue that are scheduled to be settled that day.

Fails due to insolvency. Inevitably, it occurs now and then that a broker/dealer fails to NSCC because he has gone bankrupt. In that case, NSCC immediately goes into the open market and either buys the securities it is owed by the insolvent broker/dealer or sells the securities it was scheduled to deliver to the insolvent broker/dealer. More often than not, the market has moved in such a way that NSCC takes a small loss when it does this.

NSCC self-insures itself against such losses by requiring every full settlement member to deposit with it a dollar sum, which is a function of that member's average daily settlement activity with NSCC; the result is a fund that NSCC maintains to absorb potential losses. A broker/dealer must meet the first $10,000 of its deposit obligation to NSCC in cash; it can meet the remainder by depositing U.S. government-guaranteed securities with a custodian bank. Should NSCC lose money due to a fail by a participating broker/dealer it has the right to subtract that loss from the broker/dealer's deposit with it before turning over the remainder of the deposit to the broker/dealer's bankruptcy trustee. Should the broker/dealer's deposit prove insufficient to cover NSCC's loss, NSCC may look to the deposits of other members to cover its loss, and, if need be, it may further assess its members, up to 25% of their capital, to cover its loss. In recent years, the only clearing house that has suffered a loss sufficiently large to force it to take that step was the COMEX clearing house.

Currently, NSCC has about $320 million in its defense fund, which seems more than adequate to meet any losses it might sustain. To give perspective to this number, we note that NSCC settles, on an average day, $12 to $13 million of securities on a gross basis and a mere $1 million on a net basis. By money market standards, those sums are peanuts.

Evolution of NSCC. NSCC is an evolving system that constantly seeks to do its job more efficiently. Noted one officer of NSCC, "It is inconceivable to think of equity trading being accomplished today the way it was even five years ago. Once, we feared that we might not be able to keep up with volume. Now, with our new systems, hardware and software, volume is no problem.

"If we have any problem today, it is not the back end, moving the money and the securities; all that has been automated. Rather, our remaining problem is the front end, the comparisons, which are labor-intensive to do. To the extent that we can reach into trading systems and grab trades off them at the time of execution, we can operate more efficiently and handle greater volume. Today, we get data for comparisons often on tape in machine-readable form or computer-to-computer. Nonetheless, the

comparison system is still primitive, when two guys who do a trade must each scribble the trade on a piece of paper and then give that paper to their back office, which, in turn, must record the trade some way and then pass on the trade data to us.

"It used to be that every trade on the floor of the exchange resulted in a comparison at NSCC of two reports from the two parties to the trade on the day after the trade date. Now, 35% of transactions done on the NYSE are completely automated. On the floor of the NYSE there is the DOT system, and trades done through it are reported to us already compared. Before DOT and related systems, there used to be a thick wall between trading and clearing systems. Now, the two are coming together; as a result, we get a lot of information directly from the exchanges. Even NASD, which used to be just a quote system, now has the ability to automatically execute trades; and those trades are compared before they reach us."

NSCC also has its eye on international markets. Noted the same officer of NSCC, "We have a subsidiary just to do international clearance; and in several months we expect to have a pilot link with the London Stock Exchange. We could expand that link from corporate stocks to corporate bonds and even to 'gilts' [British Treasuries] and to U.S. Treasuries. Currently, we are talking about equities with Euroclear and Cedel; also, we are in contact with Tokyo. Eventually, we expect to expand around the world."

Institutional delivery system

Trades between "professionals" (broker/dealers) come into DTC via NSCC. A second big group of trades that flow into DTC are those between a broker/dealer and an institutional investor that utilizes a custody bank. Such trades come into DTC via what's called the *institutional delivery (ID) system;* NSCC is not involved.

To illustrate how the ID system works, suppose that Aetna Insurance uses Chase as custodian and Stein Roe as an investor adviser; on a Friday, Aetna buys from Merrill, for settlement on the following Friday, 1,000 shares of XYZ stock. Merrill would immediately provide the details (price, quantity, date, etc.) of the trade to DTC and also send confirms to Aetna, Stein Roe, and Chase. DTC in turn would shoot out confirms to Stein Roe, Chase, and, probably, Aetna. Before Wednesday evening, if there were no hitch up, DTC would tell Merrill and Chase that Stein Roe had *affirmed* the trade as Merrill reported it. Thursday, Chase would look at the Aetna account to see that there were sufficient funds in the account to do the contracted trade. If so, Chase would authorize the trade for automatic settlement on Friday. (Note that if Aetna had, for example, sold securities to Merrill and if it had lent out those securities and failed

to get them back in time to make delivery, Chase would find that Aetna did not have in its account the requisite securities to make delivery to Merrill. In that case, Aetna would fail on its delivery to Merrill and the parties involved would have to settle that fail.)

Chase is able to settle, via DTC, Aetna's supposed trade with Merrill because Chase and other custody banks participate in DTC and are able to make to DTC and receive from DTC deliveries of both money and securities—the latter either in physical form or in DTC-book-entry form.

When a custody bank takes delivery of securities for a institutional customer, the normal procedure and the one DTC prefers is that the custody bank leave those securities in DTC's vault; if this were done in our Chase–Aetna example, then at settlement, when Chase paid out money for Aetna, it would receive, in its custody account at DTC, a book-entry credit for the 1,000 shares of XYZ purchased by Aetna. Simultaneously, Chase would change its records of Aetna's custody account with it to reflect the payment from that account of money and the receipt into that account of 1,000 shares of XYZ.

A retail trade

Broker/dealers deal not only with institutional customers who utilize custody banks, but with retail customers who often do not. If a retail customer bought 100 shares of XYZ from Merrill and asked Merrill to safekeep those securities for him, DTC would probably be unaware of that trade, but the physical shares being safekept would be at DTC backing book-entry credit by DTC of those shares to Merrill.

Delivery of securities into DTC is not a once and for all affair. If a customer buying 100 shares of XYZ from Merrill wants physical securities to put under his mattress, in his safe deposit box, or whatever, Merrill can withdraw shares from DTC to make physical delivery. At its vault, DTC maintains a working inventory of securities for making deliveries. To cut storage costs, DTC converts, to the extent possible, securities it holds in excess of that inventory level into jumbo certificates.

Lending securities and writing options

Besides immobilization of securities, DTC also offers other secondary services. One is the capability for a party, say, a dealer that has securities on deposit at DTC, to pledge those securities under the Uniform Commercial Code to a pledgee bank, which might then lend that dealer the value of the securities minus some margin. There are also provisions in the system for the borrowing of securities to cover fails and for the writing of covered options.

Interest and dividends

When interest or dividends are paid on securities held at DTC, the issuer wires money due on such securities to the account of DTC at U.S. Trust. DTC in turn credits the money accounts of participants appropriately.

At this point DTC operates strictly in a clearing-house-funds environment. It receives payments from broker/dealers via certified checks and hands out bank drafts. DTC has eliminated paper certificates, but it still has messengers running around N.Y.C. with paper checks. This, however, may change when, as, and if DTC gets dual-funds (clearing house and Fed funds) capability, something DTC has been working on for some time.[1]

Municipal securities

Currently, many muni bond issues are DTC-eligible, but DTC is just gearing up to handle muni notes; the latter lack a CUSIP number and typically settle at issue in Fed funds. It is estimated that there are about $750 billion of municipal securities outstanding of which about $360 billion are in DTC. For DTC to have almost 50% of all outstanding municipal securities in its vaults is quite an accomplishment; DTC did not start to deal in municipal securities until 1981, and, even today, only 300,000 of the estimated 1.5 million muni issues outstanding are DTC-eligible.

In the summer of 1984, the Municipal Securities Rule Making Board gave dealers in municipal securities a massive shove toward the depository approach to clearing by requiring that they use NSCC to compare trades in depository-eligible municipal issues. If the receiver and deliverer so elect, delivery of the securities traded may occur at DTC. Currently, NSCC does not carry out net continuous settlement for municipal issues, but that may evolve over time. The changes that are occurring today in the back offices of muni dealers took many years to evolve in equities.

Why any paper?

Why, in the middle of the 1980s, do corporations and municipal bodies go on issuing paper certificates when the federal government has ceased to do so and has demonstrated by its example the efficiency of not doing so? That is a good question. There are in fact efforts outside the Treasury world to end certificates. Treasurers of some states have, on

---

[1]Having same-day funds capability would permit DTC to proceed with its plans to add muni notes, "animals"—LIONS, CATS, TIGERS, etc.—and maybe medium-term corporate notes to its system.

new muni bond issues, issued to DTC a single global or jumbo certificate; on such issues, there are literally *no* certificates available for individual investors to hold.

The SEC has promoted a similar concept for corporate debt securities, but, as of 1987, no corporate bond issue had been sold in book-entry form only. SEC suggestions for phasing out physical corporate securities meet much resistance from many small investors. They cry, "Do not take away our certificates." Such investors often cherish certificates as tangible proof of their investments.

Another factor that slows DTC's march away from paper securities is that it has been almost too successful in what it has accomplished. Today, even on high-volume days, the Street is settling, customers are not up in arms because of back-office mistakes and delays. Consequently, there is no great pressure on DTC to push for eliminating certificates.

Other depositories

Besides DTC there are three other depositories in the United States: the Philadelphia Depository, the Pacific Securities Depository Trust Company, and the Midwest Securities Trust Company. These three organizations are all subsidiaries of a parent exchange, and they all have sister clearing corporations like NSCC. While DTC's competitors outnumber it, DTC does 90% of all transactions in immobilized securities.

THE GOVERNMENT SECURITIES CLEARING CORPORATION

Currently, trades in book-entry securities (governments and agencies) are, as we've noted, cleared on a one-by-one basis over the Fed wire. The example of DTC-NSCC suggests that the clearing of such trades could be done much more efficiently if multilateral netting were appended to the existing book-entry/Fedwire approach to clearing. While it's easy to say this, history suggests that major changes in clearing procedures occur only in response to a major crisis: An insurance crisis forced introduction of the book-entry system for governments; a back-office crisis forced introduction of the current DTC-NSCC approach to clearing corporates.

In mid-1987, a major effort was under way to introduce multilateral netting in the clearing of governments. That effort might well be described as a response to a perceived potential crisis: the Fed has proposed new caps on daylight overdraft at banks, caps that threaten to put the clearing banks out of business if clearing procedures are not changed. Obviously, no clearing banks, no government securities market.

The need for netting

Netting is sorely needed in the clearing of governments because the current approach to the clearing of such securities leads to several serious problems, a point that one dealer made quite forcefully. "Netting," said he, "shall come to pass because there is currently a *crisis* on three levels of the clearing system."

The first problem or crisis is that the Fed wire is creaking along and almost never closing on time. Part of the problem is sheer volume of trades to be cleared. A second part of the problem is the technology used; the most recent upgrading of Fedwire was described, by a dealer whose firm spares no expenses to keep its back office and communications state of the art, as the equivalent of "adding rubber tires to a horsecart." Netting would immediately cut volume and thereby reduce pressure on Fedwire. This, in turn, would create a window for the resolution of technological issues that need to be addressed.

There is no doubt in the minds of major dealers that such issues exist. "The Fed screams," noted an operations office at a major dealer, "about daylight overdraft, congestion on the wire, late items; and they are the cause! They have a system designed to handle a market that was maybe $500 billion in 1975 and is now $2 trillion. And they say to us [dealers], 'What are *you* going to do about it?' We used to have a couple of guys from the Fed in to lunch twice a year to discuss operations, and their [low] budgets for automation were blowing our minds."

A second level on which the current system for clearing governments creates crisis concerns credit risk. Currently, the biggest of the dealers and their clearing banks are eyeing each other warily on the credit-risk issue. A top dealer is wont to say to its clearing bank, "We have each day at risk through your systems and your procedures tens of billions of money and securities. If you have a problem, we are going to have a problem." Meanwhile, that same dealer's clearing bank is likely looking at that dealer and saying, "Even if you have a near-zero error rate, the normal flow of your work is so huge that we might end up on the hook for hundreds of millions of dollars." Perhaps the biggest of the dealers are getting too big for their clearing bank.

A third level on which the current system for clearing book-entry securities creates crisis concerns the daylight overdrafts currently run by clearing banks with the Fed. The Fed is currently proposing that, in March 1988, it will include in its calculation of a bank's daylight overdraft for cap purposes not only daylight overdraft created by a bank's money transfers, but daylight overdraft created by a bank's traffic on the securities wire. In addition, the Fed proposes, at the same time, to cut by 25% a bank's cap on daylight overdraft. These changes are supposed

to be made palatable to the clearing banks by the fact that the Fed is willing to reduce a bank's calculated daylight overdraft due to securities transactions by an amount equal to what it (the Fed) views as certain collateral in that bank's possession minus one or two haircuts—one for market risk and maybe one for operating risk. A big problem with this is that what the Fed proposes to count as certain collateral will include only securities it sees coming into a bank over Fedwire; the summing of the collateral available to a clearing bank will thus omit incoming physical securities, certain securities coming off repo, and so on.

A clearing bank's response to all this is, first, shock and then a politely worded letter of comment to the Fed in which it says, in effect, "If you won't count as collateral all of the securities we have to pledge against our daylight overdraft, and if, to add insult to injury, you haircut once or twice by significant-to-us amounts the collateral you do count, we will have to seriously consider getting out of the clearing business."

Threats to exit the clearing business are not mere bluffs by the clearing banks. Fed policy on daylight overdraft is making daylight overdraft a scarce and therefore valuable commodity to a bank. Suddenly, a bank finds itself facing, besides its capital/asset ratio constraint, a new daylight-overdraft constraint. For a bank that is big in a number of businesses—money transfers, custody, clearing, and maybe dealing too—all of which generate big daylight overdrafts, a natural line of thought is, "If we can't carry on all of our lines of business and live within our cap on daylight overdraft, we had better figure out what rate of profit we are earning on our use of daylight overdraft in each of our lines of business and perhaps get out of one of them." Put in economic terms, a bank that faces a capital constraint and is now asked to respect a constraint on its daylight overdraft faces a nifty little linear programming problem: how to maximize profits subject to two linear constraints. The answer might well be to exit one of its lines of business.

New caps on daylight overdraft are not the only proposal that the Fed has up its sleeve. In addition, the Fed has been kicking around the idea of limiting the size of individual securities transactions that may go over the Fed wire to $25 or $50 million each. Doing so would pare daylight overdrafts at banks because big dealers would no longer have an incentive to build inventory to make deliveries of $500 million or maybe even $800 million of a given issue to a single buyer. (Deliveries of this size do get made to money funds which have a voracious appetite for repo collateral, given the several hundred billions of money they must constantly keep invested short term.) While cutting the size of allowable single deliveries over the Fed wire sounds attractive, it would add, possibly intolerably, to congestion on the Fed wire unless a new netting system were introduced into the clearing of wireable securities.

Reasons for cooperation. While it is easy to say that a new netting system is needed for the clearing of trades in wireables, neither the Fed nor the Treasury is prepared to exercise leadership in the creation of such a system.[2] This means that the various parties who would play a role in netting—the dealers, the clearing banks, and the brokers—players who have sometimes complementary but often competing interests, must come together, design, and implement a netting system on their own. To carry out that tall order, the *Government Securities Clearing Corporation (GSCC)* has been created.

The GSCC approaches its task with some optimism because the various parties to clearing all have at this point a strong economic interest in seeing netting introduced and, therefore, a strong incentive to cooperate and to compromise. Netting promises to cut dealers' operating costs and the risks they perceive to exist in the clearing process as well. Netting promises to get the government brokers totally out of the business of clearing buys and sells. Finally, netting promises to substantially reduce daylight overdraft at clearing banks both at the dealer-bank level and at the bank-Fed level.

What trades to net. Many different sorts of trades are done in book-entry securities: brokered dealer-to-dealer trades, direct dealer-to-dealer trades, and dealer-to-customer trades. Also, such trades are done both for cash and for regular (next-day) settlement. Ideally, one would like a system, à la DTC-NSCC, that would create multilateral netting for all parties to all such trades. But such a system would be too ambitious and difficult to create all at once.

For this reason, GSCC proposes to begin by netting just brokered trades for regular settlement, which means, in effect, the trades for regular settlement that the 40 primary dealers and 13 aspiring dealers carry out through the 5 or 6 brokers of governments. Those trades are regarded as having a sufficient critical mass so that netting of them would contribute significantly to efficiency in the clearing of governments. Once such trades are netted, other classes of trades can also be added to the netting process; the agenda of GSCC is fluid.

Settlement with multilateral netting

NSCC proposes to implement multilateral netting in steps.

---

[2] A top official of the FRBNY is quoted as having said several times that the netting of trades in governments would artificially increase the velocity of trading in the government market, thereby increasing both market volatility and market risk. An incredulous operations office at a major dealer commented, "They are saying that, because there would be fewer settlement problems [with netting], traders would do more trading. Our traders have *never* been in the cage [back office]. They trade and say, 'You guys clean it up for me.'"

The beginning: comparisons. First, GSCC will introduce a system for comparing trades just as NSCC compares trades. Doing so will require a lot of cooperation from both dealers and brokers, as GSCC says it will want by midnight of each trading day information in machine-readable form on the trades that it is to compare for each participant. Some dealers and brokers currently do not get such information to their clearing bank until much later; to meet GSCC's deadline, they will have to make big changes in the way they run their operations area.

GSCC will put trades that compare (both sides agree as to what was done) into the netting process. It will kick back trades that do not compare to the parties submitting them for those parties to straighten out and clear.

It is crucial for the eventual success of GSCC that it begin by getting the comparison process working smoothly. Otherwise, even with netting, a lot of trades will end up having to be cleared in the old-fashioned way over the wire and outside of the net settlement process. For trade comparisons to work smoothly, all of the participating dealers and brokers must be educated to report their trades accurately and on a timely basis.

Step two: netting. To illustrate the netting process currently proposed by NSCC, suppose that Sali sells through a broker $10 million of bills, 5 to Merrill and 5 to Bache. The way things would work if there were no other trades in the system is that GSCC would tell Sali to forget the 10 it sold and to deliver 2 lots of 5. Sali would be instructed to deliver 5 to the account of GSCC at Manny, which would redeliver those securities to Merrill. At the same time, Sali would be instructed to deliver 5 to the account of GSCC at Sec Pac which clears for Bache. GSCC would redeliver those securities to Bache. Note that, although Sali has in effect sold securities to Bache, Sali won't know Bache nor will Bache know Sali. The system is designed to ensure the confidentiality of brokered trades.

In the real world of trading, GSCC will have to net trades among 53 dealers and 5 or 6 brokers. If all of the dealers and brokers used the same clearing bank, then a dealer would have to make or receive only one net delivery in each issue he traded. Actually, the different brokers and dealers use a number of big clearing banks, and GSCC therefore plans to have an account at each of these banks. Conceivably, a dealer who was a big net seller of an issue might have to make a delivery to GSCC's account at each of several different clearing banks—that would depend on who the buyers were and what banks they used to clear their trades. In any case, netting as conceived of by GSCC would dramatically reduce the number of trades that a participating dealer or broker would need to clear.

The netting system that GSCC plans, initially at least, for government will be less ambitious than the DTC-NSCC scheme in several respects.

First, GSCC currently has no plans to become the guarantor of interdealer trades cleared through it as is NSCC. Second, dealer-customer trades will be outside the ambit of GSCC netting.

When as and if.   Getting the GSCC system in place will require a lot of work and cooperation by different players in the clearing process. Not all dealers agree on just what issues they want addressed first. Brokers who in some ways stand to benefit most from the system are fearful that it just might lead to their being replaced by black boxes. Clearing banks would like to see their daylight overdraft fall as it would with netting, but they are concerned about what will happen to their revenues: As the number of trades cleared declines, will they have to raise clearing fees? Many questions remain unanswered, but much work is being done to put in place a netting system that will make the clearing of wireable securities significantly more efficient.

THE NEXT CHAPTER

In our final chapter, we turn to the tricky business of clearing both repos of and outright trades of mortgage-backed securities. This is one end of the clearing business that creates some royal headaches. This is prompted in part by the big fails that the clearing of certain of these securities regularly generates.

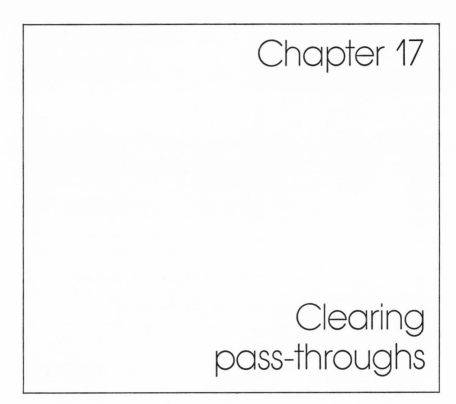

Chapter 17

Clearing
pass-throughs

PASS-THROUGHS ARE A HYBRID SECURITY, the most complex Wall Street has ever traded. The complexity of pass-throughs is such that one might almost wish to disinvent them. Pass-throughs, however, are here to stay because they have come to play a key role in providing liquidity to mortgage loans and in drawing, into the residential mortgage market, vast sums of funds from nontraditional sources.

Pass-throughs are too long-lived to be a true money market instrument. However, since they are traded and cleared by many of the same dealers and banks who clear other money market instruments, we include here a chapter on the clearing of pass-throughs.

PASS-THROUGHS: PHYSICAL VERSUS BOOK ENTRY

Currently, GNMAs come solely in physical, *registered* form. Figure 17-1 shows a GNMA certificate. Freddie Macs and Fannie Maes also used to come in registered form, but no longer. Outstanding conventional mortgage securities have largely been converted to book-entry form, and new issues of Freddie Macs and Fannie Maes are available in book-entry form only.

FIGURE 17-1
GNMA pass-through certificate

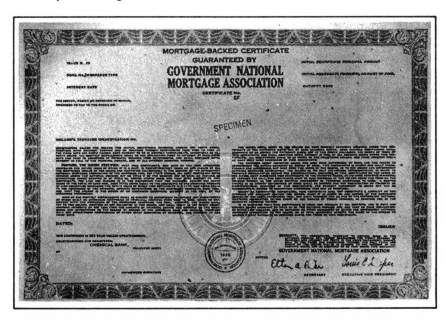

A question commonly asked, especially since Freddie Macs and Fannie Maes have successfully gone book entry, is why GNMAs were never converted to book-entry form. Part of the answer is that, until recently, the Fed wasn't soliciting more book-entry business because Fedwire lacked the capacity to handle either more issues or more transactions. It has that capacity now, but during the period that it did not, clearing banks and others invested large sums in creating facilities to clear the huge volume of GNMA trades currently done in the market. Naturally, such entities are not now going to champion the switching of GNMAs from physical to book-entry form. The impetus for such a switch would have to come from GNMA. Unfortunately, the leadership at GNMA is uncertain about how much conversion of GNMAs to book entry would benefit both issuers of and investors in GNMAs. Also, issuers do not favor a switch to book-entry form for reasons outlined below.

TRADING IN PASS-THROUGHS: CASH, FORWARD, AND RPS

GNMAs, Freddie Macs, and Fannie Maes are all traded in active, liquid markets, which are made by many of the same dealers who make the markets for Treasuries. Pass-throughs have, however, some unique quirks.

Consequently, market practices with respect to the trading, clearing, and safekeeping of pass-throughs differ sharply from those that prevail in the market for Treasuries.

The cash and secondary markets for pass-throughs

Pass-throughs trade in the cash and secondary markets *by coupon* and settlement month on a *TBA* (pool number *to be advised*) basis. This is a sharp, but easily explained, break with practices in the market for Treasuries.

By coupon/month.   In the Treasury market, any note or bond is uniquely identified by *its coupon and date of maturity;* and in trading, different Treasuries are so identified. A trader might, for example, quote bids and offers for the 10¾s of 05; and when he does so, every other trader will know specifically what issue he is quoting.

To identify a specific GNMA, or any other pass-through, one must know *its coupon and pool number.* Also, if one wants to estimate the current expected life of a pass-through, one must know, among other things, *its date of issue.* Since the universe of identifiably different GNMAs is, unlike that of identifiably different Treasuries, vast, some lumping together of different pass-throughs within particular classes of pass-throughs, for example, of different GNMAs and of different Freddie Macs, must be done to make pass-throughs tradable. In both the new-issue and secondary markets for pass-throughs, such lumping together is done *by coupon.*

TBA (to be advised).   The fact that pass-throughs trade by coupon, not by pool number, is also rooted in the way they are created and distributed. Creating pass-throughs requires time-consuming administrative work and procedures. "To sell a new Treasury issue," noted one GNMA trader, "the Treasury simply says, 'We're issuing.' And bam, they hit the Fed wire with $400 million in new bills." With mortgage-backs, things are less simple. For example, the procedures start, for GNMAs, with a mortgage banker who packages mortgage loans into pools and presents them to Ginnie Mae. Once Ginnie Mae gets the loans, it analyzes them to verify that they meet its criteria. If they do, Ginnie Mae affixes its guarantee to the pool and assigns a number to the pool; after that, Ginnie Mae gives the pool information to Chemical Bank, the transfer agent, which then prints up certificates bearing the new pool number.

A mortgage banker who assembles a pool of pass-throughs and presents them to a guarantor will, chances are, want to sell those securities before the guarantor finishes its work and assigns the pool a number. At this point, all that the mortgage banker knows is the coupon that the new pass-throughs will carry and the assumption as to which month the loans will close. Assume that Sali gives our mortgage banker

a bid for his securities. If the latter takes Sali's bid, Sali may well turn right around and sell, to investors, the pass-throughs it has just bought. If so, Sali will have to put, on its confirms to buyers, the coupon rate on the pass-throughs and, instead of a pool number, three letters: *TBA,* an acronym for [*pool number*] *to be advised.* In the *new-issues market,* pass-throughs trade, for easily understood reasons, TBA.

Pass-throughs also trade TBA in the *secondary market* where already existing pass-throughs are traded. A second reason is, as noted, that the universe of pass-throughs is so vast that some lumping together of different pass-throughs is required to make them tradable. Traders do this lumping together by treating all of an issuer's paper that carries a specific coupon (e.g., GNMA 10½s) as it were *homogeneous,* which it is not; traders of pass-throughs, in quoting bids and offers, disregard differences both in pool numbers and in dates of issue; such a trader will have, for say GNMA 10½s, just *one* bid and *one* offer. A second reason that pass-throughs trade TBA is that a pool traded for future delivery cannot be priced until after the factors for each pool (determined by preceding payments of principal) are announced each month.

Because of the different ways in which pass-throughs and Treasuries are traded, differences also exist in the ways in which the responsibilities of traders in the two sorts of shops are divided. A shop trading governments will assign, to each of its traders, Treasuries falling within a specific maturity range: Such a shop will, depending on the size of the shop and the number of traders it employs, have a short-bill trader, a long-bill trader, a short-note trader, an intermediate-note trader, and so on. In contrast, a shop that trades pass-throughs splits traders according to the coupons they trade: One guy trades 6% to 8% coupons, another trades 8½% to 10% coupons, and so on.

An investor who contracts to buy GNMA 10½s, thus, knows that he will get securities with a 10½% coupon, but he doesn't know what pool numbers he will get, nor does he know, unless he contracts to buy a coupon currently—but not previously—issued, what date of issue the paper he gets will carry. GNMA has issued paper at certain coupon levels during at least two periods: once when mortgage rates were trending up through that coupon level in the 1970s, and once again when mortgage rates were trending down through that coupon level in the 1980s.

RPs and reverses of pass-throughs

Pass-throughs, like governments and other money market instruments, are commonly financed by dealers and by investors in the RP market. If it's a dealer who borrows money, the trade is called an RP, whereas if it's an investor who borrows money, the trade is commonly called a reverse. Pass-throughs offer higher yields than Treasuries of comparable

maturity; consequently, a buyer of pass-throughs is often able to earn *positive carry* (a profitable spread) by buying and financing pass-throughs that pay a yield well above the current RP or reverse rate. Today, the big dealers in pass-throughs, such as Sali and First Boston, all run big "matched books" in pass-throughs as part of their much bigger overall matched-book operation.

A dealer is said to run *a matched book in RP and reverse* when he reverses in securities with the right hand and RPs them to investors with the left hand. He does this in part to earn a spread between the reverse rate he is paid by those who borrow from him and the somewhat lower RP rate he pays to those from whom he borrows. Dealers also use their matched books to create contrived bets on short-term interest rates; to provide financing to those of their investors who want to buy securities on credit; to cover their *short positions* (sales of securities that they do not have in position); and, sometimes, to finance their positions.

The forward market

We spoke above of what might be called the *cash markets* for pass-throughs, that is, markets in which pass-throughs are traded for delivery before the next monthly record date for a payment of interest and principal. In addition to the cash market for pass-throughs, there is also an active, brokered *forward market* for these securities. In this forward market, pass-throughs are traded for delivery at various, specified dates, each of which lies one or more months into the future.

Traders in pass-throughs seek to actively arbitrage the cash and forward markets for these securities, that is, they set up, using the cash, forward, and RP-reverse markets, multilegged trades designed to lock up a profit, albeit not always a large one. Because of this active arbitrage, forward Ginnies, for example, always sell, when carry is *positive,* at a *discount* to cash Ginnies; the amount of the discount will be greater: (1) the greater is the spread between the RP rate and the yield on cash Ginnies, and (2) the greater is the time before the forward trade settles.

Trades that involve the conversion of spot or cash pass-throughs into forward pass-throughs are referred to by pass-through traders as *dollar rolls.* On a dollar roll, a trader or investor might, for example, sell spot Ginnies, invest the proceeds in RP, and buy forward Ginnies.

Clearing trades in pass-throughs

The clearing of trades in pass-throughs gets a little confusing for several reasons. First, most trades in Ginnies and in other pass-throughs that are done to settle during the current month are actually done, for reasons described below, to settle on one of several future days of the month. A

second peculiarity of the pass-through market is that, in this market, many trades are done *both* in *registered* securities and in *book-entry* securities. Because of this situation, which is made all the more confusing because some Freddie Macs are still in registered form, one must, before one can describe how a given pass-through trade is cleared, determine whether the pass-through traded is in physical or book-entry form.

GNMA day

The reasons for GNMA day are rooted in history. When GNMAs were introduced, traders acquired the habit of settling almost all trades in them on a single day, *GNMA day,* which is the third Wednesday of the month. That date was picked to give issuers time to provide information on pools they had put into Ginnie Mae for its guarantee. Later, as other types of pass-throughs were introduced, traders adopted the habit of settling trades in them, too, on GNMA day. One reason traders did the latter was to facilitate swaps: An investor wants to sell Ginnies, buy Freddies, stay fully invested the whole time, but not have to borrow; the only way he can do this is if his two trades both settle on the same day. Actually, since settling all trades of pass-throughs on one day of the month created *nightmares* for people in dealer operations and in clearance, dealers tried, beginning in March 1986, to stagger the clearing of pass-throughs over several days: Freddies and Fannies on Monday, Ginnies on Wednesday, and certain heavily discounted pass-throughs the following week. This schedule underwent and is still undergoing further changes to spread out the clearing of pass-throughs.

CLEARING TRADES IN REGISTERED PASS-THROUGHS

The clearing of registered pass-throughs resembles in many respects the clearing of other physical money market instruments: Money and securities must change hands according to a carefully choreographed routine. Still the clearing of physical pass-throughs has its own peculiarities, of which GNMA day is but one.

Dealer operations: Registered pass-throughs

To clear a trade in registered pass-throughs, a dealer's back office must do many of the same things it must do to clear a trade in any physical security. It must clean up the trader's or salesperson's trade ticket, send the customer a confirm, and *just prior to GNMA day,* instruct both the customer and its clearing bank as to what securities are to be delivered against what money. Also, on sells to the dealer, it must track incoming

confirms and be prepared to receive, just prior to GNMA day, instructions with respect to what securities will be delivered to it and what monies it must pay out for those securities.

The mortgage-backed allocation function.   One unique task a dealer's operations people must carry out in clearing trades in physical pass-throughs is what's called the *allocation function.* During a month, a dealer in pass-throughs will typically do many buys and sells, few of which will be settled on the spot. Thus, when the forward settlement date, GNMA day, or a nearby day, comes up, the dealer has *many* trades to settle. To get paid for all of the securities he has sold, the dealer must make good delivery of these securities.

This turns out to be trickier when *registered certificates* are to be delivered than when *book-entry* securities are to be delivered. For one thing, certificates come in discrete pieces, some big, some small; a dealer must, thus, piece together a delivery of any size: find the certificates with the right coupon, and then find, among them, the right-sized pieces. According to *PSA* (*Public Securities Association*) guidelines, a dealer delivering GNMAs must give the customer no more than *three* pools *per million* of a trade. Also, the *aggregate unpaid balance* (original principal minus previous payments and prepayments of principal) on these certificates must deviate by no more than 2½% from the par amount for which the trade was done: If First Boston sells $1 million of GNMAs to a customer, it must deliver to that customer no more than three certificates, the aggregate unpaid balance of which must lie between $975,000 and $1,025,000.

When a dealer sells pass-throughs to a client, neither it nor the client has any idea of what pools will be delivered; depending on the coupon, the pools delivered could be any one of a vast number of old pools or they could be new pools. Before clearing and settling its trades in mortgage-backed securities, the dealer must go through something known as *the mortgage-backed securities allocation function.*

The department that carries out the allocation function assigns pools carrying appropriate coupons to each sell ticket for forward settlement that the dealer has accumulated over the month. Say a dealer has sold $1 million GNMA 11s to a customer for settlement on the third Wednesday in April. Several days prior to that date, he must *build that trade.*

Allocation, done manually, is tedious and complex. The dealer attempts, given what he has in inventory and what is coming in, to patch together a host of deliveries, each of which is a good delivery. Noted one dealer, "To deliver pass-throughs, we used to keep, on cards, information on our inventory by pool number, face amount, and coupon. If we had to deliver out $1 million of GNMAs 11s, we'd hunt through our files and say, 'We have Ginnie Mae pool 123. That's worth $500,000. Take that out. We have

Ginnie Mae pool 456. That's worth $200,000. We can use that. Well, we are up to $700,000. We must reach $975,000. We need one more pool of a Ginnie Mae for $275,000—that's outstanding balance, not original face." Once we got our three pool numbers, we'd have to call the client, by 3 P.M. on the 14th and give him the pool information: 'pool 123 for $500,000, pool 456 for $200,000, pool 789 for $250,000. The trade price is . . . and so on [to complete trade details]." "

A dealer wants to avoid, at all costs, fails to deliver, so he tries mightily to piece together, from his inventory and from incoming deliveries, all of the many outgoing deliveries he must make. If that won't work, he may put some of the securities he has in inventory into the transfer agent for a *denominational exchange.* Today, many dealers still do the allocation of pass-throughs by hand as we have described it, but the biggest dealers have automated the procedure. Allocation is precisely the sort of problem that begs to be solved by a computer programmed to do it.

Forty-eight hours prior to settlement date, the dealer must call, by 3 P.M., each buyer who has purchased securities from him and tell him what amounts of what pool numbers he will be getting and what money he must pay. After the dealer calls his clients, he sends computer-generated, hard-copy advices both (1) to his clients, telling them what securities to expect to receive from him and (2) to his clearing bank, instructing it what securities sales to clear for him. Meanwhile, the dealer will be receiving similar calls and hard-copy advices from parties from whom he has bought pass-throughs. In response to these messages, the dealer will tell his clearing bank what securities purchases to clear for him.

Trade calculations.   Once a dealer's operations area has determined what pass-throughs are going to be delivered to it and what pass-throughs it is going to deliver out to others, it must price all of these securities. That alone is a monumental job for a shop that's an active trader of mortgage backs.

Treasuries are easy to price. The money on a Treasury is always the product of two numbers (the agreed-upon sale price *times* face value) *plus* accrued interest. The pricing of pass-throughs is more complex. To come up with the money on a trade of pass-throughs, one must first calculate, for each certificate, its current unpaid balance. To do this, one multiplies, for each certificate to be delivered or received, the original face value of the certificate times its current *factor,* unpaid principal balance per $100 of face value (factors are published, monthly, for each pass-through pool of each issuer). Next, one multiplies that product by the price at which the trade was done. Finally, to come up with total proceeds for the trade, one must add, to that sum, interest accrued since the last payment date. A common problem in the pricing of pass-throughs

is that current pool factors are often reported incorrectly, for example, by Chemical, the transfer agent for GNMAs; when a trade is priced on the basis of an incorrect factor, it must later be *cancelled and corrected* by the dealer.

A dealer's operations people must also check the pricing of the many pass-throughs to be delivered to them on settlement day.

The clearing bank in action

Clearing trades in physical pass-throughs turns out to be, for a clearing bank, a more trying job than does the clearing of any other money market instrument. First, the dealer's clearing bank reads the hard-copy advice from the dealer instructing it what pass-throughs to deliver against what money. The bank also gets other instructions from the dealer telling it what securities it should expect to receive for the dealer's account and what monies it should pay for these securities.

A dealer's clearing bank, reading a particular delivery instruction, will say, "Ah ha, First Boston wants us to deliver, to XYZ Inc., GNMA pools 123, 456, and 789 for which the monies are. . . ." On GNMA day, the bank will, if it has been safekeeping these securities for First Boston, retrieve them from its vault, and deliver them, against payment, either to First Boston's customer or to that customer's agent. Alternatively, if First Boston directs its clearing bank to deliver out securities it [First Boston] is supposed to receive on GNMA day, its clearing bank will do that, too, provided the securities come in on time.

When a clearing bank clears physical pass-throughs, it must go through much the same steps it does when it clears, say, CDs or BAs. It must accept securities in over the window, count and verify those securities, and then pay for them. These securities then go to the dealer's account manager at the clearing bank; he, in turn, uses the securities, together with any of the dealer's securities that have been taken out of the clearing bank's vault, to build deliveries per the client dealer's instructions. These deliveries are made against receipt of a stamped delivery bill and, it is hoped, a later receipt of money equal to the correct sales price.

Naturally, clearing bank personnel generate a lot of time-stamped slips as they move securities around the clearing bank's operations area, into and out of its vault, and off-premise to make a delivery. No clearing bank wants to lose track of millions of dollars of GNMAs if it can help it.

The headaches.   For a clearing bank, clearing physical pass-throughs is an unparalleled headache because peaking in the work load is so great that everything must be done at breakneck speed. On one business day a month, the clearing bank must not only receive a vast number of

deliveries of pass-throughs, but it must, partly by using pass-throughs delivered to its dealer client, make an equally vast number of deliveries of pass-throughs.

Most of the time clearing banks are glad to get more business from dealers whom they deem creditworthy. However, pass-throughs are another story. These days, clearing banks hate to get more GNMA or other physical, pass-through business. A bank that takes on such business must process mountains of trades during just a few days a month. This creates, for the bank, a problem: How, during the rest of the month, when the volume of pass-throughs to be cleared is near nil, is the bank to employ productively the people who labor feverishly two days a month to clear pass-through trades that settle en masse either on GNMA day or on an adjacent day.

Self-clearing.   Partly because of the problem of getting a clearing bank to commit to do GNMA business, partly to save clearing costs, and partly to maximize winnings in the fails game, some dealers in pass-throughs, Sali included, have developed a set-up whereby they clear their own trades in pass-throughs.

Fails

Most, if not all, parties to the GNMA clearing process would like to see fails held to a minimum, but, in fact, fails occur in large numbers on GNMA day. Some are avoidable; others, probably, are not. Some avoidable fails are caused by customers. Despite all of the effort that dealers put into the allocation function, deliveries of pass-throughs to customers routinely fail. For such a trade to go through, the customer must advise its clearing agent that it has bought securities X for money Y from dealer Z and direct its agent to clear that trade. Customers often forget to do this. When a customer does so, a fail, costly to him, occurs.

Some unavoidable fails occur because there is too little time in the day to clear all the deliveries, sometimes daisy chains of deliveries, that must clear so that every pass-through trade that is supposed to clear actually clears. In a typical situation, A is scheduled to deliver, to B, securities that B is scheduled to deliver to C who, in turn, is scheduled to deliver those same securities to D. A does not know C or D and, probably, could not care less whether C manages to make his delivery to D. Along the daisy chain of deliveries, all anyone cares about is shoving out all of the securities he can, given what securities he has in inventory and what securities have already been delivered to him.

Every dealer wants to end up having more fails that earn him money than fails that cost him money. Thus, GNMA delivery days end up

resembling, for all the world, a bunch of kids playing hot potato: Toss the hot potato (pass-throughs) to the next kid before you burn your fingers (experience a costly fail). Given the volume of pass-throughs that are put through the clearing process, it always occurs that some dealers receive deliveries of securities too late in the day to have time to redeliver those securities elsewhere. When this occurs, the dealer who gets the hot potato too late fails and ends up out money.

RPs of pass-throughs also generate, as noted below, a lot of fails. From a dealer's point of view, there is one bright side to pass-through-related fails; Sali and some other dealers manage, it is said, to finance their total dealing operations in GNMAs, an expensive business, with the money they make on fails.

Reregistration

Whenever physical pass-throughs are delivered, by a clearing bank or by a dealer who self-clears, the normal procedure is for the securities to be delivered in bearer form. This may mean one of two things: (1) the assignment form on the back of the certificate has been executed in blank, or (2) a bond power executed in blank has been attached to the certificate. For a top, creditworthy customer, an IBM or a Metropolitan Life, a dealer might agree to deliver to that customer, against payment, certificates registered in the customer's name rather than bearer paper. A dealer would, however, never agree to that for a smaller dealer or investor; the credit risk would be too great. If a customer wants its dealer to register securities it has bought in its name, that dealer will, normally, require that the customer first fully pay for the securities.

Customers to whom pass-through certificates are delivered on or around GNMA day have adequate time to put that paper into the transfer agent so that, by the record date, it is registered in the name either of the investor or of the nominee of the investor's custodial agent. On GNMAs, for example, Chemical promises 48-hour turnaround time on transfer requests. Sometimes, around settlement time for GNMAs, Chemical fails, due to volume, to meet that turnaround time, by several days. However, if a customer gets his securities delivered to him on time, and if he acts promptly, he will have adequate time to get his securities through transfer before the next record date.

One problem that crops up, occasionally, with respect to transfer is that, even though Chemical issues, at the end of a month, new GNMA certificates that bear the name of the new holder of record and that are dated or back-dated to the record date for that month, the principal and interest payments made the following month on these certificates are sent to the former registered holders of the certificates. When this occurs, yet more claim forms must go out.

On physical pass-throughs, most dealers try to transfer into their name, prior to the last business day of the month, every security they have added to their inventory. Dealers want to ensure that principal and interest payments on such paper come to them, not to prior registered holders of the paper. Nonetheless, there is a lot of claiming of interest and principal going on on the Street that wouldn't occur if every dealer ran a tight back-office operation.

Risk of theft.   Theft of pass-through certificates is not much of a problem these days. Noted one dealer, "If we lost a GNMA today that was in the name of First Boston, we would immediately contact the transfer agent, Chemical, and tell them to put a stop on the certificate. The party who stole the securities would receive no principal and interest payments; these would continue to go to First Boston. He would also be unable to reregister the security because of the stop we would put with the transfer agent. Finally, if he were to walk into a bank and try to use the certificate as collateral for a loan, the bank would check whether the certificate was stolen [recall our discussion in Chapter 12 of the Securities Information Center], and, bingo, the thief would be caught. The systems we have in place today for these types of problems work very efficiently, once proper action is taken by the party from whom the securities were taken.

"Back in the 60s when the book-entry system was begun, the communications that existed weren't what they are today. Information on stolen securities did not get around to everyone back then. If you reported a lost or stolen security, a flyer might appear two weeks later; there was no service to publish information on stolen securities. Fortunately, things are different today. Every GNMA day, messengers are running around the Street with *billions and billions* of Ginnie Maes." Most of the Ginnie Maes are, by the way, endorsed in blank, which makes them bearer paper.

Going book-entry

Because of the big and growing problems created by the clearance of physical Ginnie Maes, everyone on the Street has agreed for some time that Ginnie Maes ought to go book-entry. In 1987, the dealers finally made a concerted effort to get Ginnies into the *Mortgage-Backed Securities Clearing Corporation* (*MBSCC*), which is tied to the Midwest Clearing Corporation. According to the original plan, every Ginnie Mae issue was to be made depository-eligible by June 1987, and rules were to be established that every issue that could settle depository had to settle that way. The Public Securities Association tried to push this by

saying that, once a Ginnie Mae issue became depository-eligible, a dealer to whom that issue was delivered in physical rather than book-entry form was supposed to pay in clearing house (next-day) funds, rather than in immediately available Fed funds.

MBSCC had some initial success in comparing trades in pass-throughs, but the movement of Ginnie Maes into a depository began haltingly at best. Everyone blamed the problem on someone else. Some dealers said custody banks were torpedoing the depository—joining it only slowly—because they stood to earn more as long as Ginnies stayed physical. Others put the blame on issuers of Ginnie Maes, who service these securities and who happen to operate on thin margins; issuers, it was said, stood to gain from keeping Ginnies in physical form because they got more float on payments passed through on physical Ginnies than they would get on payments passed through on Ginnies in a depository. The one sure thing is that the MBSCC was, for whatever reason or reasons, getting off in mid-1987 to a slow and uncertain start. Some went so far as to say it was stillborn.

CLEARING TRADES IN BOOK-ENTRY PASS-THROUGHS

The dealer and clearing-bank operations involved in clearing trades in book-entry pass-throughs (Freddie Macs and Fannie Maes) are almost identical to those described in Chapter 11 where we talked about how trades of wireable securities are cleared. One difference, exception makes the rule: In the case of book-entry pass-throughs, settlements tend to be bunched on several days of the month, one for Freddies and one for Fannies.

A comparison of how Ginnies and Freddies are cleared demonstrates to all parties—investors, dealers, and clearing banks—the advantages of issuing securities in book-entry form. First, there is no expensive shuffling of certificates from place to place and no counting and verifying several or more times of stacks of certificates. Second, since book-entry securities are fungible and divisible, allocation, at settlement time, requires, for book-entry pass-throughs, little or none of the assembling of this and that piece that is required to build a delivery of Ginnies. Third, delivery of a book-entry pass-through causes a coincident change in the list of holders of record of that security; thus, when book-entry securities change hands, there is no fee and no expenditure of time involved in reregistration. Finally, with book-entry securities, the fails generated by incorrect paper work with respect to reregistration and by incorrect reregistration—as occurs, sometimes, on RPs of Ginnies—are eliminated.

CLEARING RPS OF PASS-THROUGHS

The huge amounts of RPs of pass-throughs, which are done daily by the major dealers in pass-throughs, are cleared just like outright buys and sells of pass-throughs.

Lots of investors won't take pass-throughs as collateral, and for this reason dealers pay, to repo pass-throughs, a rate that's a spread above the RP rate on Treasuries. Normally, the reverse rate on pass-throughs is a spread above the RP rate on such securities.

On term RPs of pass-throughs, dealers generally deliver out RP collateral, whether the collateral is in physical or book-entry form. On overnight RPs, however, they rely heavily on investors whom they have cultivated and who are willing to do trust-me or tri-party RPs with them. If a dealer's clearing bank charges him $25 a certificate to clear GNMAs, clearing a $50-million RP of GNMAs that might, topside, amount to 150 certificates, would cost the dealer, if he made delivery, $3,750 just in bank fees; and, on top of that, he would have to pay a like fee on leg two of the RP. A dealer who delivered collateral on overnight RPs of pass-throughs would also incur a lot of other in-house costs, and even that might not be the end of his costs: delivering a bunch of pass-through certificates to an investor in RP creates endless opportunities for both the dealer and the investor to make costly mistakes.

Dealers who are big in mortgage backs do a substantial chunk of their matched-book business in pass-throughs. Today, it looks attractive to many hungry investors, such as S&Ls, to buy mortgage-backed securities with next to no money, finance them, and earn a spread. As long as interest rates do not back up, that's a great play. If rates do back up, it's a quick way to go bankrupt.

Clearing RPs of physical pass-throughs

Given the way RPs of Treasuries are handled by the Street, it was natural, when GNMAs—and later other pass-throughs—were born and began to be repoed, for the Street to say, "Monthly payments of principal and interest on pass-through collateral shall go to the giver of the collateral who truly owns these securities."

That sounds straightforward. Yet, the distribution of principal and interest payments to the correct party in an RP frequently creates problems: one sort if the pass-throughs are in *registered* form, another sort if the pass-throughs are in *book-entry* form.

The way an RP of registered, pass-through securities is supposed to work is that the borrower of money attaches an endorsed stock power to the securities he gives as collateral, but the securities remain, throughout the term of the RP, registered in his name. If this procedure

is followed, the owner of the pass-throughs will continue to receive monthly payments of principal and interest on his securities throughout the term of the RP. Also, the giver of collateral will get back, at the end of the RP, the *identical certificates* he gave out as collateral at the beginning of the RP.

Often, however, RPs of registered pass-throughs do not work so smoothly. To illustrate why, we assume that First Boston takes in, from an S&L, GNMAs registered in the name of the S&L and RPs them to, say, IBM. That's a typical matched-book trade. IBM's custodial agent could and should just hold the GNMA collateral it gets with the attached stock power. Often, however, it does not do so. The clerical person who receives the GNMA certificates is programmed: "I get a certificate; it is a Ginnie Mae; if it's for the IBM account, I put it into Chemical Bank, the transfer agent, for registration in IBM's name." The clerk does not go the extra step and say, "Hey, this is a repo; I simply put the security in the vault. Only on a purchase must I register the security in IBM's name."

Incorrect reregistering of a pass-through that has been repoed creates two problems. First, monthly payments of principal and interest that occur during the term of the RP or perhaps after it—there's a lag between record and payment dates—will go to the wrong party; and the rightful recipient of those payments will have to file a claim to get his money. If, moreover, he does not get his money for some time, as often occurs, the time pattern of the series of payments his securities generate will be slowed and the return he earns on them will, thereby, be *lowered*.

Incorrect reregistration of a repoed pass-through also causes a second problem: fails to deliver when the RP comes off. Suppose IBM tries, at the end of its RP, to redeliver to First Boston GNMA certificates that have been incorrectly transferred into its name. First Boston will say, "Sorry, you have the right face amount, the right pool numbers, but the wrong owner of record. We can't accept those securities until you transfer them back into the name of the guy who reversed them into us because he's not going to take securities registered in your name." So IBM fails for a couple of days on its redelivery of collateral to First Boston, and First Boston fails on its redelivery of collateral to the S&L from whom it originally got the collateral. This fail earns extra income for the S&L, which gets, for several days, *free* financing; it also costs IBM money because it is IBM who provides that free financing.

A giver of collateral registered in his name has several reasons for insisting that the securities returned to him be registered in his name. First, if he accepted, versus payment, securities registered in the name of some other party, he would expose himself to a significant credit risk, unless, of course, those securities had, attached to them, properly executed bond powers. Second, even the latter alternative is unattractive, for, while it would expose the original giver of collateral to no credit risk, it would

force him to go to the trouble and expense of getting his collateral transferred back into his name. On an RP of registered securities, good delivery requires that the securities returned be registered in the same name in which they were registered when they went out.

When a physical security is put into transfer, a new certificate bearing a new certificate number—the old certificate number is canceled—is always issued. This explains why, on an RP of physical pass-throughs, the giver of securities may get back certificates bearing new certificate numbers. This, as noted, will occur on an RP of physical, registered mortgage backs whenever the receiver of collateral mistakenly registers, due to a clerical error, the collateral in his name. Such mistakes, which occur routinely, often generate fails when the parties attempt to execute leg two of the RP.

On an RP of other registered securities, the same mistake that occurs on RPs of physical pass-throughs might occur. If it did, the giver of collateral would eventually get back a certificate with a new number.

Clearing RPs of book-entry pass-throughs

The putting of Freddie Macs into book-entry form has eliminated the problem of incorrect transfer that often occurs in connection with RPs of GNMAs and other physical pass-throughs. On each leg of an RP of book-entry Freddie Macs, ownership records change, at appropriate tiers of the book-entry system, automatically and simultaneously with the transfer of the securities repoed.

However, RPs of book-entry Freddie Macs create a problem of their own. Unlike Treasuries, such securities throw off payments of principal and interest once a month and then only days after a record date. As a result, principal and interest payments on book-entry Freddie Macs that have been repoed are constantly being made with a lag, which does not exist on Treasuries, to a past holder of collateral. It drives everyone's operations people mildly insane to have to determine which payments from which entities on which Freddie Macs they ought to be claiming today.

The whole problem is complicated by the fact that the cash flow that a pass-through throws off in any month is unique to both the pool and the month; it is not, as in the case of a straight coupon security, a nice fixed sum, 5% or whatever of face value. To make matters still worse, the current pool factors, on which operations people rely for claiming payments of principal and interest due their firm on pass-throughs, often contain, when they are published each month, errors. Because of the above, the Street would dearly love to have the Fed track who is getting whose principal and interest payments on which book-entry Freddie Macs and Fannie Maes and reroute the payments to the correct parties. So far, the Fed has said, "Sorry boys, that's a job we're unwilling to take on."

Glossary

Common money market and bond market terms

Accretion (of a discount): In portfolio accounting, a straight-line accumulation of capital gains on discount bonds in anticipation of receipt of par at maturity.

Accrued interest: Interest due from issue or from the last coupon date to the present on an interest-bearing security. The buyer of the security pays the quoted dollar price plus accrued interest.

Active: A market in which there is much trading.

Actuals: The cash commodity as opposed to the futures contract.

Add-on rate: A specific rate of interest to be paid. Stands in contrast to the rate on a discount security, such as a Treasury bill, that pays *no* interest.

After-tax real rate of return: Money after-tax rate of return minus the inflation rate.

Agencies: Federal agency securities. See also **Agency bank.**

Agency bank: A form of organization commonly used by foreign banks to enter the U.S. market. An agency bank cannot accept deposits or extend loans in its own name; it acts as an agent for the parent bank. Term often used on the Street to refer both to foreign bank agencies and branches.

Agent: A firm that executes orders for or otherwise acts on behalf of another (the principal) and is subject to its control and authority. The agent may receive a fee or commission.

279

Agent bank: A commercial bank that does the following for an issuer of, say, commercial paper: prints up notes, delivers them out against money, and redeems them at maturity—all pursuant to the issuer's instructions.

All-in cost: Total costs, explicit and other. Example: The all-in cost to a bank of CD money is the explicit rate of interest it pays on that deposit *plus* the FDIC premium it must pay on the deposit *plus* the hidden cost it incurs because it must hold some portion of that deposit in a non-interest-bearing reserve account at the Fed.

All or none (AON): Requirement that none of an order be executed unless all of it can be executed at the specified price.

Amortize: In portfolio accounting, periodic charges made against interest income on premium bonds in anticipation of receipt of the call price at call or of par value at maturity.

AP (agreement to pledge loan): Loans used by dealers who need to finance physical securities that they self-clear. Such a dealer sends to his bank a list of the collateral he is pledging against his loan from the bank.

Arbitrage: Strictly defined, buying something where it is cheap and selling it where it is dear; e.g., a bank buys 3-month CD money in the U.S. market and sells 3-month money at a higher rate in the Eurodollar market. In the money market, often refers: (1) to a situation in which a trader buys one security and sells a similar security in the expectation that the spread in yields between the two instruments will narrow or widen to his profit, (2) to a swap between two similar issues based on an anticipated change in yield spreads, and (3) to situations where a higher return (or lower cost) can be achieved in the money market for one currency by utilizing another currency and swapping it on a fully hedged basis through the foreign exchange market.

Asked: The price at which securities are offered.

Away: A trade, quote, or market that does not originate with the dealer in question, e.g., "the bid is 98–10 away (from me)".

Back contracts: Futures contracts farthest from expiration.

Back discount rate: Yield basis on which short-term, non-interest-bearing money market securities are quoted. A rate quoted on a discount basis understands bond equivalent yield. That must be calculated when comparing return against coupon securities.

Back-end computer: Computer that performs applications function on date it receives. Mostly, it debits this and credits that.

Back up: (1) When yields rise and prices fall, the market is said to back up. (2) When an investor swaps out of one security into another of shorter current maturity (e.g., out of a 2-year note into an 18-month note), he is said to back up.

Bank line: Line of credit granted by a bank to a customer.

Bank wire: A computer message system linking major banks. It is used not for effecting payments, but as a mechanism to advise the receiving bank

of some action that has occurred, e.g., the payment by a customer of funds into that bank's account.

Banker's acceptance (BA): A draft or bill of exchange accepted by a bank or trust company. The accepting institution guarantees payment of the bill.

BANs: Bond anticipation notes are issued by states and municipalities to obtain interim financing for projects that will eventually be funded long term through the sale of a bond issue.

Basis: (1) Number of days in the coupon period. (2) In *commodities* jargon, basis is the spread between a futures price and some other price. A money market participant would talk about *spread* rather than basis.

Basis point: One-one hundredth of 1%.

Basis price: Price expressed in terms of yield to maturity or annual rate of return.

Bear market: A declining market or a period of pessimism when declines in the market are anticipated. (A way to remember: "Bear down.")

Bearer security: A security the owner of which is not registered on the books of the issuer. A bearer security is payable to the holder.

Best-efforts basis: Securities dealers do not underwrite a new issue, but sell it on the basis of what can be sold. In the money market, this usually refers to a firm order to buy or sell a given amount of securities or currency at the best price that can be found over a given period of time; it can also refer to a flexible amount (up to a limit) at a given rate.

Bid: The price offered for securities.

Blind broker: A broker who acts as principal and does not give up names to either side of a brokered trade. Blind brokering of securities is common, whereas blind brokering of Fed funds and Euro time deposits would be infeasible.

Block: A large amount of securities, normally much more than what constitutes a round lot in the market in question.

Bond power: Assignment form that, when properly executed and attached to a registered security, puts that security into negotiable form (makes it acceptable for good delivery).

Book: A banker, especially a Eurobanker, will refer to his bank's assets and liabilities as its "book." If the average maturity of the liabilities is less than that of the assets, the bank is running a **short** and **open** book.

Book-entry securities: The Treasury and federal agencies are moving to a *book-entry* system in which securities are not represented by engraved pieces of paper but are maintained in computerized records at the Fed in the names of member banks, which, in turn, keep records of the securities they own as well as those they are holding for customers. In the case of other securities for which there is a book-entry system, engraved securities do exist somewhere in quite a few cases. These securities do not move from holder to holder but are usually kept in a central clearinghouse or by another agent.

Book value: The value at which a debt security is shown on the holder's balance sheet. Book value is often acquisition cost ± amortization/accretion, which may differ markedly from market value. It can be further defined as "tax book," "accreted book," or "amortized book" value.

Broker: A broker brings buyers and sellers together for a commission paid by the initiator of the transaction or by both sides; he does not position. In the money market, brokers are active in markets in which banks buy and sell money and in interdealer markets.

Bull market: A period of optimism when increases in market prices are anticipated. (A way to remember: "Bull ahead.")

Buy-back: Another term for a repurchase agreement.

Calendar: List of new bond issues scheduled to come to market soon.

Call: An option that gives the holder the right to buy the underlying security at a specified price during a fixed time period.

Callable bond: A bond that the issuer has the right to redeem prior to maturity by paying some specified call price.

Carry: The interest cost of financing securities held. (See also **Negative** and **Positive carry.**)

Cash commodity or security: The actual commodity or security as opposed to futures contracts for it.

Cash management bill: Very short-maturity bills that the Treasury occasionally sells because its cash balances are down and it needs money for a few days.

Cash market: Traditionally, this term has been used to denote the market in which commodities were traded for immediate delivery, against cash. Since the inception of futures markets for T bills and other debt securities, a distinction has been made between the cash markets in which these securities trade for immediate delivery and the futures markets in which they trade for future delivery.

Cash price: Price quotation in the cash market.

Cash settlement: In the money market, a transaction is said to be made for cash settlement if the securities purchased are delivered against payment in Fed funds on the same day the trade is made.

Certificate of deposit (CD): A time deposit with a specific maturity evidenced by a certificate. Large-denomination CDs are typically negotiable.

CHIPS: The New York Clearing House's computerized Clearing House Interbank Payments System. Most Euro transactions are cleared and settled through CHIPS rather than over the Fed wire.

Circle: Underwriters, actual or potential as the case may be, often seek out and "circle" retail interest in a new issue before final pricing. The customer circled has basically made a commitment to purchase the note or bond *or* to purchase it if it comes at an agreed-upon price. In the latter case, if the price is other than that stipulated, the customer supposedly has first offer at the actual price.

Clear: A trade carried out by the seller delivering securities and the buyer delivering funds in proper form. A trade that does not clear is said to fail.

Commercial paper: An unsecured promissory note with a fixed maturity of no more than 270 days. Commercial paper is normally sold at a discount from face value.

Competitive bid: (1) Bid tendered in a Treasury auction for a specific amount of securities at a specific yield or price. (2) Issuers, municipal and public utilities, often sell new issues by asking for competitive bids from one or more syndicates.

Confirmation: A memorandum to the other side of a trade describing all relevant data.

Convertible bond: A bond containing a provision that permits conversion to the issuer's common stock at some fixed exchange ratio.

Corporate bond equivalent: See **Equivalent bond yield.**

Corporate taxable equivalent: Rate of return required on a par bond to produce the same after-tax yield to maturity that the premium or discount bond quoted would.

Coupon: (1) The annual rate of interest on the bond's face value that a bond's issuer promises to pay the bondholder. (2) A certificate attached to a bond evidencing interest due on a payment date.

Cover: Eliminating a short position by buying the securities shorted.

Covered call write: Selling calls against securities owned by the call seller.

Covered interest arbitrage: Investing dollars in an instrument denominated in a foreign currency and hedging the resulting foreign exchange risk by selling the proceeds of the investment forward for dollars.

Credit risk: The risk that an issuer of debt securities or a borrower may default on his obligations, or that payment may not be made on sale of a negotiable instrument.

Cross hedge: Hedging a risk in a cash market security by buying or selling a futures contract for a similar but not identical instrument.

CRTs: Abbreviation for the cathode-ray tubes used to display market quotes.

Current coupon: A bond selling at or close to par; that is, a bond with a coupon close to the yield currently offered on new bonds of similar maturity and credit risk.

Current issue: In Treasury bills and notes, the most recently auctioned issue. Trading is more active in current issues than in off-the-run issues.

Current maturity: Current time to maturity on an outstanding note, bond, or other money market instrument; for example, a 5-year note 1 year after issue has a current maturity of 4 years.

Current yield: Coupon payments on a security as a percentage of the security's market price. In many instances the price should be *gross* of accrued interest, particularly on instruments where no coupon is left to be paid until maturity.

Cushion bonds: High-coupon bonds that sell at only a moderate premium because they are callable at a price below that at which a comparable non-callable bond would sell. Cushion bonds offer considerable downside protection in a falling market.

CUSIP number: *CUSIP* is an acronym for the *Committee on Uniform Identification Procedures.* Treasury securities, most federal credit agency securities (including mortgage backs), municipal bonds, corporate stocks, and corporate bonds all have identifying CUSIP numbers.

Custody bank: A commercial bank that holds securities of any sort in custody for an investor of any ilk.

Day trading: Intraday trading in securities for profit as opposed to investing for profit.

Daylight overdraft: Intraday overdraft that a bank runs with the Fed or that a bank customer runs with a bank. Foreign banks typically run big daylight overdrafts with their U.S. correspondent banks. A daylight overdraft exposes the institution that extends it to a credit risk.

Dealer: A dealer, as opposed to a broker, acts as a principal in all transactions, buying and selling for his own account.

Dealer loan: Overnight, collateralized loan made to a dealer financing his position by borrowing from a money market bank.

Debenture: A bond secured only by the general credit of the issuer.

Debt leverage: The amplification in the return earned on equity funds when an investment is financed partly with borrowed money.

Debt securities: IOUs created through loan-type transactions—commercial paper, bank CDs, bills, bonds, and other instruments.

Default: Failure to make timely payment of interest or principal on a debt security or to otherwise comply with the provisions of a bond indenture.

Delivery bill: A multi-part bill that says, in effect, "Pay us 'X' dollars for these 'Y' securities." When a physical security is sold, a delivery bill is delivered along with the security.

Delivery month: A month in which a futures contract expires and delivery may be taken or made.

Demand line of credit: A bank line of credit that enables a customer to borrow on a daily or an on-demand basis.

DI (Depositing Institution): DIs comprise commercial banks, S&Ls, savings banks, credit unions, foreign bank branches, in the U.S., etc.

Difference check: The amount of money that changes hands, by check or wire, when two trades are settled by a pairoff.

Direct paper: Commercial paper sold directly by the issuer to investors.

Direct placement: Selling a new issue not by offering it for sale publicly, but by placing it with one or several institutional investors.

Discount basis. See **Bank discount rate.**

Discount bond: A bond selling below par.

Discount paper: See **Discount securities.**

Discount rate: The rate of interest charged by the Fed to member banks that borrow at the discount window. The discount rate is an add-on rate.

Discount securities: Non-interest-bearing money market instruments that are issued at a discount and redeemed at maturity for full face value; e.g., U.S. Treasury bills.

Discount window: Facility provided by the Fed enabling member banks to borrow reserves against collateral in the form of governments or other acceptable paper.

Disintermediation: The investing of funds that would normally have been placed with a bank or other financial intermediary directly into debt securities issued by ultimate borrowers; e.g., into bills or bonds.

Distributed: After a Treasury auction, there will be many new issues in dealers' hands. As those securities are sold to retail, the issue is said to be distributed.

Diversification: Dividing investment funds among a variety of securities offering independent returns.

DK: To DK (don't know) a trade is to reject it because it fails to correspond in some way to a purchase that the receiver anticipates getting.

Documented discount notes: Commercial paper backed by normal bank lines plus a letter of credit from a bank stating that it will pay off the paper at maturity if the borrower does not. Such paper is also referred to as **LOC** (letter of credit) **paper.**

Dollar bonds: Municipal revenue bonds for which quotes are given in dollar prices. Not to be confused with "U.S. Dollar" bonds, a common term of reference in the Eurobond market.

Dollar price of a bond: Percentage of face value at which a bond is quoted.

DTC: Depositing Trust Company.

Due bill: An instrument evidencing either the obligation of a seller to deliver securities sold to the buyer or a letter repo agreement (see *Letter Repo*).

Dutch auction: Auction in which the lowest price necessary to sell the entire offering becomes the price at which all securities offered are sold. This technique has been used in Treasury auctions.

DVP: Delivery versus payment. Method of clearing a securities trade.

Edge Act corporation: A subsidiary of a U.S. bank set up to carry out international banking business. Most such "subs" are located within the United States.

Elbow: The elbow in the yield curve is the maturity area considered to provide the most attractive short-term investment; e.g., the maturity range in which to initiate a ride along the yield curve.

Eligible banker's acceptance: In the BA market an acceptance may be referred to as eligible because it is acceptable by the Fed as collateral at the discount window and/or because the accepting bank can sell it without incurring a reserve requirement.

Equivalent bond yield: Annual yield on a short-term, non-interest-bearing security calculated so as to be comparable to yields quoted on coupon securities.

Equivalent taxable yield: The yield on a taxable security that would leave the investor with the same after-tax return he would earn by holding a tax-exempt municipal; for example, for an investor taxed at a 50% marginal rate, equivalent taxable yield on a muni note issued at 3% would be 6%.

Eurocurrency deposits: Deposits made in a bank or bank branch that is not located in the country in whose currency the deposit is denominated. Dollars deposited in a London bank are Eurodollars; German marks deposited there are Euromarks.

Eurodollars: U.S. dollars deposited in a U.S. bank branch or a foreign bank located outside the United States.

Excess reserves: Balances held by a bank at the Fed in excess of those required.

Exchange rate: The price at which one currency trades for another.

Exempt securities: Instruments exempt from the registration requirements of the Securities Act of 1933 or the margin requirements of the Securities and Exchange Act of 1934. Such securities include governments, agencies, municipal securities, commercial paper, and private placements.

Exercise: To invoke the right to buy or sell granted under terms of a listed options contract.

Exercise price: The price at which an option holder may buy or sell the underlying security. Also called the striking price.

Extension swap: Extending maturity through a swap, e.g., selling a 2-year note and buying one with a slightly longer current maturity.

Fail: A trade is said to fail if on settlement date either the seller fails to deliver securities in proper form or the buyer fails to deliver funds in proper form.

Fails game: The strategies dealers use to attain a positive fail ratio and to thereby make money on fails.

Fed funds: See **Federal funds.**

Fed wire: A Federal Reserve communications and settlement system that links Fed banks and offices to DI that want to link up to the Fed. Fed wire is used to transfer money and book-entry securities.

Federal credit agencies: Agencies of the federal government set up to supply credit to various classes of institutions and individuals; e.g., S&Ls, small business firms, students, farmers, farm cooperatives, and exporters.

Federal Deposit Insurance Corporation (FDIC): A federal institution that insures bank deposits, currently up to $100,000 per deposit.

Federal Financing Bank: A federal institution that lends to a wide array of federal credit agencies funds it obtains by borrowing from the U.S. Treasury.

Federal funds: (1) Non-interest-bearing deposits held by member banks at the Federal Reserve. (2) Used to denote "immediately available" funds in the clearing sense.

Federal funds rate: The rate of interest at which Fed funds are traded. This rate is currently pegged by the Federal Reserve through open-market operations.

Federal Home Loan Banks (FHLB): The institutions that regulate and lend to savings and loan associations. The Federal Home Loan Banks play a role

analogous to that played by the Federal Reserve Banks vis-à-vis member commercial banks.

Figuring the tail: Calculating the yield at which a future money market instrument (one available some period hence) is purchased when that future security is created by buying an existing instrument and financing the initial portion of life with a term RP.

Firm: Refers to an order to buy or sell that can be executed without confirmation for some fixed period.

Fixed-dollar security: A nonnegotiable debt security that can be redeemed at some fixed price or according to some schedule of fixed values (e.g., bank deposits and government savings bonds).

Fixed-rate loan: A loan on which the rate paid by the borrower is fixed for the life of the loan.

Flat trades: (1) A bond in default trades flat; that is, the price quoted covers both principal and unpaid, accrued interest. (2) Any security that trades without accrued interest or at a price that includes accrued interest is said to trade flat.

Flex repo: A repo for a variable (usually declining) sum done for some period, often several years.

Float: The difference between the credits given by the Fed to banks' reserve accounts on checks being cleared through the Fed and the debits made to banks' reserve accounts on the same checks. Float is always positive, because in the clearing of a check, the credit sometimes precedes the debit. Float adds to the money supply.

Floating-rate note: A note that pays an interest rate tied to current money market rates. The holder may have the right to demand redemption at par on specified dates.

Floating supply: The amount of securities believed to be available for immediate purchase, that is, in the hands of dealers and investors wanting to sell.

Flower bonds: Government bonds that are acceptable at par in payment of federal estate taxes when owned by the decedent at the time of death.

Foreign bond: A bond issued by a nondomestic borrower in the domestic capital market.

Forward Fed funds: Fed funds traded for future delivery.

Forward market: A market in which participants agree to trade some commodity, security, or foreign exchange at a fixed price at some future date.

Forward rate: The rate at which forward transactions in some specific maturity are being made; e.g., the dollar price at which DM can be bought for delivery three months hence.

Free box: Securities that a dealer has in his clearing and that he has not pledged as collateral for a dealer loan or for an RP.

Free delivery: Delivery of securities with no offsetting payment of funds.

Free reserves: Excess reserves minus member bank borrowings at the Fed.

Full-coupon bond: A bond with a coupon equal to the going market rate and consequently selling at or near par.

Front-end computer: Computer that performs a communications traffic cop function.

Futures market: A market in which contracts for future delivery of a commodity or a security are bought and sold.

General obligation bonds: Municipal securities secured by the issuer's pledge of its full faith, credit, and taxing power.

Give up: The loss in yield that occurs when a block of bonds is swapped for another block of lower-coupon bonds. Can also be referred to as "after-tax give up" when the implications of the profit (loss) on taxes are considered.

Glass-Steagall Act: A 1933 act in which Congress forbade commercial banks to own, underwrite, or deal in corporate stock and corporate bonds.

Go-around: When the Fed offers to buy securities, to sell securities, to do repo, or to do reverses, it solicits competitive bids or offers, as the case may be, from all primary dealers. This procedure is known as a go-around.

Good delivery: On *the Street* this term refers to delivery of the *correct* security in an *acceptable* form (e.g., in the case of a registered security, with a properly executed bond power attached).

Good funds: A market expression for immediately available money; i.e., Fed funds.

Good trader: A Treasury coupon issue that can readily be bought and sold in size. If a trader can short $10 or $20 million of an issue and sleep at night, that issue is said to be a good trader.

Governments: Negotiable U.S. Treasury securities.

Gross spread: The difference between the price that the issuer receives for its securities and the price that investors pay for them. This spread equals the selling concession plus the management and underwriting fees.

GSI (Government Securities, Inc.): Some dealers that deal in both SEC-regulated and exempt securities have formed a GSI subsidiary in which they deal only in exempt securities, primarily governments and agencies.

Haircut: Margin in an RP transaction; that is, the difference between the actual market value measured at the bid side of the market and the value used in an RP agreement.

Handle: The whole-dollar price of a bid or offer is referred to as the *handle*. For example, if a security is quoted 101–10 bid and 101–11 offered, 101 is the handle. Traders are assumed to know the handle, so a trader would quote that market to another by saying he was at 10–11. (The 10 and 11 refer to 32nds.)

Hedge: To reduce risk, (1) by taking a position in futures equal and opposite to an existing or anticipated cash position, or (2) by shorting a security similar to one in which a long position has been established.

Hit: A dealer who agrees to sell at the bid price quoted by another dealer is said to *hit* that bid.

In the box: This means that a dealer has a wire receipt for securities indicating that effective delivery on them has been made. This jargon is a holdover from the time when Treasuries took the form of physical securities and were stored in a rack.

Indenture of a bond: A legal statement spelling out the obligations of the bond issuer and the rights of the bondholder.

Interest rate exposure: Risk of gain or loss to which an institution is exposed due to possible changes in interest rate levels.

Investment banker: A firm that engages in the origination, underwriting, and distribution of new issues.

Joint account: An agreement between two or more firms to share risk and financing responsibility in purchasing or underwriting securities.

Junk bonds: High-risk bonds that have low credit ratings or are in default.

Letter repo: Nondelivery repo confirmed by letter.

Letter RP: A nondelivery (of collateral RP) RP, the general conditions of which may be outlined by a letter or other document.

Leverage: See **Debt leverage.**

LIBOR: The London Interbank Offered Rate on Eurodollar deposits traded between banks. There is a different LIBOR rate for each deposit maturity. Different banks may quote slightly different LIBOR rates because they use different reference banks.

Lifting a leg: Closing out one side of a long-short arbitrage before the other is closed.

Line of credit: An arrangement by which a bank agrees to lend to the line holder during some specified period any amount up to the full amount of the line.

Liquidity: A liquid asset is one that can be converted easily and rapidly into cash without a substantial loss of value. In the money market, a security is said to be liquid if the spread between bid and asked prices is narrow and reasonable size can be done at those quotes.

Liquidity diversification: Investing in a variety of maturities to reduce the price risk to which holding long bonds exposes the investor.

Liquidity risk: In banking, risk that monies needed to fund assets may not be available in sufficient quantities at some future date. Implies an imbalance in committed maturities of assets and liabilities.

Locked market: A market is said to be locked if the bid price equals the asked price. This can occur, for example, if the market is brokered and brokerage is paid by one side only, the initiator of the transaction.

Lockup CDs: CDs that are issued with the tacit understanding that the buyer will not trade the certificate. Quite often, the issuing bank will insist that it keep the certificate to ensure that the understanding is honored by the buyer.

Long: (1) Owning a debt security, stock, or other asset. (2) Owning more than one has contracted to deliver.

Long bonds: Bonds with a long current maturity.

Long coupons: (1) Bonds or notes with a long current maturity. (2) A bond on which one of the coupon periods, usually the first, is longer than the others or than standard.

Long hedge: *Purchase* of a *futures* contract to lock in the yield at which an anticipated cash inflow can be invested.

Make a market: A dealer is said to make a market when he quotes bid and offered prices at which he stands ready to buy and sell.

Margin: (1) In an RP or a reverse repurchase transaction, the amount by which the market value of the securities collateralizing the transaction exceeds the amount lent. (2) In futures markets, money buyers and sellers must put up to assure performance on the contracts. (3) In options, similar meaning as in futures for sellers of put and call options.

Marginal tax rate: The tax rate that would have to be paid on any additional dollars of taxable income earned.

Market value: The price at which a security is trading and could presumably be purchased or sold.

Marketability: A negotiable security is said to have good marketability if there is an active secondary market in which it can be easily resold.

Match fund: A bank is said to match fund a loan or other asset when it does so by buying (taking) a deposit of the same maturity. The term is commonly used in the Euromarket.

Matched book: If the distribution of the maturities of a bank's liabilities equals that of its assets, it is said to be running a *matched book*. The term is commonly used in the Euromarket.

MBSCC: Mortgage-Backed Securities Clearing Corporation.

Money market: The market in which short-term debt instruments (bills, commercial paper, bankers' acceptances, etc.) are issued and traded.

Money market (center) bank: A bank that is one of the nation's largest and consequently plays an active and important role in every sector of the money market.

Money market fund: Mutual fund that invests solely in money market instruments.

Money rate of return: Annual return as a percentage of asset value.

Mortgage bond: Bond secured by a lien on property, equipment, or other real assets.

Municipal (muni) notes: Short-term notes issued by municipalities in anticipation of tax receipts, proceeds from a bond issue, or other revenues.

Municipals: Securities issued by state and local governments and their agencies.

Naked position: An unhedged long or short position.

Negative carry: The net cost incurred when the cost of carry exceeds the yield on the securities being financed.

Negative fail ratio: A dealer is said to have a negative fail ratio if his fails to others exceed fails to him. In this case, the dealer is losing money on fails.

Negotiable certificate of deposit: A large-denomination (generally $1 million) CD that can be sold but cannot be cashed in before maturity.

Negotiated sale: Situation in which the terms of an offering are determined by negotiation between the issuer and the underwriter rather than through competitive bidding by underwriting groups.

New-issues market: The market in which a new issue of securities is first sold to investors.

New money: In a Treasury refunding, the amount by which the par value of the securities offered exceeds that of those maturity.

Nominee: See **Street name.**

Noncompetitive bid: In a Treasury auction, bidding for a specific amount of securities at the price, whatever it may turn out to be, equal to the average price of the accepted competitive bids.

Note: Coupon issues with a relatively short original maturity are often called *notes.* Muni notes, however, have maturities ranging from a month to a year and pay interest only at maturity. Treasury notes are coupon securities that have an original maturity of up to 10 years.

NSCC: National Securities Clearing Corporation.

OD (Overdrawn): A bank that runs a daylight overdraft at the Fed is OD at the Fed.

Odd lot: Less than a round lot.

Off-the-run issue: In Treasuries and agencies, an issue that is not included in dealer or broker runs. With bills and notes, normally only current issues are quoted.

Offer: Price asked by a seller of securities.

One-man picture: The price quoted is said to be a one-man picture if both the bid and ask come from the same source.

One-sided (one-way) market: A market in which only one side, the bid or the asked, is quoted or firm.

Open book: See **Unmatched book.**

Open repo: A repo with no definite term. The agreement is made on a day-to-day basis and either the borrower or the lender may choose to terminate. The rate paid is higher than on overnight repo and is subject to adjustment if rates move.

OPM (Other People's Money): In the course of their varied transactions, dealers may end up holding temporarily balances of customers' money, OPM.

Opportunity cost: The cost of pursuing one course of action measured in terms of the foregone return offered by the most attractive alternative.

Option: (1) **Call option:** A contract sold for a price that gives the holder the right to buy from the writer of the option, over a specified period, a specified amount of securities at a specified price. (2) **Put option:** A contract sold for a price that gives the holder the right to sell to the writer of the contract, over a specified period, a specified amount of securities at a specified price.

Original maturity: Maturity at issue. For example, a 5-year note has an original maturity at issue of 5 years; 1 year later, it has a current maturity of 4 years.

Over-the-counter (OTC) market: Market created by dealer trading as opposed to the auction market prevailing on organized exchanges.

Paper: Money market instruments, commercial paper, and other.

Paper gain (loss): Unrealized capital gain (loss) on securities held in portfolio, based on a comparison of current market price and original cost.

Par: (1) Price of 100%. (2) The principal amount at which the issuer of a debt security contracts to redeem that security at maturity, *face value.*

Par bond: A bond selling at par.

Pass-throughs: Securities backed by a pool of mortgages that pass through monthly to the holders of the securities interest and principal payments made on the underlying pool of mortgages.

Paydown: In a Treasury refunding, the amount by which the par value of the securities maturing exceeds that of those sold.

Pay-up: (1) The loss of cash resulting from a swap into higher-price bonds. (2) The need (or willingness) of a bank or other borrower to pay a higher rate to get funds.

Perfected interest: Having an ownership interest that will stand up in court. State UCCs (Uniform Commercial Codes) state what steps a buyer must take to perfect his interest in an item he has purchased.

Pickup: The gain in yield that occurs when a block of bonds is swapped for another block of higher-coupon bonds.

Picture: The bid and asked prices quoted by a broker for a given security.

Play for fail: A dealer is said to play for fail when he leaves unfinanced some of the securities due to be delivered to him because he anticipates that some of these securities will fail to come in.

Plus: Dealers in governments normally quote bids and offers in 32nds. To quote a bid or offer in 64ths, they use pluses; for example, a dealer who bids 4+ is bidding the handle plus $\frac{1}{32} + \frac{1}{64}$, which equals the handle plus $\frac{3}{64}$.

Point: (1) 100 basis points = 1%. (2) One percent of the face value of a note or bond. (3) In the foreign exchange market, the lowest level at which the currency is priced. Example: "One point" is the difference between sterling prices of $1.8080 and $1.8081.

Portfolio: Collection of securities held by an investor.

Position: (1) To go long or short in a security. (2) The amount of securities owned (long position) or owed (short position).

Positive carry: The net gain earned when the cost of carry is less than the yield on the securities being financed.

Positive fail ratio: A dealer is said to have a positive fail ratio if fails to him exceed his fails to others. In that case, the dealer is earning money on fails.

Premium: (1) The amount by which the price at which an issue is trading exceeds the issue's par value. (2) The amount that must be paid in excess of par to call or refund an issue before maturity. (3) In money market parlance, the fact that a particular bank's CDs trade at a rate higher than others of its class, or that a bank has to pay up to acquire funds.

Premium bond: Bond selling above par.

Prepayment: A payment made ahead of the scheduled payment date.

Presold issue: An issue that is sold out before the coupon announcement.

Price risk: The risk that a debt security's price may change due to a rise or fall in the going level of interest rates.

Prime rate: The rate at which banks lend to their best (prime) customers. The all-in cost of a bank loan to a prime credit equals the prime rate plus the cost of holding compensating balances.

Principal: (1) The face amount or par value of a debt security. (2) One who acts as a dealer buying and selling for his own account.

Private placement: An issue that is offered to a single or a few investors as opposed to being publicly offered. Private placements do not have to be registered with the SEC.

Prospectus: A detailed statement prepared by an issuer and filed with the SEC prior to the sale of a new issue. The prospectus gives detailed information on the issue and on the issuer's condition and prospects.

Proving: Reconciling ins and outs of money and securities to a daily statement provided to a bank by the Fed, to a dealer by his clearing bank.

Put: An option that gives the holder the right to sell the underlying security at a specified price during a fixed time period.

PVD (Payment versus delivery): Method of clearing a securities trade.

RANs (Revenue anticipation notes): These are issued by states and municipalities to finance current expenditures in anticipation of the future receipt of nontax revenues.

Rate risk: In banking, the risk that profits may decline or losses occur because a rise in interest rates forces up the cost of funding fixed-rate loans or other fixed-rate assets.

Ratings: An evaluation given by Moody's, Standard & Poor's, Fitch, or other rating services of a security's creditworthiness.

Real market: The bid and offer prices at which a dealer could do size. Quotes in the brokers market may reflect not the real market, but pictures painted by dealers playing trading games.

Red herring: A preliminary prospectus containing all the information required by the Securities and Exchange Commission except the offering price and coupon of a new issue.

Refunding: Redemption of securities by funds raised through the sale of a new issue.

Registered bond: A bond whose owner is registered with the issuer.

Regular-way settlement: In the money and bond markets, the regular basis on which some security trades are settled is that delivery of the securities purchased is made against payment in Fed funds on the day following the transaction.

Reinvestment rate: (1) The rate at which an investor assumes interest payments made on a debt security can be reinvested over the life of that security.

(2) Also, the rate at which funds from a maturity or sale of a security can be reinvested. Often used in comparison to *give up* yield.

Relative value: The attractiveness—measured in terms of risk, liquidity, and return—of one instrument relative to another, or for a given instrument, of one maturity relative to another.

Reopen an issue: The Treasury, when it wants to sell additional securities, will occasionally sell more of an existing issue (reopen it) rather than offer a new issue.

Repo: See **Repurchase agreement.**

Repurchase agreement (RP or repo): A holder of securities sells these securities to an investor with an agreement to repurchase them at a fixed price on a fixed date. The security "buyer" in effect lends the "seller" money for the period of the agreement, and the terms of the agreement are structured to compensate him for this. Dealers use RP extensively to finance their positions. Exception: When the Fed is said to be doing RP, it is lending money, that is, increasing bank reserves.

Reserve requirements: The percentages of different types of deposits that member banks are required to hold on deposit at the Fed.

Retail: Individual and institutional customers as opposed to dealers and brokers.

Revenue bond: A municipal bond secured by revenue from tolls, user charges, or rents derived from the facility financed.

Reverse: See **Reverse repurchase agreement.**

Reverse repurchase agreement: Most typically, a repurchase agreement initiated by the lender of funds. Reverses are used by dealers to borrow securities they have shorted. Exception: When the Fed is said to be doing reverses, it is borrowing money, that is; absorbing reserves.

Revolving line of credit: A bank line of credit on which the customer pays a commitment fee and can take down and repay funds according to his needs. Normally the line involves a firm commitment from the bank for a period of several years.

Risk: Degree of uncertainty of return on an asset.

Roll over: Reinvest funds received from a maturing security in a new issue of the same or a similar security.

Round lot: In the money market, round lot refers to the minimum amount for which dealers' quotes are good. This may range from $100,000 to $5 million, depending on the size and liquidity of the issue traded.

RP: See **Repurchase agreement.**

Run: A run consists of a series of bid and asked quotes for different securities or maturities. Dealers give to and ask for runs from each other.

S&L: See **Savings and loan association.**

Safekeep: For a fee, banks will safekeep (i.e., hold in their vault, clip coupons on, and present for payment at maturity) bonds and money market instruments.

Sale repurchase agreement: See **Repurchase agreement.**

Savings and loan association: Federal- or state-chartered institution that accepts savings deposits and invests the bulk of the funds thus received in mortgages.

Savings deposit: Interest-bearing deposit at a savings institution that has no specific maturity.

Scale: A bank that offers to pay different rates of interest on CDs of varying maturities is said to "post a scale." Commercial paper issuers also post scales.

Scalper: A speculator who actively trades a futures contract in the hope of making small profits off transitory upticks and downticks in price.

Seasoned issue: An issue that has been well distributed and trades well in the secondary market.

Secondary market: The market in which previously issued securities are traded.

Sector: Refers to a group of securities that are similar with respect to maturity, type, rating, and/or coupon.

Securities and Exchange Commission (SEC): Agency created by Congress to protect investors in securities transactions by administering securities legislation.

Serial bonds: A bond issue in which maturities are staggered over a number of years.

Settle: See **Clear.**

Settlement date: The date on which trade is cleared by delivery of securities against funds. The settlement date may be the trade date or a later date.

Shell branch: A foreign branch—usually in a tax haven—which engages in Eurocurrency business but is run out of a head office.

Shop: In street jargon, a money market or bond dealership.

Shopping: Seeking to obtain the best bid or offer available by calling a number of dealers and/or brokers.

Short: A market participant assumes a short position by selling a security he does not own. The seller makes delivery by borrowing the security sold or reversing it in.

Short bonds: Bonds with a short current maturity.

Short book: See **Unmatched book.**

Short coupons: Bonds or notes with a short current maturity.

Short hedge: *Sale* of a *futures* contract to hedge, for example, a position in cash securities or an anticipated borrowing need.

Short sale: The sale of securities not owned by the seller in the expectation that the price of these securities will fall or as part of an arbitrage. A short sale must eventually be covered by a purchase of the securities sold.

Sinking fund: Indentures on corporate issues often require that the issuer make annual payments to a sinking fund, the proceeds of which are used to retire randomly selected bonds in the issue.

Size: Large in size, as in "size offering" or "in there for size." What constitutes size varies with the sector of the market.

Skip-day settlement: The trade is settled one business day beyond what is normal.

Specific issues market: The market in which dealers reverse in securities they want to short.

Spectail: A dealer that does business with retail but concentrates more on acquiring and financing its own speculative position.

Spot market: Market for immediate as opposed to future delivery. In the spot market for foreign exchange, settlement is two business days ahead.

Spot rate: The price prevailing in the spot market.

Spread: (1) Difference between bid and asked prices on a security. (2) Difference between yields on or prices of two securities of differing sorts or differing maturities. (3) In underwriting, difference between price realized by the issuer and price paid by the investor. (4) Difference between two prices or two rates. What a commodities trader would refer to as the *basis*.

Stop (a): An owner of a physical security that has been mutilated, lost, or stolen will request the issuer to place a stop (transfer) on the security and to cancel and replace the security.

Stop-out price: The lowest price (highest yield) accepted by the Treasury in an auction of a new issue.

Street name: A security is said to be in *street name* when it is registered in the name of a *nominee*. Nominees are shell partnerships whose sole function is to act as nominee, to pass through payments of interest and dividends, etc.

Sub right: Right of substitution—to change collateral—on a repo.

Subject: Refers to a bid or offer that cannot be executed without confirmation from the customer.

Subordinated debenture: The claims of holders of this issue rank after those of holders of various other unsecured debts incurred by the issuer.

Swap: (1) In securities, selling one issue and buying another. (2) In foreign exchange, buying a currency spot and simultaneously selling it forward.

Swing line: See **Demand line of credit.**

TABs (tax anticipation bills): Special bills that the Treasury occasionally issues. They mature on corporate quarterly income tax dates and can be used at face value by corporations to pay their tax liabilities.

Tail: (1) The difference between the average price in Treasury auctions and the *stop-out* price. (2) A *future* money market instrument (one available some period hence) created by buying an existing instrument and financing the initial portion of its life with term RP.

Take: (1) A dealer or customer who agrees to buy at another dealer's offered price is said to take that offer. (2) Eurobankers speak of taking deposits rather than buying money.

Take-out: (1) A cash surplus generated by the sale of one block of securities and the purchase of another, e.g., selling a block of bonds at 99 and buy-

ing another block at 95. (2) A bid made to a seller of a security that is designed (and generally agreed) to take him out of the market.

TANs: Tax anticipation notes issued by states or municipalities to finance current operations in anticipation of future tax receipts.

Technical condition of a market: Demand and supply factors affecting price, in particular the net position—long or short—of dealers.

Technicals: (1) Supply and demand factors influencing the cash market. (2) Value or shape of technical indicators.

Tenor: Maturity.

Term bonds: A bond issue in which all bonds mature at the same time.

Term Fed funds: Fed funds sold for a period of time longer than overnight.

Term loan: Loan extended by a bank for more than the normal 90-day period. A term loan might run five years or more.

Term RP (repo): RP borrowings for a period longer than overnight, may be 30, 60, or even 90 days.

Thin market: A market in which trading volume is low and in which consequently bid and asked quotes are wide and the liquidity of the instrument traded is low.

Throttle: Slowing of the rate at which Fed wire processed incoming messages. Throttle was caused by heavy traffic on Fed wire.

Throughput: The number of transactions a computer system can handle per unit of time.

Tight: An issue is said to be tight when it is hard to obtain and expensive to borrow. Big shorts in an issue make it "tight."

Tight market: A tight market, as opposed to a thin market, is one in which volume is large, trading is active and highly competitive, and spreads between bid and ask prices are narrow.

Time deposit: Interest-bearing deposit at a savings institution that has a specific maturity.

Trade date: The date on which a transaction is initiated. The settlement date may be the trade date or a later date.

Trade on top of: Trade at a narrow or no spread in basis points to some other instrument.

Trading paper: CDs purchased by accounts that are likely to resell them. The term is commonly used in the Euromarket.

Treasurer's check: A check issued by a bank to make a payment. Treasurer's checks outstanding are counted as part of a bank's reservable deposits and as part of the money supply.

Treasury bill: A non-interest-bearing discount security issued by the U.S. Treasury to finance the national debt. Most bills are issued to mature in 3 months, 6 months, or 1 year.

TT&L account: Treasury tax and loan account at a bank.

Turnaround: Securities bought and sold for settlement on the same day.

Turnaround time: The time available or needed to effect a turnaround.

Two-sided market: A market in which both bid and asked prices, good for the standard unit of trading, are quoted.

Two-way market: Market in which both a bid and an asked price are quoted.

Underwriter: A dealer who purchases new issues from the issuer and distributes them to investors. Underwriting is one function of an investment banker.

Unmatched book: If the average maturity of a bank's liabilities is less than that of its assets, it is said to be running an unmatched book. The term is commonly used in the Euromarket. Equivalent expressions are **open book** and **short book.**

Variable-price security: A security, such as stocks or bonds, that sells at a fluctuating, market-determined price.

Variable-rate CDs: Short-term CDs that pay interest periodically on *roll* dates; on each roll date the coupon on the CD is adjusted to reflect current market rates.

Variable-rate loan: Loan made at an interest rate that fluctuates with the prime.

Visible supply: New muni bond issues scheduled to come to market within the next 30 days.

When-issued trades: Typically there is a lag between the time a new bond is announced and sold and the time it is actually issued. During this interval, the security trades, **wi,** "when, as, and if issued."

Wi: When, as, and if issued. See **When-issued trades.**

Wi wi: T bills trade on a wi basis between the day they are announced and the day they are settled. Late Tuesday and on Wednesday, two bills will trade wi, the bill just auctioned and the bill just announced. The latter used to be called the wi wi bill. However, now it is common for dealers to speak of the just auctioned bill as the 3-month bill and of the newly announced bill as the wi bill. This change in jargon resulted from a change in the way interdealer brokers of bills list bills on their screens. Cantor Fitz still lists a new bill as the wi bill until it is settled.

Without: If 70 were bid in the market and there was no offer, the quote would be "70 bid without." The expression *without* indicates a one-way market.

Write: To sell an option.

Yankee bond: A foreign bond issued in the U.S. market, payable in dollars, and registered with the SEC.

Yankee CD: A CD issued in the domestic market (typically in New York) by a branch of a foreign bank.

Yield curve: A graph showing, for securities that all expose the investor to the same credit risk, the relationship at a given point in time between yield and current maturity. Yield curves are typically drawn using yields on governments of various maturities.

Yield to maturity: The rate of return yielded by a debt security held to maturity when both interest payments and the investor's capital gain or loss on the security are taken into account.

Index